RHEA

ZEUS   POSEIDON   HADES

EILEITHYIA   HEBE   HEPHAESTUS

DIONYSUS   ATHENA   HERMES   APHRODITE

L TREE

GODS

THE
ODYSSEY

OF
HOMER

GREEK MYTHS

Texts from the Stories by
Gustav Schwab

Essay, Chapter Introductions, and Glossary by
Michael Siebler

Illustrations by
Clifford Harper

TASCHEN

—INTRODUCTION—

The Gods and Heroes of Ancient Greece
by Michael Siebler
8

THE MYTHS

—APPENDIX—

INTRODUCTION

by Michael Siebler

The Gods and Heroes of Ancient Greece

The most celebrated Greek and Roman myths are still very much with us. We encounter the epic plots and their protagonists everywhere, often without being aware of this – in spoken language, our everyday lives, and the cultures that have formed us.

Take the Trojan Horse, whose ominous function designates malware on computers, or the travails of Odysseus, whose name has become synonymous with protracted wanderings marked by considerable upheavals. Then there is the Achilles heel: a crucial physical weakness or fatal character flaw. A "herculean task" can only be accomplished by hard physical or mental labor (p. 110). The "Oedipus complex" is a term Sigmund Freud introduced to psychoanalysis. The very constellations of the night sky such as Cassiopeia and Perseus (pp. 48–57), and the 1968 Stanley Kubrick film *2001: A Space Odyssey* keep the names of ancient mythological characters and events alive.

What is so special about these tales from long ago? Why do they still give wings to the creative imaginations of writers, artists, composers, stage and film directors, cartoonists, and the inventors of computer games? What continues to drive interest in them in an era dominated by rationality and technology, with no place for fairy tales and myths? There's a simple answer to that: The classical myths deal with nothing less than all that being human implies – human existence, society, and culture – usually projected onto the gods, who, as we are well aware, knew all there was to know about human affairs.

These myths provide us with the entire panoply of human feelings and characteristics, all facets of the human condition: all variants of conflict resolution, including questions of life and death, love and hatred, pain, courage, luck good and bad, hubris, revenge, jealousy, betrayal, humanity, mercy, piety, cruelty, cunning, altruism, accountability, and much more. The fascination of ancient myths, the quality that makes them immortal – and this despite what we term "progress" – rests mainly on the fact that human experience has not changed in fundamentals since antiquity, and that mythology can express it vividly, in memorable verbal and visual imagery.

Gustav Schwab's Collection of Myths

Events and adventures from a mythic past continue to whet the curiosity and inspire the imaginations of generation after generation of young readers especially, and this is due in large part to a Swabian pastor, who also taught secondary school and wrote books. Without *Gods and Heroes: Myths and Epics of Ancient Greece* (*Sagen des klassischen Altertums*), written by Gustav Schwab (1792–1850, p. 13), and published in three volumes between 1838 and 1840, the realm of the ancient gods and heroes would not be literally at readers' fingertips in all those bookcases and on so many library shelves (p. 14). He ensured that these tales would not be forgotten. The Schwab collection was an instant hit, a publishing triumph that has fundamentally and lastingly shaped our knowledge and interpretation of Greco-Roman mythology. In fact, Schwab deserves the credit for providing readers in the German-speaking countries with what might well be the definitive complete version of the most famous myths of classical antiquity in his collected tales.

When Gustav Schwab began writing them down, he had at his disposal all the skills needed for retelling the classical myths in an accessible way: a profound knowledge of ancient

Greek and Latin as well as experience both as an educator and a writer. From 1817 on he taught classical languages in Stuttgart. In 1825 he was hired by Leipzig publishers F. A. Brockhaus to work on *Blätter für literarische Unterhaltung* (Papers for Literary Entertainment) and in 1828 by the Stuttgart publishing house Johann Friedrich Cotta to edit *Morgenblatt für gebildete Stände* (Morning Paper for the Educated Classes). Schwab had already dabbled in retelling old tales as a literary genre with *Buch der schönsten Geschichten und Sagen* (The Book of the Most Beautiful Tales and Myths), printed at the suggestion of Samuel Gottlieb Liesching (1786–1864), another Stuttgart publisher. Liesching would be Schwab's mentor while he was writing *Gods and Heroes: Myths and Epics of Ancient Greece*.

The three-volume work was widely acclaimed and successful so soon after it was published for two reasons. On the one hand, Schwab gave many curious readers anxious to widen their knowledge easy access to traditional Greco-Roman mythology: Until then, engaging with it had required sound knowledge of the classical languages and the relevant sources in Greek and Roman literature and history. Schwab was determined that young readers in particular should not be deterred by the prosody of the *Iliad* or the exalted linguistic register of Greek tragedy.

He stated his aims very clearly in a preface to the first edition of the first volume: "The vitality inherent in this imagery is so powerful that it does not even seem to depend on the perfection of the art form in which we possess much of the content dealt with by the greatest poets, but rather the simplest representation suffices for its greatness to be revealed, even to those for whom the art form must be an obstacle to promoting comprehension." That was why he wanted to try to "retell the most beautiful and significant myths of classical antiquity from the ancient writers, preferably the poets, in a simple way, divested of the glory of artistic representation yet, *wherever possible, in their own words*." In Schwab's view, it was "a lovely quality peculiar to the myths and heroic epics of classical antiquity that they appeal to scholars and the untutored alike although they might view them with different eyes. Whereas the scholar plumbs in them the wellsprings of human knowledge, the basic tenets of religion and philosophy, and the dawning of history, unsophisticated viewers are enchanted by the revelation of the most richly drawn characters, the spectacle of Nature and the spirit world in the nascent state, as it were."

The second, no less important aspect was the fact that Schwab took the trouble of shaping something novel and great from a virtually intractable mass of source material that had been variously transmitted in celebrated poetry and plays or preserved for posterity in scattered commentaries and versions retold in late antiquity with a wealth of variants, chronologically divergent additions and embellishments of the mythological material. The importance and value of Schwab's interweaving of such diverse strands of mythological tradition to create a collection of complete tales cannot be overstated. Schwab explained his methodology, justifying it in his preface to the second volume by illustrating his approach with the most magnificent ancient epic, the Myth of Troy, "in fact from the foundation of the city to its fall, consequently with completeness the like of which was never attained in this narrative form in the sources." To bring off this masterstroke, Schwab had to "resort for a fluid narrative to the turgidly flowing streams

Far left
Alfred Renz
*Cover illustration depicting Oedipus
and the Sphinx,* 1925

Near left
Oscar Woite
*Cover illustration for the fifteenth edition
of Schwab's anthology,* 1883

Right
Gustave Moreau
Prometheus, oil on canvas, 1868
*Prometheus sits bound to the Caucasus
Mountains, with vultures to his side
and at his feet.*

of that rhetorical hotchpotch we possess from a much later time under the names of Dictys Cretensis and Dares Phrygius. However, their account, from which the bits most easily reconcilable with *Homer* were selected, forms merely the basic historical warp or the chain of events whereas the most celebrated poets of Greco-Roman antiquity – Sophocles, Euripides, Horace, Ovid *et al.* – contributed the brilliantly hued woof of their imagination to the weave." Thus Schwab describing his approach in simple metaphorical language. Readers aware of the parlous state of the transmitted source material, on the other hand, will soon realize that the author undertook a task of sheer Herculean proportions – with all the minor flaws inherent in such a decidedly subjective process of selection and individual approach to the subject.

Gustav Schwab's admirable and courageous achievement lies in having conveyed the mythological content via the ancient form of simple narration and having so consciously selected in advance the content he wanted to cover from stories that never really ended. In so doing, he met a need for something that, thanks to Schwab, no longer exists for us as such: retelling the most famous myths of antiquity in chronological order to form a complete narrative cycle.

And that explains why the myths and epics were published in a narrative sequence of unprecedented scope. The first volume acquaints readers with myths predating the Trojan War, such as the Argonauts, the Heracles cycle and the hero's famous labors, and the myths of Theseus (pp. 124–129) and Oedipus (pp. 130–137). The second volume encompasses the myths associated with Troy from the foundation of the city to its fall. The best-known part recounts the grudge Achilles nursed against

Agamemnon, the high-handed commander of the Greek forces, and the death of Hector. This part is described in the roughly 16,000 lines of hexameter that make up the *Iliad,* the epic usually attributed to Homer (pp. 138–179). Incredibly, this episode takes place in only fifty-one days of the war fought at the gates of Troy for ten years. Finally, in the third volume Schwab turns to the adventures of the heroes returning home from Troy. The best known of these tales deals with the wanderings of Odysseus, which have come down to us in the *Odyssey,* a Homeric epic comprising more than 12,000 lines of hexameter (pp. 180–249). Again, a ten-year timespan is eschewed: It would have covered the time Odysseus spent on his wanderings before he reached Ithaca, his home, and could embrace his son Telemachus and his wife Penelope after twenty years. Instead, the *Odyssey,* too, has a limited narrative focus: in this case, just forty days. One part of Schwab's third volume is about the return of the Greek heroes to Greece. The other deals with the flight of Aeneas from the burning walls of Troy. In the *Aeneid* Virgil tells the story of his adventures in Carthage and Italy, where his descendants would ultimately found Rome on the Tiber.

The extensive body of work Schwab produced to educate the youth of his day, as well as adults, is part and parcel of the tradition of sweeping education reforms carried out by Wilhelm von Humboldt (1767–1835) at secondary school and university level. Humboldt was a true polymath, and his boundless enthusiasm for Greco-Roman antiquity represented a sound foundation on which the education reforms he instituted in Prussia in 1809–10 might rest. Aimed at broadening the school curriculum, they targeted a pupil intake from all walks of life regardless of social class.

GVSTAVE·MOREAV·1868· PROMETHEVS·

Those years saw the groundwork laid for publishing an increasing number of popularizing anthologies that conveyed the rudiments of the humanities and ancient history to pupils at an early stage in their education, thus sparing them the need for struggling with endless lines of hexameter in the original Greek and Latin. And Schwab's collection of tales drawn from classical mythology and the heroic epics definitely belonged to that genre because in his day, being familiar with classical mythology was a reliable indicator of a well-furnished mind. No wonder this book enjoyed pride of place on many a table laden with presents at Christmas and other festive occasions – and still does.

A classic in its own right and translated into seventeen languages, Schwab's collection of myths and epic tales went through innumerable editions and revisions, even by other writers long after his death. It also had a lasting impact on educated adult readers, who engaged with it seriously. Distinguished scholars, including Ernst Beutler (1885–1969), a professor of German literature and Goethe specialist, as well as Ernst Pfuhl (1876–1940) and Karl Schefold (1905–1999), classical archaeologists, were among those charged by reputable publishing houses with revising these new editions and selecting suitable illustrations for them. In addition, new illustrations were prepared specially for the Schwab myth collection. Whereas the original three-volume had only one illustration per volume, as the decades passed artists were commissioned to produce a larger number of suitable illustrations. The present book features a choice selection of these works.

Hermann Hesse (1877–1962), Nobel laureate and, like the author of the *Myths and Epics of Ancient Greece*, a native of Swabia, wrote in a review of the Schwab edition revised by

Ernst Beutler: "Here we can linger at leisure in the land of the Greeks and Trojans innocently and undeterred by the bickering and squabbling of philologists and read about the wrath of Achilles and the misfortunes of Icarus in good German without notes and commentaries. With this fine book of myths, the Swabian poet, whose poetry we have laid aside and forgotten, has deservedly attained in this fine book of myths, which every pupil taking Latin at school should own and be more thoroughly conversant with than the complete or abridged Ploetz *Encylopaedia of World History*, the immortality, entirely unsought and unsung, which some might have thought such an overly diligent poetaster incapable of."[1] In the *Bibliothek der Weltliteratur* (Library of World Literature) that Hesse collated in 1929, he touted Schwab's book as the best collection of ancient myths available. The writer Rudolf Borchardt (1877–1945) described his first encounter with classical mythology as follows: "I could read at a very early age and had well-thumbed books early on. One of my earliest memories is being angry at having to lay aside my book to to make an appearance with my siblings for guests; the book was *Gods and Heroes: Myths and Epics of Ancient Greece* by good old Schwab, which meant the world and endless bliss to me, the only world I had that was all my own..."[2]

The Myth of Troy Reflected in History

The impact Greco-Roman mythology continues to make on European civilization is undeniable. Every issue that affected the ancient Greeks and Romans is still being addressed by literature, the visual arts, and music. The world of the ancient myths has been subjected to thorough reflection and interpretation.

Yet how much weight was actually attached to myths in antiquity and what role did such epics and traditions play in daily life then? Might a myth have even had a bearing on politics? The Myth of Troy and the Trojan War is probably the prime example of how an ancient tradition, lost in the mists of time, might have influenced political decision-making, indeed might have made the difference between war and peace.

Even though the question of whether the Trojan War as described in Homeric epic and other literary sources ever took place, whether there is a core of historical truth to the tales about the city and its destruction, is still the subject of heated debate, in antiquity no one doubted the historicity of the conflict fought out before the walls of Troy. Even then, however, there was no real certainty about when the Greek conquest of the city was supposed to have taken place. The dates that have come down to us vary between 1334 BC and 1135 BC. The *Parian Chronicle* (*Marmor parium*) inscribed on Parian marble even gives the day Troy was conquered and destroyed as June 5, 1209 BC. This purely fictional date did not hinder the historian Thucydides (ca. 455–450 BC), whose work on the Peloponnesian War is regarded as ushering in the era of critical historiography, from viewing the Trojan War as the first joint expedition undertaken by Hellenic forces against a foreign foe.

Shortly before crossing the straits separating Asia from Europe on his campaign against Greece in 480 BC, Xerxes, King of the Persians (ca. 519–465 BC), visited the ruins of Ilion, as Troy was also called. He may well have viewed the excursion as effective political propaganda aimed at the Greeks that might also be interpreted as the prelude to retribution for the blow once struck against the East by the West. Roughly

a century and a half later, Alexander the Great (356–323 BC) also took time to visit Troy before setting out on his retaliatory strike against the Persians in 334 BC. As Plutarch (ca. 45–125 AD) tells it in his biography of Alexander, who was an ardent admirer of Homer, Alexander "sacrificed to Athena at Ilion, and honored the memory of the heroes who were buried there with solemn libations, especially Achilles, whose gravestone he anointed. And with his friends, as the ancient custom is, he ran naked about the tomb and crowned it with garlands, declaring how happy he esteemed him [Achilles], in having so faithful a friend [Patroclus] while he lived, and when he was dead, so famous a poet [Homer] to proclaim his actions."[3]

For Rome, as an emerging world power, the mythical descent of the Romans from Aeneas, who by the will of the gods escaped the inferno of Troy on fire with his father, Anchises, and his son, Ascanius (Iulus), represented historical reality. This tradition was regarded as so uncontestably real that it was seamlessly incorporated in the realpolitik practiced by the Romans, who otherwise tended to be practical and objective. Some power politicians put it to very sophisticated use. Gaius Julius Caesar (100–44 BC) and his adopted son, later the emperor Augustus (63 BC–14 AD), were the most effective appropriators of the Myth of Troy for personal and familial self-aggrandizement. The Julian family venerated Venus, Aphrodite in Greek mythology, as their divine ancestress. As legend has it, the love goddess was Aeneas's mother. By 68 BC, Julius Caesar, then only thirty-two years old, was putting emphasis on the family's descent from Venus in the funeral oration he gave for his aunt Julia. Later he would honor the mythic homeland of his ancestors by enlarging the imperial domains.

Left
Caravaggio
Head of the Medusa, oil on canvas, 1597/98
*The painting of Medusa's severed head was
one of many representations of the Gorgon to
adorn ornamental shields in the 16th century.*

Right
Arthur Rackham
*Bellerophon vaults over the three-headed
Chimera, aided by the wings of Pegasus,* 1922

In late antiquity Troy as a place was gradually forgotten. However, the myth of the Trojan War, with its heroes and their dramatic stories, lived on in collective memory to lead to remarkably dubious interpretations and political acts of aggression. What had once been part of the general education of the Roman elite now informed the thinking of the tribes engaged in the Barbarian Invasions and later inspired the Knights Templars and the Crusaders. The stories associated with the Matter of Troy also found their way into Christian medieval art. Since knowledge of ancient artworks was limited, the mythology was given a contemporaneous makeover. Just as the Romans had once exploited the Myth of Troy for their ancestral mythology, other European powers now began to discover the advantages of such cultural appropriation. Identification with the unifying myth enabled affiliation with the Roman civilization they admired. This step in turn allowed them military superiority to underpin claims to political power as the rightful heirs to the fallen Inperium Romanum.

The account of the visit to Troy paid in 1462 by Sultan Mehmed II (1432–1481), the conqueror of Constantinople, indicates the extent to which the Trojan War was still – or once again – viewed as an East-West conflict. In keeping with Greek and Roman tradition, the Sultan visited the ruins, where, like his great predecessors, he sacrificed at the tomb of Achilles.

The best-known historical figure now associated with Troy may be Heinrich Schliemann (1822–1890). The Mecklenburg merchant's unshakable faith in Homer's veracity and the existence of myth-enshrouded Troy led him to seek the theater of operations in which the Trojan War took place – and he ultimately found it for archaeology. In 1870 he began excavating on the Mound of Hisarlik on the west coast of Turkey. Scholars still disagree on what the excavations undertaken by Schliemann and later archaeologists have brought to light, yet it remains an indisputable fact that Schliemann did find the place which in antiquity was equated with Troy, "sacred Ilios."

Living with Myths: Athens

Scholars have been focusing on classical mythology again for some years now. New questions about mythology and the stories associated with it from ancient Greece have given rise to fresh knowledge and astonishing insights. Unsurprisingly, once again interest centers on fifth-century Athens, the cradle of democracy, quintessentially synonymous with ancient Greek civilization.

After the city of Athens and its temples had been razed to the ground in 480–479 BC by the Persians – events that were unprecedentedly traumatic for the citizens of the city – the decisive Athenian victory in the sea battle off Salamis in 480 BC (p. 316), ushered in a new era for Athens. The Greek city-state had defeated Persia, a world power, not once but twice: in 490 BC at Marathon and ten years later off the coast of Attica and at Plataea. In the following years Athens, like Sparta, grew into a hegemonic power. The classical period represented an age of matchless Athenian cultural ascendency, which has shaped not only our conception of classical art but even in antiquity was viewed as the absolute high point of Greco-Roman civilization. The names of the Athenian statesman Pericles (ca. 490–429 BC) and the sculptor Phidias (ca. 500/490–430/420 BC) are indissolubly linked with the classical period.

INTRODUCTION

Under the auspices of perhaps the most ambitious cultural agenda the West has ever known, a new Athens, more resplendent than ever, arose from the rubble and ashes of the destroyed city. Athens and its citizens were the most resourceful of all Greeks when it came to luring mainstream cultural and intellectual trendsetters to their city. There are very good reasons for believing that Pericles was the planner and driving force behind the complete remake of Athens and the Attic peninsula by commissioning Phidias, the legendary artist and maker of the celebrated gold and ivory statues of Athena Parthenos on the Acropolis and Zeus in Olympia, to head the project. A subtly sophisticated narrative web of relief panels and sculptures on temples and statues in shrines and elsewhere eventually overlaid Athens and Attica, all interlinked as if by an invisible ribbon. The focus was on the figurative sculpture that decorated the temples on the Acropolis and the statues set up there. What all these works had in in common was that they proclaimed the myth and the greatness of Athens. Above all, they narrated the myths and adventurous tales associated with Athena, the titular patron and tutelary deity of their city, who also features in Gustav Schwab, which over the course of centuries had been forgotten and only now are being brought to light from the obscurity of the scant visual and verbal sources that have been handed down.

Like other Olympian gods, Athena was not without flaws and was held accountable for her actions. However, as is so often the case in Greek mythology, mortals, guilty or innocent, were often the ones who had to take the rap. The most harrowing drama for both Athena and her mortal charges was probably the fate of Erechtheus, her adopted son. His death – Zeus paralyzed Erechtheus with his thunderbolt so Poseidon could impale him on his trident – resulted from a dispute between Athena and Poseidon about who was entitled to rule over Athens and Attica. Erechtheus lived on in the rocks of the Acropolis, transformed into a serpent. The most compelling illustration of the myth was probably the lost gold and ivory cult statue of Athena Parthenos by Phidias, which featured Erechtheus, the son who had "been lost and found again" as a serpent between the goddess and her shield, fondly turned towards his adoptive mother.

The resurrection or rebirth of her son consoled Athena, and the orgy of violence and human sacrifice became the foundation for the reconciliation between the city of Athens and its powerful foe, Poseidon. Athena remained the patron deity of Athens and Attica but the god of the sea was also venerated on the Acropolis from then on. Athens was saved from destruction only by the restoration of friendly relations between Athena and Poseidon. It was the basis for the city's rise to unparalleled greatness and power, which indisputably was at its zenith in the fifth century BC. No wonder that politics, religion, and myth, as well as art and literature, have drawn on such a rich store of multireferential material.

These and other tales from Attica are in no way inferior to the epic story of Jason and Medea or the heroic adventures at Troy. Of one thing we can be certain: Had Gustav Schwab had access to the comprehensive findings related to the mythology and tales associated with the Attic myth of Athena, divine patron of Athens, retrieved by archaeology since his time, he would not have hesitated to include this myth, too, in his collection of the most beautiful myths and epics of classical antiquity.

Left
Giuseppe Cesari
Perseus and Andromeda, oil on slate, 1592
*The Ethiopian princess Andromeda is
rescued by the hero on a winged horse, with
the Gorgon's head clutched in his left hand.*

Right
William Russell Flint
*Theseus fends off a group of Nereids or
sea-nymphs in a retelling of his exploits from*
The Heroes *by Charles Kingsley, 1912*

The Antique Heroes gave rise to Modern Superheroes

In the twentieth century the reception of the classical heroic myths assumed a special form manifest in the superhero comic genre that figures so prominently in pop culture. During the late nineteenth century comics gained popularity as newspaper supplements before developing into a form of entertainment in their own right. In the 1930s and 1940s, a novel genre emerged in the U.S., superhero comics, which attracted a wide readership and still appeals to a broad public.

The earliest and best-known character featured in this genre is Superman, who is still the iconic archetype of the superhero. Superman, who was developed as a character in the early 1930s, was an instant hit with his first appearance in *Action Comics* magazine in 1938. Other superheroes in comics soon followed him to universal fame, such as Batman, launched by *DC Comics* in 1939, and Spider-Man, featured in *Marvel Comics* since 1962. A mere three years after Superman, the first female superhero appeared on the scene in DC Comics in 1941: Wonder Woman. Like a fearless Amazon, Wonder Woman has combated evil in countless comics, comic strips, and movies since then. Alongside these solitary superhero characters, superheroes acting as teams have emerged, including the *Marvel Comics* Avengers from the early 1960s. The most recent film about them, *The Avengers* (2012), was a box-office super hit.

The character traits and iconographic features that distinguish superheroes are patently reminiscent of the heroes and demigods of Greco-Roman mythology because modern superheroes, like their ancient forebears, possess courage, a combative spirit, and a sense of justice along with the superhuman powers and abilities (such as being able to fly) they deploy in battling evil and monsters threatening humanity. And like the ancient hero Heracles, who is unmistakable because he is always depicted wearing the skin of the Nemean Lion he slew and flayed (pp. 110–119), Superman and other superheroes invariably wear an unusual costume, which is easy to identify and usually includes a cape.

Like Achilles, who was virtually invincible except for a single vulnerable spot on his body – the "Achilles heel" that bears his name – Superman is for all intents and purposes invulnerable. His powers are only weakened by proximity to the fictional mineral kryptonite.

The comic-book stories about American superheroes are still being adapted for television serials, movies, and computer games, and they have devoted fans the world over. Recreations of the superhero outside the U.S. have not, on the other hand, attained the status of their American templates nor have they succeeded in retaining their appeal over the long term. The sole exception might be Asterix the Gaul, a comic-book character created by René Goscinny and Albert Uderzo in 1959. Asterix, who lives in a small Gaulish village in Julius Caesar's day and is constantly engaged in acts of resistance against the Roman occupation, imbibes a magic potion to become a superhero. He and his friend Obelix embark on a number of fantastic adventures in ancient Gaul.

Classical Mythology in Art

The classical myths have continued to inspire not only writers but also painters, sculptors, composers, stage and film directors, and creatives in many other fields. The impact made by Schwab's works after the mid-nineteenth century is, of

INTRODUCTION

course, a moot question; their influence need not have been negligible, far from it in fact. From the mass of adaptations, re-creations, retellings, and interpretations, consider the following works of world literature: *Ulysses*, the great James Joyce (1882–1941) novel, a conceptional borrowing from the *Odyssey*; *Cassandra*, a socio-critical novel by Christa Wolf (1929–2011) published simultaneously in the then GDR and the Federal Republic of Germany in 1983, and *The Firebrand* (1987), a bestselling Marion Zimmer Bradley (1930–1999) fantasy novel that retells the story of the Trojan War from the viewpoint of Priam's daughter Cassandra.

Twentieth-century plays were also often based on the myths associated with the Trojan War and the Fall of Troy. Notable examples are the *Mourning Becomes Electra* cycle by Eugene O'Neill (1888–1953); *La guerre de Troie n'aura pas lieu* (*The Trojan War will not Take Place*) by Jean Giraudoux (1882–1944); *The Odyssey: A Modern Sequel* by Nikos Kazantzakis (1883–1957), the author of *Zorba the Greek*; the *Atriden-Tetralogie* (Iphigenia in Aulis, The Death of Agamemnon, and Electra) by Gerhart Hauptmann (1862–1946); and *Philoktet* (*Philoctetes*) by Heiner Müller (1929–1995). Spectacular operas based on classical mythology include *Orfeo ed Euridice* by Christoph Willibald Gluck (1714–1787), *Il ritorno d'Ulisse in patria* by Claudio Monteverdi (1567–1643), *Les Troyens* by Hector Berlioz (1803–1869), and *Elektra* by Richard Strauss (1864–1949).

The twentieth-century film industry has also repeatedly drawn on the seemingly inexhaustible treasure trove of the Trojan myth cycle, and other related epics. The best-known of these films is probably Wolfgang Petersen's (*1941) *Troy*, starring Brad Pitt as Achilles. Pier Paolo Pasolini (1922–1975)

contributed *Edipo re* and *Medea* with Maria Callas (1923–1977) famously playing the lead role. Kirk Douglas (1916–2020) was Odysseus in the fantasy-adventure film *Ulysses*, while the *Aeneid* was serialized by Franco Rossi (1919–2000).

The visual arts are teeming with representations taken from classical mythology. Artists working in all period styles, painters, and sculptors, have welcomed motifs from Greco-Roman myths. A few standouts in such a rich tradition memorably document the period styles in which they were executed as well as the artists' individual thematic approaches to ancient subject matter: the gallery of epic heroes drawn from Homer, *Homer nach Antiken gezeichnet* (p. 22), by Johann Heinrich Wilhelm Tischbein (1751–1829), taking famous ancient sculptures as his models; *Hector Taking Leave of Andromache* by Angelica Kauffmann (1741–1807), *Jason with the Golden Fleece* by the Danish sculptor Bertel Thorvaldsen (1770–1844), *The Trojan Horse* by Lovis Corinth (1858–1925), *Odysseus und Kalypso* (p. 28 r.) by Max Beckmann (1884–1950); *Pan im Schilf* (p. 29) and *Odysseus und Polyphem* (p. 16) by Arnold Böcklin (1827–1901), and *La Minotauromachie*, Pablo Picasso's (1881–1973) most important print, a signature work which expresses the enduring fascination the mythological figure of the Minotaur had for him and was preceded by a cover for the first issue of the Surrealist art magazine *Minotaure*.

Greco-Roman mythology also played a role in book illustration. The present edition of the *Myths and Epics* unites famous artists and works from the "Golden Age" of book illustration that was in its heyday in the late nineteenth and early twentieth centuries. New technologies made it possible to print more illustrations in books and magazines. In the English-speaking

Hendrick Goltzius fecit et sculpsit. A° 1589.

Far Left
Gustav Klimt
Pallas Athene, oil on canvas, 1898
The goddess of wisdom, art, and handcraft depicted with a breastplate of a gorgoneion.

Near left
Max Beckmann
Odysseus and Calypso, oil on canvas, 1943
Calypso offers Odysseus the gift of eternity.

Right
Arnold Böcklin
Pan in the Reeds, oil on canvas, 1858
Pan plays his flute on the riverbank.

countries more artists – inspired by movements such as the Pre-Raphaelite Brotherhood, the Arts and Crafts movement, and Art Nouveau/Jugendstil – produced numerous book illustrations, which are just as expressive and elegant today as they ever were. This remarkable band of artists, whose works illustrating the Greek myths are featured in this book, includes Walter Crane (1845–1915), Charles Edmund Brock (1870–1938), Edmund Dulac (1882–1953), John Flaxman (1755–1826), Sir William Russell Flint (1880–1969), Clément Gontier (1876–1918), Arthur Rackham (1867–1939), Gustaf Tenggren (1896–1970), Milo Winter (1888–1956), and Newell Convers Wyeth (1882–1945) as well as the distinguished women illustrators Virginia Frances Sterrett (1900–1931) and Helen Stratton (1867–1961) – to mention just a few of the artists compiled in this publication.

They not only illustrated classics of English and American literature, such as the works of Shakespeare, Robert Louis Stevenson, Oscar Wilde, Charles Dickens, Lewis Carroll, and Nathaniel Hawthorne (p. 19), but also devoted themselves to mythological material, showcasing major figures and pivotal scenes from the Greek myths: Pandora and her box (pp. 33, 36), the touching elderly lovers Philemon and Baucis (p. 251), Odysseus disguised as a beggar (p. 234), Medea on a dragon-drawn chariot (p. 95), King Midas surrounded by his golden treasures (p. 302), and the dramatic battle between Theseus and the Minotaur (pp. 129, 288). All these illustrations attest that the passing years have not dimmed the brilliant legacy of Gustav Schwab's Greek myths.

THE MYTHS

by Gustav Schwab

PROMETHEUS AND PANDORA

*A fate addressed by artists and poets again and again since antiquity:
Prometheus steals fire from the gods and brings it to mankind. Retribution for
this deed follows at once, and is horrific: Zeus has Prometheus fettered to a rock
in the Caucasus. The father of the gods sends Pandora to the mortals and she
pours out all the evils of the world from her box.*

Illustrations by Gustaf Tenggren, Milo Winter, and Walter Crane

PROMETHEUS AND PANDORA

Heaven and earth were created: the sea flowed back and forth along the earth's shores where fish played; twittering birds flew through the air and the ground was thronged with animals. But as yet there was no creature whose body was so designed that the spirit might create within it a home from which to rule the surrounding world. Then Prometheus, offspring of an ancient dynasty of gods overthrown by Zeus, descended to earth. As the son of Iapetus, earthborn son of Uranus, Prometheus was clever and quick-witted. Knowing full well that the seeds of heaven lay dormant in the soil, he scooped up some clay, which he moistened with water from the river and shaped it into an image to match that of the gods who ruled the world. To bring this clod of earth to life, he borrowed both good and bad traits from within all manner of creatures and embedded them in the heart of his human creation. Among the immortals, Prometheus had a good friend, Athena, Goddess of Wisdom. She admired the ingenuity of this son of a Titan and breathed the celestial spirit into the still unfinished being.

The first humans were thus created and soon they reproduced in vast numbers across the earth. However, they did not immediately understand how to use their noble limbs and the divine spark within them. They had eyes, but did not see, and ears, but did not hear. Like phantoms, they wandered aimlessly around, not knowing how to rely on their own resourcefulness. They knew nothing about the arts of quarrying and cutting stone, firing clay to make bricks, and cutting beams from trees chopped down in the forest. Nor did they know how to apply all these skills together to build houses for themselves. Scurrying about like ants in sunless underground caves, they noticed no signs of the arrival of winter, nor of spring in full bloom, nor trees weighed down with the fruits of summer. None of their activities were ever planned. But then Prometheus came

to help. He taught them to observe the rising and setting of the heavenly bodies; he taught them how to count and how to write; he taught them how to yoke animals together to ease the burden of labor in their communities. He trained horses to wear reins and pull wagons and he built boats with sails fit to travel by sea. He also attended to other aspects of people's lives. In the past, when a man fell ill, he knew nothing about possible remedies, nor about what he could or could not eat or drink. He had no knowledge of any salve that might soothe a wound. In truth, the lack of medicines meant people would die in great distress. Thus, Prometheus showed them how to mix mild remedies to treat all sorts of disease. Then he interpreted their dreams and taught them how to foretell the future, by reading signs such as birds in flight and the entrails of sacrificial animals. Furthermore, he showed them that beneath the soil they could discover ores, such as iron and silver, as well as gold. In short, he introduced them to the arts of life and all the comforts it could offer.

Meanwhile, Zeus and his children had recently seized power in heaven, having dethroned his father Cronus and toppled the older generation of gods, who were Prometheus's ancestors.

Now the new gods were taking an interest in the new creation – man. They demanded veneration in return for the protection they were willing to grant him. At Mecone in Greece, mortals and immortals met together to determine man's rights and obligations. At this meeting, Prometheus spoke as man's advocate, thus ensuring that the gods did not impose too heavy a price for protecting the beings he had created. On their behalf, the Titan's son then used his astuteness to seduce the gods. He slaughtered a huge bull and invited them to choose whichever parts they preferred. However, in cutting up the sacrificial beast, he had placed the pieces in two piles. On one side he heaped the meat, the entrails and the fat, which he covered with the animal's hide, placing its stomach on top. On the other side he

Page 33
No sooner had she reached Epimetheus than she quickly lifted the lid.

placed the bare bones, artfully concealed in the hard, white suet gathered from inside the bull. This was the largest pile. Zeus, all-seeing Father of the Gods, knew precisely what he had done and remarked, "Son of Iapetus, illustrious king and good friend, how unfairly you have divided the portions!" Now Prometheus was quite sure his trick had been successful. Smiling to himself, he replied, "Illustrious Zeus, greatest of the immortal gods, select whichever piece your heart bids you to choose." Zeus chose to conceal his anger. Instead he grasped the suet with both hands, tearing it apart to reveal the bare bones and making it seem as though he had only now discovered the deception. In anger he said, "I see very well, my friend, son of Iapetus, that you have not yet forgotten the art of deception!"

Zeus decided to take revenge on Prometheus and his trickery by refusing mortals the gift they needed to perfect their civilization – fire. However, the sly son of Iapetus knew how to handle this. He took a long stalk of pithy fennel and as he approached the passing chariot of the sun, he held the stalk towards it until it was set ablaze.

FROM THEN ON, ALL KINDS OF MISERY INVADED LAND, SEA, AND AIR.

With this kindling he returned to earth and soon sent brushwood blazing towards the sky. As he watched the flames rising upwards among the people, the bringer of thunder felt pain in his innermost soul. He immediately grasped that since mortals no longer lacked fire, he had to confront them with a new evil. He commissioned the fire god Hephaestus, famed for his artistic skills, to fashion an image of a beautiful young woman. Athena herself, who had become envious of Prometheus and had since withdrawn her favors, cast a shimmering white robe across the woman's figure and covered her face with a flowing veil, which the maiden held apart with both hands. Athena then crowned the maiden's head with fresh flowers bound together by a band of gold. Hephaestus was closely involved with the work and, to please his father, used his artistic talent to produce colorful animal-shaped trimmings. Hermes, the messenger god, instilled language into the beautiful creation, while Aphrodite furnished her with charm. In the guise of something wonderful, Zeus had created a ferocious stroke of evil. He named the young maiden Pandora, which meant "recipient of gifts from all around," since each of the immortals had bestowed upon her an ill-omened offering to be passed on to the mortals. Zeus then led the maiden down to earth where both mortals and gods strolled at leisure, all of them filled with admiration for this incomparable creature. Prometheus had warned his sibling never to accept offerings from the ruler of Olympus and to return them at once, before they could cause harm among mortals. Nevertheless Epimetheus – whose name meant "mindless" – warmly welcomed the beautiful young woman. He did not feel the presence of anything evil until it was right upon him. Until that moment, under the guidance of his brother Prometheus, human society had lived free of adversity, without backbreaking work or distressing disease. But the woman held in her hands her gift, packed in a large, lidded box. No sooner had she reached Epimetheus than she quickly lifted the lid, immediately releasing a multitude of trials and tribulations which would spread at high speed across the earth. The only thing of value, hidden at the bottom of the box, was hope. Even so, at the father of the gods' instruction, Pandora shut the lid so that hope might never escape. From then on, all kinds of misery invaded land, sea, and air. Day and night, disease spread secretly and silently among mortals, for Zeus had given them no voice. The earth was besieged by hordes of pestilences and death, which before had only slowly crept up on mortals now moved as if on wings.

Now Zeus addressed the matter of taking revenge on Prometheus. He handed the miscreant over to Hephaestus and his servants Kratos and Bia, whose names meant "force" and "violence." The pair were ordered to drag Prometheus to the Scythian wastelands and to hang him there above a

PROMETHEUS AND PANDORA

Pandora had a gift, a large lidded box.

terrifying abyss, shackled to a rock face of the Caucasus Mountains with unbreakable chains. Hephaestus obeyed his father's orders reluctantly, for he loved the Titan's son, a child of the gods, a descendant of his own great-grandfather Uranus and hence his own kin. Speaking compassionate words, much to the disgust of his more malicious servants, he carried out his gruesome task. Now Prometheus was forced to hang horror-struck, upright, sleepless and unable to bend his weary knees. "You will send out protests and sighs, but they will all be in vain," Hephaestus told him. "For Zeus's design is unrelenting. All of those who have seized power for themselves are heartless. Zeus brought down his father Cronus, thus toppling the ancient dynasty of the gods, and seized Olympus by force (Iapetus and Cronus were brothers, Prometheus and Zeus were siblings)." In fact, the prisoner's sufferings were intended to last forever, or for at least thirty thousand years. Although he moaned aloud, calling upon winds, rivers, springs and ocean waves, Mother Earth and the all-seeing zodiac to witness his pain, his spirit remained unbroken. "Whoever among us has learned to recognize the invincible power of necessity must bear whatever fate decrees," he said. Nor did he give in to the threats of Zeus, always refusing to explain his sinister prediction that a new union between the king of the gods and the goddess Thetis would almost certainly lead to his downfall and destruction. Zeus was true to his word. Each day he sent an eagle to feed on the captive's liver which, however much the bird of prey consumed, always grew back again. This torture was designed to last until such time as there arrived another who, of his own free will, would be ready to suffer in Prometheus's place.

Such a moment arrived sooner than the condemned son of the Titans had expected. After many years hanging from the cliff, along came Heracles who was on his way to search for the golden apples of the Hesperides. Heracles sought advice about his intended quest from Prometheus, but when he saw the descendant of the gods shackled to the Caucasian Mountains, he was filled with pity. He saw how the eagle perched on the unfortunate Prometheus's knees and devoured his liver. Laying his lion's skin on the ground, he bent his bow and shot his arrow into the cruel bird, tearing it away from the liver of its anguished victim. He then loosened Prometheus's chains and led him away. Then to comply with Zeus's conditions, he brought the centaur Chiron, who offered to die in Prometheus's place, even though he could claim immortality. However, the son of Cronus's ruling had to be obeyed in full. Since Prometheus had been condemned to spend a much longer time chained to the cliff-face, he would always be obliged to wear an iron ring set with a small stone from that same cliff. Thus, Zeus could still boast that his enemy remained shackled to a mountain in the Caucasus.

EUROPA

How a continent acquired its name:
Zeus disguises himself as a handsome bull and abducts Europa,
the daughter of a Phoenician king, taking her on his back to Crete.
There she gives birth to Minos, later king of Crete. Aphrodite tells
Europa that the foreign continent will bear her name in the future.

Illustrations by Edmund Dulac and Virginia Frances Sterrett

EUROPA

The next day she sailed through endless waters seated on the beast.

It was in the land of Tyre and Sidon that Europa, daughter of King Agenor, grew up in the quiet seclusion of her father's palace. It was here, in the midnight hours, that mortals were often visited by dreams, some of them strange but seemingly sent straight from heaven. In one such dream, it seemed to her that two parts of the world, Asia and the part lying opposite, came to her in the guise of women, each fighting to claim her as their own. One of the women had a foreign-looking face, while the other, Asia, shared the appearance and gestures of Europa's own country-women. Full of tender enthusiasm and warmth, this woman insisted that *she* was the one who had borne and nurtured Europa, her lovely little daughter. The stranger then wrapped her strong arms around the child as if to abduct her and hurried away, while Europa felt no desire to struggle and escape. "Come with me, my darling," said the stranger, "and I shall take you to Zeus, bearer of the shield of Athena, for you are destined to be with him." With beating heart, Europa awoke and sat up from her couch, for her night-time vision had been as clear as day. For a long time she remained upright and motionless on the bed, staring straight ahead to where the two women stood before her wide-open eyes. At last her lips moved as she spoke nervously to herself. "What god has sent me this vision?" she asked. "What kind of extraordinary dream startled me while

I slept safe and sound in my father's house? Who was the strange woman I saw in my dream? What new kind of longing did she arouse in my heart? How lovingly she approached me, and even when she carried me away by force she looked at me and smiled at me like a loving mother! May the gods be showing my dreams as a good omen."

Morning had come and the pale light of day blended with the nocturnal glow of Europa's dreams, driving the visions from her mind and bringing her back to the usual tasks and pleasures that were part of a young girl's life. Soon she was surrounded by friends and playmates, girls of her own age, the daughters of noble houses. Together they danced, sang, and observed the rites of sacrificial offerings. This time they invited their young mistress to come for a walk with them to a meadow where girls from the neighborhood went to enjoy the many kinds of flowers scattered among the grass and to hear the sound of surf washing against the shore.

But they could not delight in the flowers for long. As predicted in her dream of the night before, fate suddenly intruded upon Europa's carefree girlhood. Zeus, son of Cronus, shot by the arrow of Aphrodite, goddess of love, the only one of the immortals able to triumph over the invincible father of the gods, was moved by young Europa's beauty. Even so, overwhelmed by his fear of Hera's jealous wrath, he could scarcely hope to arouse the senses of the innocent maiden, so he cunningly devised a plot. He changed himself into a bull. But what a bull! Nothing like the beast that moves across a commonplace field, bowed under a yoke and hauling an overloaded wagon. No, this one was a splendid specimen, with bulging neck muscles and massive shoulders. His horns were small and delicate as though fashioned by hand and more transparent than genuine jewels. His body was colored yellow-gold, but right in the middle of his forehead there shimmered a silvery-white mark, resembling the curved shape of the crescent moon. His eyes of brilliant blue rolled in their sockets, gleaming with desire. The handsome creature wandered through the lush grass. His horns were no threat, his flashing eyes aroused no fear. He was the very picture of gentleness. Europa and her maidens admired the animal's noble figure and his peaceful demeanor. They wanted to look at him more closely and stroke his glittering back. The bull appeared to be aware of this and gently moved closer until he could stand right in front of Europa. Startled at first, she took several steps backwards, but when the beast stood motionless and calm, she summoned up the courage to approach him and hold her bouquet of flowers to his foaming mouth, from which he breathed out the scent of ambrosia. The bull lovingly licked the flowers presented to him and the tender feminine hand that had wiped the foam from his lips and began to stroke him tenderly. The maiden became evermore enchanted by the noble creature and even dared to plant a kiss on his shining forehead. At this, the beast let out a joyous bellow, yet he did not roar like other common bulls but made a sound like the notes of a Lydian flute, reverberating down a mountain valley. Then he crouched down at the feet of the beautiful princess, looking at her longingly, then turning his head as if to show her his broad back. Europa then called to her maidens. "Come closer, my dear playmates, it will be fun for us to climb onto the back of this handsome bull. I think there is

ZEUS, SHOT BY THE ARROW OF APHRODITE, WAS MOVED BY YOUNG EUROPA'S BEAUTY.

room for four of us. He looks so tame, so gentle and so charming. Not at all like other bulls. I truly believe he has the same power of reason as a human. All he lacks is speech." As she spoke, she took the wreaths of flowers one by one from the hands of her companions and hung them on the bull's lowered horns. Then, with a smile on her face, she sprang on to his back, while her friends stood watching, hesitating and full of uncertainty.

As for the bull, having seized the maiden he desired, he leaped from the ground. At first he moved slowly and steadily as he carried her, but fast enough for prevent her friends keeping pace with him. With the meadow behind him and the deserted beach ahead, he doubled his speed. He now seemed less like a gently trotting bull than a galloping steed. And before Europa knew what was happening, he leapt into the sea and swam away with his quarry. With her right hand, the maiden clutched one of his horns and with the left hand steadied herself on his back. The wind filled her gown as if it were a sail. Fearfully, she looked back at the land she had left behind and called out to her comrades, but to no avail. As they sailed with the water lapping against the bull's side, she raised her dainty feet for fear of soaking them. But the bull floated like a ship. Soon the shore disappeared from view, the sun set, and in the darkness the unfortunate girl could see nothing around her but waves and stars. And so the journey continued. The next day she sailed through endless waters seated on the beast, who so cleverly cut through the waves that not a drop fell on his beloved captive. Finally, towards evening, they reached a faraway land. The bull swung himself ashore, then gently slipped the young woman off his back and into the shade of the vaulting bows of a tree, before disappearing from sight. In his place there appeared a handsome godlike man. He explained that he was the ruler of the island of Crete and would protect her if she surrendered herself to him. Amid feelings of loneliness and despair, Europa

EUROPA

He cut through the waves so cleverly that not a drop fell on his beloved captive.

gave him her hand as a token of agreement, and Zeus accomplished his wish.

Numbed after a long sleep, Europa awakened when the morning sun already stood high in the heavens. She found she was alone, looking around as if lost and trying to find her way home. "Father, father!" she called with a piercing cry of pain, then had second thoughts. "How can I, a pampered daughter, even dare to speak the word 'father'? What madness has made me forget the love between parent and child?" She looked around again, as if thinking back to what had happened. "Where did I come from and where have I come to?" she wondered. "Death alone is too light a penalty for a virgin like me. But am I really awake? Am I lamenting a real dishonor? No, I am certainly innocent of everything and my mind is being taunted by something trivial, something only seen in a dream which will soon disappear during one's early morning sleep! And how could I possibly have decided to swim the endless seas riding on the back of a monster rather than gather flowers in the safest of places?" As she spoke, she drew the palm of her hand across her eyelids, as if to erase the abhorrent fantasy. But when she looked around, unfamiliar trees and rocks surrounded her and a strangely foaming tide crashed onto an unrecognized shore and against the tall, unyielding cliffs. "Oh, if someone could bring the bull to me

now," she cried in despair, "how I would delight in tearing away his flesh and not rest until I had broken the horns of the monster who once I found so lovable. But to wish is all in vain! After I have shamelessly left home, what more can I do but die? If not all the gods have abandoned me, let them send me a lion or a tiger! Perhaps they will be attracted by my beauty and I need not wait until starvation devours the glow of my cheeks."

In this way the unfortunate young woman tortured herself with thoughts of death, unable to summon up the courage to die. Then suddenly she heard a mocking whisper and turned around quickly, fearing the presence of an eavesdropper. Standing before her in supernatural splendor was the goddess Aphrodite with her small son, Eros, God of Love, next to her with his bow lowered. A smile hovered on the lips of the goddess, who then said, "Forget your anger and discontent, sweet maiden! The bull you so detest will come and hold out his horns so that you may break them in pieces. Take comfort, Europa! I was the one who sent you the dream you had in your father's house. He who abducted you was Zeus. You are the mortal spouse of the undefeatable god and your name will be immortal. For the strange continent to which you were taken shall henceforth be called Europe!"

CADMUS

Founding a city in an extraordinary way:
Apollo orders Cadmus, king in Phoenicia, to establish the city of Thebes in central Greece.
What seems like a straightforward undertaking is, however, beset with difficulties.
Cadmus first has to subdue a dragon and sow its teeth, with unexpected consequences.
He does succeed in the end.

Illustrations by Virginia Frances Sterrett

CADMUS

Cadmus was the son of Agenor, king of Phoenicia and Europa's brother. When his sister was carried away by Zeus, in the guise of a bull, her father sent Cadmus and his brothers in search of her, telling them they would not be allowed to return without her. For a long time, he journeyed in vain across the world, unable to hunt down the devious god Zeus. Having lost hope of ever finding his sister and fearing his father's anger, Cadmus sought the counsel of Phoebus Apollo and asked in which land he might dwell for the rest of his life. Apollo advised him, "In a lonely meadow, you will meet a cow who has never borne a yoke. You must let her lead you to a place where she chooses to rest among the grass. There you must build ramparts to surround a city which you will name Thebes." Cadmus had scarcely left the Castalian Spring, site of Apollo's oracle, when he came upon a green field where a heifer, with a neck showing no sign of having labored under the yoke, was grazing. Silently praying to Phoebus, he slowly followed in the animal's tracks. She had already waded across the ford of the River Cephissus, continuing on to a wide strip of land where she stopped and filled the air with her lowing. Then, looking at Cadmus and his attendants, she finally laid down on the lush grass.

Full of gratitude, Cadmus threw himself down and kissed the unfamiliar earth. There he prepared to make an offering to Zeus. He ordered his servants to search for a living spring to provide water for his offering to the god. They found such a place, an ancient wood where none of the trees at its center had ever been hewn by axes. There, rocks linked bushes and undergrowth to create a vault across a gorge running with spring water. Hidden in this cavern lay a vicious dragon. Its scarlet crest could be seen from afar and fire spurted from its eyes. Its body was bloated with venom and it was armed with three sizzling tongues and a mouth filled with three rows of teeth. Just as the Phoenicians entered the grove and lowered their pitcher into the rippling water, the azure dragon suddenly thrust its head out of its cave and let out a terrifying hiss. The urns slid from the servants' hands and their blood ran cold. The dragon coiled its scaly body, drew backwards, ready to strike, and reared to half its height to see across the wood. Then it plunged towards the Phoenicians. Some it killed with its teeth, others by twisting its body around them and crushing them to death, and the rest it killed by poisoning them with its evil spittle and its putrid breath.

Cadmus did not know why his servants were taking so long. Finally, he went in search of them. Wearing a skin he had torn from a lion, he armed himself with a lance, a javelin and an even better weapon – a valiant heart. Immediately upon entering the grove, he saw the bodies of his murdered servants and above them the enemy, its body bloated and its tongue lapping up its victims' blood. "My poor friends," he wailed, "I shall either be your avenger or your companion in death!" With that, the hero grabbed a piece of rock and hurled it at the dragon. The stone was large enough to have shaken walls and towers, but the dragon stood unscathed, its thick black hide and solid scales protected it like a suit of armor. Then he threw his javelin which struck the monster, the iron point sinking deep into its entrails. Roaring with pain, the dragon turned its head backwards, crushing the shaft of the javelin but sinking the point into its body. A stroke of the sword caused the beast's anger to mount, its throat swelling and more foam

CADMUS

Page 43
He told them they would not be allowed to return without Europa.

Page 44
Silently praying to Phoebus, he slowly followed in the animal's tracks.

Below
Full of gratitude, Cadmus threw himself down and kissed the unfamiliar earth.

*Its thick black hide and solid scales
protected it like a suit of armor.*

gushing from its poisonous jaws. Straight as an arrow, the dragon burst forth until its breast crashed against the trunks of the trees. The son of Agenor sidestepped the oncoming attack, letting the dragon sink its teeth into the tip of his spear. At last, blood began to flow from the monster's throat, staining the green grass around it. But it was only a minor wound and the dragon still escaped every thrust, so preventing its adversary from striking again. Soon, however, Cadmus buried his sword in the dragon's throat, so deeply that it came out on the other side, piercing an oak tree so deeply that the beast was nailed to the trunk. The tree was dragged downwards by its weight, moaning as it felt the tip of the monster's tail tearing against its bark. At last the enemy was defeated.

For a long time Cadmus fixed his eyes upon the slaughtered dragon. When he stopped and looked around him, he saw Pallas Athena, who had descended from heaven and was now bidding him to immediately turn over the soil and bury the monster's teeth, thereby sowing the seed of a future race. Obeying the goddess's instructions, he plowed a wide furrow in the ground and began scattering the seeds all along it. All at once the clods of earth began to move and there emerged first the point of a

"I SHALL EITHER BE YOUR AVENGER OR YOUR COMPANION IN DEATH!"

lance, then a helmet with a crest of colorful plumes, followed by shoulders, chest and limbs, as a fully-armed warrior sprang from the soil. The same happened in many places at once, and an entire crop of armed men appeared before the Phoenician's very eyes.

The son of Agenor was so startled that he made ready to fight another foe. But one of the earthborn adversaries called to him, "Lay down your arms. Do not intervene in a domestic feud!" The speaker immediately raised his sword against another warrior and was at the same time struck down by a flying javelin. The thrower of the deadly weapon was in turn fatally wounded. The combatants on both sides engaged in bitter battle until almost all of them lay on the ground, convulsed in the throes of death, and Mother Earth drank the blood of the sons she had so recently borne. Only five remained. One of them – who was later called Echion – was the first to throw down his arms at Athena's bidding. The others followed his example.

In the company of these five earthborn warriors, Cadmus, the stranger from Phoenicia, built the city as commanded by the oracle of Phoebus Apollo, and, as the latter had ordered, named it Thebes.

PERSEUS

Even the sons of gods do not always have it easy:
Perseus, son of Zeus and Danae, must decapitate Medusa, the terrible Gorgon.
Anyone who looks Medusa in the face is turned to stone. But Athena helps
Perseus to accomplish the task, and Pegasus, a winged horse, springs fully
formed from Medusa's bleeding neck.

Illustrations by William Russell Flint and Henry Justice Ford

Perseus, son of Zeus, and his mother Danae were locked in a chest and cast into the sea by his grandfather, King Acrisius of Argos. All this because an oracle had announced to the monarch that his grandson would murder him and seize the throne. Zeus guided them through stormy seas until they landed on the island of Seriphos, ruled by two brothers, Dictys and Polydectes. Dictys was fishing when he saw the chest floating towards land and dragged it ashore. Both brothers treated the lost souls with great affection. Polydectes made the mother his wife and carefully raised Zeus's son.

When Perseus was fully grown, his stepfather encouraged him to go in search of adventure and to achieve something that would bring him fame and admiration. The brave young man was willing and soon they both agreed that Perseus should seek out the Medusa, slice off her terrible head and bring it home to the king on Seriphos. Perseus set off and, guided by the gods, found his way to a far-off region where Phorcys, father to many hideous monsters, lived. First, he met three of his daughters, known as the Graeae, or Gray Sisters, since they had been gray-haired since birth. Between them, they had only one eye and one tooth, which each took her turn to use. Perseus robbed them of both and when they pleaded with him to return their most essential possessions, he agreed to do so on one condition – that they showed him the way to the nymphs. These magical nymphs each had a pair of winged shoes, a satchel and a helmet made of dog hide. Wearers of such items could fly to wherever they wished, see whatever or whoever they wished to see, without themselves being seen. Phorcys's daughters directed Perseus to the nymphs and he returned their tooth and eye. The nymphs told Perseus what he needed to know and gave him what he wanted. He threw the satchel over his shoulder, fastened the winged shoes around his ankles, and set the helmet on his head. Hermes also lent him a

ONLY THE THIRD DAUGHTER, MEDUSA BY NAME, WAS MORTAL.

sickle-shaped shield of hardened steel and, thus equipped, he flew towards the ocean where Phorcys's other three daughters, the Gorgons, lived. Only the third daughter, Medusa by name, was mortal, which was why Perseus had been sent to cut off her head. He found the Gorgons sleeping. Instead of skin, they were covered with dragons' scales and their heads sprouted snakes instead of hair. Their teeth were like the tusks of a boar, their hands were of metal, and their wings of gold enabled them to fly. Perseus knew that anyone who looked at them would be turned to stone, so he stood with his back to the sleeping creatures and saw all three reflected on his hard, glittering shield and singled out the Medusa. Athena guided his hand and he cut off the monster's head effortlessly. No sooner had he done this when there sprang from her body Pegasus, the winged horse, followed by a giant named Chrysaor, both offspring of Poseidon. Perseus hid the Medusa's head in his satchel, walking backwards as he had when he first appeared. Meanwhile, the Medusa's sisters had awakened and risen from their couch. They caught sight of their dead sister's body and rose upon their wings to pursue her killer. But the nymphs' helmet made Perseus invisible and they could not see him. As he flew above the earth, Perseus was tossed back and forth like a rain cloud. As he swept across the sandy wastes of Libya, drops of blood from the Medusa's head trickled down to the earth below, where they changed into many-colored serpents. Since then, Libya has been infested by poisonous vipers and adders. Perseus then flew further westward and finally landed in the realm of King Atlas, where he intended to rest awhile. The king owned an orchard where he cultivated golden fruits, guarded by a mighty dragon. The conqueror of the Gorgon sought shelter there for a single night, but in vain. Atlas, fearing for his golden treasures, hard-heartedly threw him out of the palace. This enraged Perseus, who said, "Since you have no wish to do as I ask, it is I who shall offer you a gift!" Turning his head aside, he drew the Gorgon's head from his satchel and held it

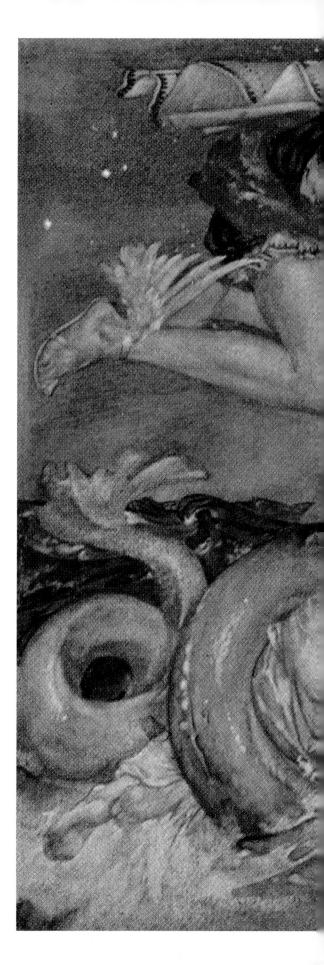

Wearers of such items could fly to wherever they wished, see whatever or whoever they wished to see, without themselves being seen.

out to King Atlas. The king was instantly turned to stone, and because of his gigantic stature he was transformed into a mountain. His beard and the hair on his head became forests; shoulders, hands and bones became rocky ridges and his head became a peak rising high into the clouds. Perseus bound his winged sandals back on his feet, strapped on his satchel, put on his helmet and leapt into the air. As he flew, he came upon the coast of Ethiopia, where King Cepheus ruled. There he saw a girl chained to a cliff that jutted into the sea. If her hair had not been ruffled by a light breeze, if her eyes were not overflowing with tears, he would have thought she was a statue hewn from marble. So enchanted was he by her beauty that he almost forgot to move his wings. "Tell me, sweet maiden," he called, "why are you, who deserves to wear quite different jewels, bound in chains? Tell me the name of your country and tell me your own name!" Shackled as she was, the young woman remained silent and shy, afraid to speak to a stranger. Had she been able to move, she would have covered her face with her hands. All she could do was to let her eyes fill with tears. At last, fearing that the young man would think she was hiding some guilt of her own, she replied. "I am Andromeda, daughter of Cepheus, king of Ethiopia. My mother boasted to the sea nymphs, who are daughters of Nereus, that she was more beautiful than them. This enraged the Nereids and their friend, the sea god, released a flood and with it a shark that devours everything in its path. An oracle promised that we would be saved from danger if I, the king's daughter, were thrown to feed the fish. My father was urged by his people to seize the opportunity to rescue them. So, in desperation, he had me chained to the cliff."

She had barely spoken the final words when the waves rushed in and from the depths of the sea there rose a monster whose vast torso stretched across the surface of the water. The girl screamed aloud and at once her parents ran towards her, both of them in despair, her mother's sorrow made deeper by her feelings of guilt. They threw their arms around their daughter but had nothing to offer her but tears and cries of anguish. Then the stranger spoke. "There will be plenty of time for tears later, but we must act now. I am Perseus, son of Zeus and Danae, I have triumphed over the Gorgon and can fly through the air on

*The nymphs told Perseus what he needed to
know and gave him what he wanted.*

magic wings. Even if the maiden were free and had choice in the matter, I would make you no mean son-in-law! Now, in offering to save her, I also ask for her hand. Do you accept my terms?" Who could have hesitated in such circumstances? The delighted parents promised him not only their daughter but also their kingdom as her dowry.

As they considered the situation, the monster was approaching like a fast-moving galley and would soon be a stone's throw away. Then suddenly, thrusting his foot against the ground, the young man took off into the air. The beast sped forward, furiously scenting the presence of an enemy about to steal its prey. Perseus dove from the sky like an eagle, swooping down onto the shark's back. He took the sword that killed the Medusa and plunged it into the shark's back up to the hilt. Hardly had he withdrawn the blade when the fish leapt high into the air and dived back into the water, rampaging in every direction like a boar pursued by a pack of hounds. Perseus dealt the creature one wound after another until stream of black blood gushed from its throat. Now the demigod's wings were soaking wet and Perseus did not dare rely on his waterlogged plumage.

Fortunately, he caught sight of a reef, whose highest point rose above the sea. Supporting himself with his left hand against a rock face, while with his right he drove the blade three or four times into the creature's guts. The sea carried the massive corpse away and soon it disappeared under the water. Meanwhile, Perseus leapt ashore, climbed the cliff and loosened the bonds of the young maiden, who welcomed him with looks of gratitude and love. He led her to her jubilant parents, whose golden palace was about to welcome him as the bridegroom. The wedding feast was still hot and the carefree hours flew by for the parents, the bridegroom and the unfettered bride, when suddenly the palace courtyards were filled with a muffled but furious uproar. Phineus, brother of King Cepheus, who once had wooed his niece Andromeda but abandoned her in her hour of need, had arrived with a band of armed warriors to renew his claims. Brandishing his spear, he marched into the wedding hall and yelled at the astonished Perseus, "I am here to avenge the theft of the bride who was torn away from me. Neither your wings nor your father Zeus can help you escape from me!" Even as he spoke, he aimed his spear. King Cepheus

PERSEUS

Perseus dove from the sky like an eagle.

rose and called to his brother. "Brother, are you mad? What outrageous notions have led you to behave in this way? Perseus did not steal your beloved. You yourself gave her up when we were forced to consent to her killing, and you stood by as she was put in chains and did nothing to help her, neither as her uncle nor her lover. Why did you not seize the prize from the cliff yourself? Due to this man, the rescue of my daughter will comfort me in my old age. Now leave the man who has nobly won her in peace!"

Phineus did not reply but merely shot angry glances at his brother and at his rival, as if attempting to decide which of the two he should aim at first. Finally, after a brief hesitation, he hurled his spear at Perseus with a force inspired by anger. But he missed, and the weapon buried its point in a cushion. Then Perseus leapt to his feet and flung his javelin towards the door through which Phineus had forced his way in. The javelin would have pierced the latter's breast, had he not escaped by diving behind a household shrine. The shot struck one of Phineus's followers in the forehead and the intruder's entourage were now engaged in hand-to-hand fighting with wedding guests who had long since risen from the table in fear. The battle was long and violent, but the guests were far outnumbered by the intruders. At last Perseus, with his bride and her parents standing close to him for protection, found himself surrounded by Phineus's warriors. Their arrows raced through the air like hailstones in a storm. To cover his back, Perseus leaned against a column. From this vantage point, he watched the host of foes as they moved forward, and he killed them one after another. Only when he realized that valor alone was not enough to defeat them did he resort to the most infallible means at his disposal. "I have no choice," he announced. "I shall seek the help of an old enemy. Those who consider me a friend, please turn away now." With these words, he reached into the satchel that even now he wore across his shoulders, drew out the Medusa's head and held it up to the first approaching attacker. The man took one look and sardonically shouted, "Go find someone else to shock with your miracle." But even as he raised his hand to throw the javelin, he turned to stone. The same happened to one man after another. With only two hundred survivors, Perseus lifted the Gorgon's head high into the air so that all might see it. And all two hundred were transformed into solid rock. Moving among the dead,

Meanwhile, Perseus leapt ashore, climbed the cliff, and loosened the bonds of the young maiden.

Phineus called his friends by name and touched with disbelief the bodies of those closest to him. They had all turned to marble. Seized with horror, his defiance turned to humiliation. "Just leave me my life," he pleaded. "The bride and the kingdom shall be yours," he cried, turning away a countenance fraught with despair. Mourning the deaths of his new friends, Perseus showed no mercy. "Traitor!" he roared in anger. "I shall erect an enduring monument to you in the house of my parents-in-law!" As hard as he had tried to look away, Phineus was forced to turn his eyes towards the indescribably hideous head.

HIS BODY FROZE, THE TEARS IN HIS EYES TURNED TO STONE.

His body froze, the tears in his eyes turned to stone. He stood bolt upright, his neck stiffening, his hands dangling by his sides, in the manner of a servant expected to undertake humble, menial tasks. Now, nothing could prevent Perseus from taking home his beloved wife, Andromeda. Long, happy days were ahead of them and he was reunited with his mother, Danae. However, he still had to fulfill his responsibility for the fate of his grandfather, Acrisius. His fear of the oracle had driven Acrisius to take shelter in an alien land ruled by the king of the Pelasgians. Here, Acrisius was watching an athletic competition when suddenly, Perseus appeared. He was on his way to Argos and had stopped to greet his grandfather and to compete in the games. By terrible misfortune, a discus thrown by his grandson struck Acrisius on the head. The young man soon became aware of what he had done. In deep mourning, he buried his grandfather outside the city and went on to exchange the kingdom of Argos, bequeathed to him by Acrisius, for the kingdoms of Tiryns and Midea, ruled by his cousin, Megapenthes. From then on, he was no longer pursued by others who envied him. Andromeda bore him many splendid sons, in whom their father's glory lived on.

DAEDALUS AND ICARUS

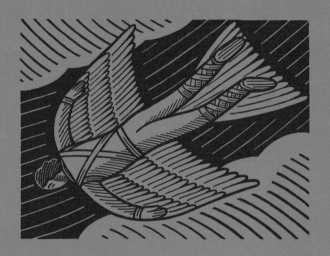

Heedless arrogance, with tragic consequences:
Daedalus, celebrated architect of the legendary labyrinth on Crete, plans
to flee with his son, Icarus, from the island on wings he has constructed of wax
and feathers. Icarus ignores his father's warnings, and blithely soars sunward.
The sun's heat melts his waxen wings and Icarus plunges into the sea.

Illustrations by Constance N. Baikie and Charles Edmund Brock

DAEDALUS AND ICARUS

"Always fly the middle course, dear boy."

Daedalus of Athens, son of Metion, great-grandson of Erechtheus, was also a member of the family of the Erechtheides. Master builder and architect, stone carver and sculptor, he was one of the most accomplished artists of his era. His works were admired in many parts of the world, and those who saw his statues described them as "living," "moving," and "seeing." Admirers saw them as sentient beings, rather than mere images. While earlier masters sculpted statues with eyes closed and hands dangling loosely down the sides of the body, he was the first to endow his creations with open eyes, outstretched hands, and feet that appeared to walk. While Daedalus was a consummate craftsman, his attitude towards his art was vain and self-satisfied – a failing that was to lead him into misconduct and eventual despair. He taught his own artistic skills to his sister's son, Talus, but found that the pupil was far more talented than his tutor. At a very young age, Talus had invented the potter's wheel. Later, using the jaws of a snake he had come across and killed, he found the reptile's jawbone could cut through a small plank of wood. He then made an iron version of the tool, with a row of zigzagging teeth carved along the edge, thus gaining recognition as the inventor of the saw. This was before he created the first wood-turning lathe by joining two metal arms, one of which stayed still while the other turned. His reputation grew further still as he continued to design other ingenious craft tools, all without the help of his master, who began to fear that

Talus's renown would outshine his own. Overwhelmed by jealousy, Daedalus surreptitiously murdered the young man by throwing him down from the Acropolis in Athens. However, when a passerby caught him digging his nephew's grave, he claimed to be burying a snake. Even so, Areopagus, the supreme court of Athens, tried him for murder and found him guilty. Daedalus escaped and at first wandered as a fugitive around Attica before fleeing to Crete, where King Minos offered him sanctuary, friendship, and the high regard due to a famous artist. The king also commissioned him to build a dwelling for the Minotaur – a hybrid creature of evil parentage with the head and shoulders of a bull and the body of a man. The idea was to design a space that would leave those who entered completely bewildered. Drawing on his innate inventiveness, Daedalus decided to build a labyrinth, a structure of tortuous twists and turns to disconcert the eyes and feet of any stranger who might arrive there. The countless corridors intertwined with each other like the tangled course of the Phrygia's River Maeander, which desperately struggles forward and backward, often colliding with its own waves. When building was complete and Daedalus set out to inspect the finished work, even he had difficulty in finding his way back to the threshold of that circuitous structure of his own invention. The Minotaur dwelt at the very heart of the labyrinth where every nine years he feasted on seven young boys and seven young maidens, whom, under the terms of an ancient agreement, Athens was obliged to send as a tribute to the king of Crete.

DAEDALUS AND ICARUS

Meanwhile, the long exile from his beloved homeland was becoming an ever-increasing burden for Daedalus, who grew more and more tortured by the idea of spending his entire life on an island surrounded by sea and ruled by a tyrant who trusted no one, not even his friends. A man of inventive spirit, he contemplated a means of escape. After lengthy consideration, he exclaimed with joy, "I have found the way out! Even if Minos prevents me from escaping by land or sea, there is still the air, over which he has no control! Powerful he may be, he does not rule the air, so that will be my chosen way out!" No sooner said than done. Daedalus's resourcefulness led him to seek help from nature. He began by arranging bird feathers according to size, in such a way that they seemed to have grown naturally to increasing lengths. He then bound the feathers together, in the middle with linen thread, on the ends with wax. Then he bent them into a barely perceptible curve, making them look like wings. Daedalus had a son named Icarus. The boy stood beside his father, watching him at work and lending him a juvenile hand. Then he reached out for the feathers, whose down stirred with the breeze, before kneading between his thumb and forefinger the yellow wax that his skillful father used. The latter simply stood by and watched, smiling at his child's ineptness. After giving a finishing touch to the work, Daedalus fitted the wings to his own body, briefly balancing himself before floating up into the air, light as a bird. Then, having returned to the ground, he instructed young Icarus how to use the wings he had fashioned specially for him. "Always fly the middle course, dear boy," he said. "If you fly too low, your wings will touch the sea and the water will weigh you down and pull you into the waves. If you

"IF YOU FLY TOO LOW, THE WATER WILL PULL YOU INTO THE SEA. IF YOU CLIMB TOO HIGH, YOU WILL COME TOO CLOSE TO THE SUN AND CATCH FIRE."

climb too high into the air, your plumage will come too close to the sun and catch fire. So fly between sea and sun and always follow me from close behind." With this warning, he bound the wings to the boy's shoulders, but as he did so, his old man's hands trembled and fearful tears trickled onto them. He took the boy in his arms and kissed him for what would be the last time.

Now the two of them were lifted by their wings. The father flew ahead, like a mother bird leading her tender fledglings from the nest and into the air for the first time. He beat his wings with precision and artistry, in the hope that his son might follow his lead, from time to time looking back to see how the boy was faring. At first all went well. Soon they passed the island of Samos on their left, before flying over Delos and Paros. They had seen several coasts disappear when young Icarus, full of daring and now convinced he had mastered the art of flying, ceased to follow his father and headed up into higher zones. But there was no escaping the threatened punishment. Now too close to the sun's powerful rays, the wax holding the feathers in place melted and before Icarus knew it, his wings dissolved and fell from his shoulders. The ill-fated boy tried to fly with his bare arms, but they could not keep him airborne and suddenly he plunged down into the sea. His father's name was on his lips but before he could speak it, the deep blue sea had closed over him. It all happened so quickly that when Daedalus looked back, as he had been doing from time to time, he no longer saw his son. "Icarus, Icarus," he called despairingly through the empty space. "Where in the sky should I search for you?" At last, casting his fear-filled eyes downwards, he saw feathers floating in the water. At once he descended and, laying

DAEDALUS AND ICARUS

*The father flew ahead, like a mother bird
leading her tender fledglings from the nest
and into the air for the first time.*

his wings aside, he paced dejectedly back and forth along the water's edge until the waves washed his son's body onto the sand. Now Talus's murder was avenged. The time had come for the inconsolable father to bury his child. The boy's body had been swept ashore on an island and it was there that he was laid to rest. In eternal memory of that tragic event, the island became known as Icaria.

After burying his son, Daedalus left the island and traveled to the great island of Sicily. This island was ruled by King Cocalus, who gave his visitor the same warm welcome he had once received from Minos of Crete. The people of Sicily greatly admired Daedalus's work. For many years, one of Sicily's most appreciated sights was the artificial lake he had created, from which a wide river flowed into the nearby ocean. And on a rocky plateau so steep it was impossible to storm, where there was only space for a few trees, he built a walled city. Winding up to the ramparts was a path so narrow that only three or four men were needed to defend the fortress. It was in this impregnable stronghold that King Cocalus chose to keep his most treasured possessions.

The third work that Daedalus had accomplished on the island of Sicily was a deep cave. There, he controlled so skillfully the steam from subterranean fires that the usually cold, damp grotto felt as comfortable as a mildly heated room, where the visitor's body perspired gently without having to tolerate excessive heat. He also extended Aphrodite's temple on Mount Eryx. There, he fashioned a golden honeycomb to be dedicated to the goddess, so ingeniously molded that the cells could have been the work of the bees themselves.

Now King Minos, from whose island Daedalus had fled in secret, heard that the master builder had escaped to Sicily and decided to pursue him with a large contingent of warlords. He armed a vast fleet and sailed with them from Crete to Agrigento. There he disembarked his land forces and sent a message to King Cocalus, calling upon him to extradite the fugitive. Cocalus, however, was enraged at the demand made by this tyrannical foreigner and looked for ways and means to bring about his downfall. He made it seem that he was willing to do as the Cretan wished and proposed that the two kings should meet to discuss the matter. On arrival at the meeting, Minos was cordially received. A warm bath was prepared so that he might rest after his journey. However, as he lay in the tub, Cocalus commanded that boiling water be poured over him until he was scalded to death. Afterwards, Minos's warriors buried him with great pomp and splendor, building a temple to Aphrodite close to his grave. Daedalus remained with King Cocalus, who always treated him kindly. Many famous masters came to consult with him and he also founded a school of sculpture in Sicily. Even so, after his son crashed to his death, Daedalus was never happy again. And while, through the work of his hands, he turned the land that had sheltered him into a place of serenity and laughter, he himself passed into old age a sorrowful and troubled man. He died on the island of Sicily, and there he was laid to rest.

THE ARGONAUTS
JASON AND PELIAS
THE REASON WHY THE ARGONAUTS SET FORTH ON THEIR VOYAGE

What destiny can hold for mortals:
love and hatred, heroic feats, devious scheming, joyful life, and cruel death.
The tale begins with Jason being sent by his uncle, Pelias, to steal the Golden Fleece in
Colchis so he will be eligible to inherit the throne. Athena helps Jason to build the Argo and
forge plans for the expedition, on which he is supported by renowned Greek heroes.

Illustrations by William Russell Flint

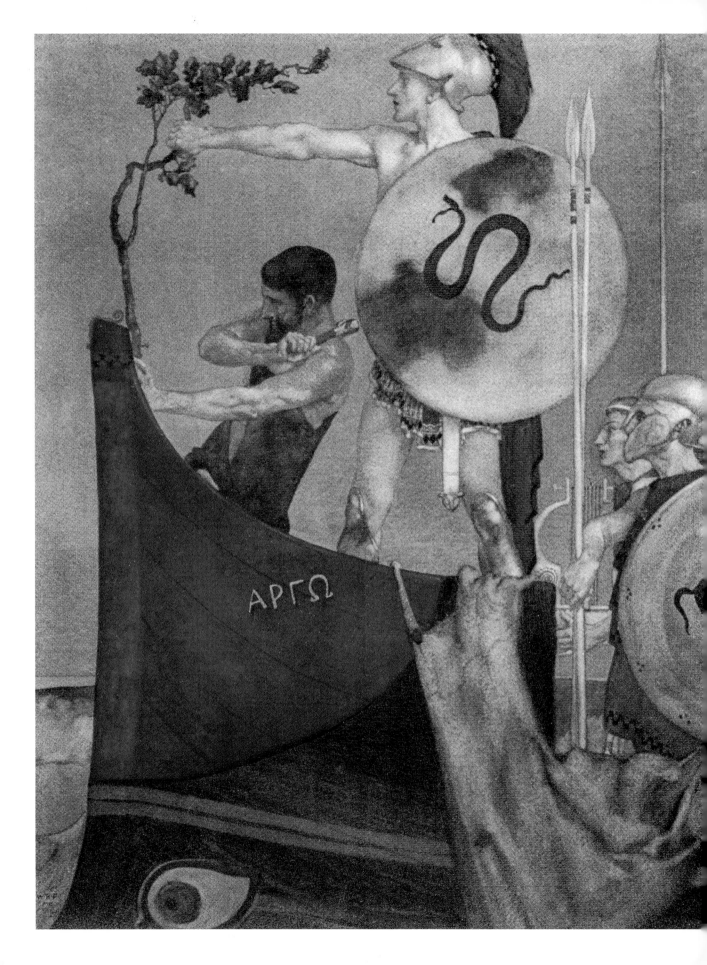

Page 63
Jason, after twenty years of being taught and reared by Chiron, set out in secret to his homeland, Iolcus.

Left
Jason was to lead the entire expedition.

Jason was the son of Aeson and grandson of Cretheus. Cretheus founded the city and kingdom of Iolcus on a bay in the land of Thessaly, which he bequeathed to his son Aeson. However, his younger son Pelias seized the throne. Aeson died and his child Jason was sent to live in safety with Chiron the centaur, who had educated many fine young heroes, one of which Jason would become under his tuition. As Pelias grew older, he became increasingly troubled by an oracle's ominous warning to beware a man wearing only one shoe. While Pelias tried in vain to fathom the meaning of such an admonition, Jason, after twenty years of being taught and reared by Chiron, set out in secret to his homeland, Iolcus, to reclaim his hereditary right to the throne. Following the tradition among the heroes of old, he came armed with two spears, one to throw, the other to thrust. Over his traveling attire, he wore the pelt of a panther he had strangled and his long, uncut hair hung loose over his shoulders. Along the way, he came upon a wide river where he met an old woman who begged him to help her across. This was Hera, Queen of the Gods and King Pelias's enemy. Jason did not recognize her in her disguise, but out of pity for an elderly person, he lifted her and waded across the river, carrying her in his arms. On the way, one of his shoes stuck in the mud. Even so, he simply strode onwards until he arrived at Iolcus, where he found his uncle Pelias in the marketplace, making a solemn offering to Poseidon, the sea god. All those present marveled how handsome and majestic Jason had become, even believing that Apollo or Ares had suddenly appeared in their midst. Then, while offering the sacrifice, the king caught sight of the stranger and to his horror noticed that only one of his feet was shod. When the religious ritual was over, he approached the newcomer and, hiding his trepidation, asked him his name and his country. Jason replied boldly but gently that he was Aeson's son, brought up in Chiron's cave, and had now come to visit his father's house. Shrewdly, Pelias concealed his unease and listened seemingly sympathetically to Jason's words. He ordered that the visitor be guided all around the palace, and Jason looked wistfully at what had once been his childhood home. He then celebrated his reunion with his kinsmen with five days of jovial feasting. On the sixth, the revelers left the tents put up for guests and came together before King Pelias. In a voice gentle and unassuming, Jason said to his uncle, "You are aware, Your Majesty, that I am the son of the rightful king and everything you possess belongs to me. Nevertheless, I shall allow you to keep all the herds of sheep and cattle and all the fields you seized from my parents. I demand no more from you than the regal throne and scepter that were once my father's." Pelias thought rapidly and answered in a friendly fashion. "I am willing to fulfill your demands. However, in return, you must grant a request of mine and carry out a task on my behalf. I am too old even to attempt it, but you, as a young man, can accomplish it with ease. For a long time, the shadow of Phrixus has been haunting my dreams. He orders me to appease his soul by travelling to Colchis, where Aeetes rules, to bring back the fleece of the golden ram. I see you as the one who will be glorified for carrying out this mission. When you return with your precious spoils, the kingdom and scepter shall be yours."

"WHEN YOU RETURN WITH YOUR PRECIOUS SPOILS, THE KINGDOM AND SCEPTER SHALL BE YOURS."

This was the story of the Golden Fleece: Phrixus, son of Athamas, king of Boeotia, had much to endure from Ino, his evil stepmother and his father's concubine. To save him from her evil machinations, his own mother, Nephele, abducted him with the help of his sister Helle. She sat her two children on the back of a winged ram with a fleece of pure gold, a gift

A favorable wind swelled the sails and soon the port of Iolcus was left behind.

she had received from the god Hermes. Brother and sister rode on the magical creature through the air over land and sea. But the girl was overcome by dizziness and plunged to her death in the sea, known ever since as the Sea of Helle, or Hellespont. Phrixus arrived safely in Colchis, a land on the coast of the Black Sea. Here he was warmly welcomed by King Aeetes, who gave him the hand of one of his daughters in marriage. Phrixus sacrificed the ram to Zeus in gratitude for enabling him to continue his flight, and then presented the fleece to King Aeetes as a gift. The monarch himself consecrated it to Ares, nailing it to a tree in a grove sacred to the war god. Since an oracle had revealed that his life depended on his guardianship of the fleece, Ares chose a particularly evil-looking dragon to stand guard over his precious possession. Throughout the world, the fleece was regarded as a matchless treasure, which many heroes and princes yearned to possess, and its fame had long since reached Greece. Pelias was not mistaken to hope he could tempt his nephew Jason by promising him such rich plunder. Jason was indeed willing to go. However, he failed to see that his uncle intended for him to die in the attempt. He gave his solemn word to undertake the bold assignment, in which Greece's most famous heroes were called upon to collaborate. In a shipyard at the foot of Mount Pelion, under the supervision of the goddess Athena, Greece's finest shipbuilder constructed a splendid vessel using a type of wood that would not be rotted by sea water. The ship with space for fifty oars, was named after its inventor, Argos, son of Arestor. It was the first long ship which the Greeks had dared to launch on to the open sea. Fixed to the masthead was a gift from Athena, a piece of wood cut from an oak in the Grove of Dodona, where sacred trees possessed the gift of prophecy. The ship was adorned with many elaborate wooden carvings, but was still so light that the heroes could carry it on their shoulders for twelve days at a time. When construction was finished and the Argonauts were assembled around it, they cast lots to decide where each man would be placed. Jason was to lead the entire expedition; Tiphys was the helmsman and eagle-eyed Lynceus the pilot. The glorious hero Heracles sat in the bow of the ship, while Peleus, father of Achilles, and Telamon, father of Ajax, occupied the stern. Among those boarded in other parts of the vessel were Castor and Pollux, sons of Zeus; Neleus, father of Nestor; Admetus, husband of pious Alcestis; Meleager, slayer of the Calydonian boar; Orpheus, the superb singer; Menoetius, father of Patroclus; Theseus, later to be crowned king of Athens and his friend Pirithous; Hylas, the young comrade of Heracles; Poseidon's son, Euphemus; and Oileus, father of Ajax the Lesser.

GREECE'S MOST FAMOUS HEROES WERE CALLED UPON TO UNDERTAKE THIS BOLD ASSIGNMENT.

Jason had consecrated his ship to Poseidon and before departure, the Argonauts made a solemn offering while praying to the deity and the other gods of the sea.

When they had all taken their places aboard the ship, the anchor was weighed. The fifty rowers began to dip their oars in and out of the sea with a regular rhythm, a favorable wind swelled the sails and soon the port of Iolcus was left behind. The sweet sounds of Orpheus's lyre and his enchanting voice kindled the bravery of the Argonauts, as they cheerfully raced past peninsulas and islands. But on the second day a storm arose, driving them into the harbor of the island of Lemnos.

THE ARGONAUTS

PHINEUS AND THE HARPIES

Saved from starvation:
On their expedition to the Black Sea, the Argonauts help the blind Phineus.
Resembling birds of prey, the Harpies snatch his food to eat it themselves or defile it
with their excrement. Zeus comes to the rescue and pursues the Harpies through the sky.
Although the winged monsters are not slain, they will no longer plague Phineus.

Illustration by Arthur Rackham

By morning the feasting was over and they continued their journey. After a few adventures they dropped anchor off the land of Bithynia, close to the seafront where King Phineus, son of the hero Agenor, now dwelt. The king had been afflicted by a great misfortune. Because he had misused the gift of prophesy bestowed to him by Apollo, in his old age he been stricken by blindness. Moreover, the harpies, repulsive mythical monsters, part woman, part bird, would not allow him to eat his meals in peace. They stole as much food as they could and polluted what remained in such a revolting manner that no one could even go near it. But Phineus found consolation in a prediction made by the oracle of Zeus. When the sons of Boreas arrived aboard the ship driven by Greek oarsmen, said the oracle, Phineus could once more enjoy his food in peace. On learning of the ship's arrival, he immediately left his chamber. No more than skin and bone, a mere shadow of his younger self, his frail old limbs trembling, he leant on a staff to support his faltering steps and, on reaching the Argonauts, he dropped exhausted to the floor. Appalled by his state of health, the seafarers gathered around him. When the monarch sensed them close to him, he summoned up all his strength and pleaded with them, "Oh gallant heroes, if you truly are those whose arrival the oracle prophesied, I beg you to help me. For the vengeful gods have not only robbed me of my eyesight; they have sent me these loathsome birds to deny me the food I need in my old age! You will not be helping a stranger, for I am a Greek – Phineus, son of Agenor. I was once king of Thrace. The sons of Boreas are the younger brothers of Cleopatra, who was my wife at that time. They must be members of your crew and will help to save me."

THE HARPIES, REPULSIVE MYTHICAL MONSTERS, PART WOMAN, PART BIRD, WOULD NOT ALLOW HIM TO EAT HIS MEALS IN PEACE.

On hearing this revelation, Boreas's son Zetes threw himself into the arms of the king and promised him that he and his brother would free him from the torment of the harpies. They then went to prepare the last meal that the marauding creatures would consume. The king had barely touched the food when, like a sudden storm, they came down from the clouds, wings flapping furiously, and greedily swooped on to his platter. The heroes yelled at them, but the harpies refused to budge until they had swallowed the last crumb. They then shot into the air, leaving behind them a nauseating stench. Zetes and Calais, sons of Boreas, pursued them with swords drawn. Zeus lent the heroes wings and indefatigable strength, of which they were in dire need, for the harpies flew faster than the strong west wind. But the sons of Boreas were close behind them and at times could almost grab them with their hands. They were finally near enough to strike them dead, when suddenly Iris, Zeus's messenger, appeared out of the ether and warned the two heroes, "Take note, you sons of Boreas, it is not permitted for harpies sent by Zeus to be slain by the sword. But I swear to you by the Styx, as do all the great gods, that these predatory birds shall no longer distress the son of Agenor." The brothers abandoned the chase and returned to the ship.

Meanwhile, the Greek heroes devoted their time to attending to the needs of the aged Phineus. They prepared a sacrificial meal at which they made the starving old man their guest. He wolfed down vast amounts of fresh, unspoiled food. To him it felt as if he were satisfying his hunger in a dream. While the company waited all night for the return of the sons of Boreas, King Phineus made them a prophecy in gratitude for their kindness to him. "First of all," he said, "in a narrow strait you will come

The heroes yelled at them, but the harpies refused to budge.

upon two steep, rocky islands. Their roots do not reach the bottom of the sea, so that they float freely in the water. Often the current drives them towards one another and the waves between them swell with terrifying strength. If you do not want every single one of you to be crushed to death, row through them as fast as a dove flies. Then you will come to the shores of the land of the Mariandyni, where the entrance to the underworld stands. You will sail past many headlands, rivers and coasts, cities founded for women by the Amazons, and the land of the Chalybes, who dig iron from the earth by the sweat of their brows. Finally, you will reach the coast, where the River

Phasis sends its mighty whirlpools flowing into the sea. There you will catch sight of the towers of King Aeetes's stronghold. Here, the Golden Fleece lies spread across the topmost boughs of an oak tree, guarded by a dragon which never sleeps."

The heroes trembled with fear as they listened to the old man and were about to question him further when the sons of Boreas descended from above and into their midst, delighting the king with a heartening message from Iris. Deeply moved and full of gratitude, Phineus bade farewell to his rescuers as they sailed onwards to new and even greater adventures.

THE ARGONAUTS
MEDEA PROMISES TO HELP THE ARGONAUTS

Love at first sight, doomed to end in tragedy:
Medea, daughter of the king in Colchis, falls madly in love with Jason as soon as
she lays eyes on him. Although King Aeetes is unwilling to give up the Golden Fleece, her
passion for the leader of the Argonauts ensures the success of their mission. Medea uses
her magic powers to accomplish what seems to be impossible.

Illustrations by Willy Pogany

Early in the morning, the heroes held a meeting. Jason rose to his feet and said, "If you, my brave companions, are willing to take my advice, you will remain on board, peacefully but with weapons at the ready. Meanwhile, the sons of Phrixus, two more from among you, and I will make our way to the palace of King Aeetes. On arrival I shall politely ask him if he is willing to hand the Golden Fleece over to us. I have no doubt that he is confident enough to refuse, but this is one way in which we can discover what we need to do."

Finally, Aeetes appeared with his wife Idyia, both of them wondering why their daughters could be heard rejoicing while at the same time weeping. Soon the entire courtyard was buzzing with excitement, with slaves busy slaughtering a fine bullock for the new guests, others splitting dry wood for the fire or boiling cauldrons of water. But, unnoticed by all those present, Eros hovered high overhead. He took an arrow that would inflict pain from his quiver and dropped down to Earth. Then, crouching behind Jason, he drew his bow and shot the arrow at Medea, daughter of the king. No one, least of all Medea herself, saw the dart flying through the air, but it burned like a flame as it struck her beneath her breast. Like one beset by some dire disease, she gasped for air while casting furtive glances at Jason in all his youthful splendor. She abandoned every other thought. Her soul was seized by a feeling of sweet sorrow, her face turning from pale to red.

During the feast, King Aeetes's grandsons told him about the fate which had overtaken them, then quietly asked him about the strangers. "I shall not hide it from you, Grandfather," Argus whispered. "These men have been sent on this dangerous mission by a king whose burning desire is to drive them out of their native land and defraud them of their possessions. They are instructed to ask you for the Golden Fleece that belongs to our father Phrixus." The noblest among these men, he told Aeetes, all belonged to the same dynasty as Jason.

The king was both horrified by what he had heard and enraged by the words of his grandsons. Deep down he could not decide whether to have the visitors slain immediately, or first test their strength. On reflection, the latter seemed the better solution and he spoke to them somewhat more peaceably than before. "Why the need to speak with such fear, stranger? If you who desire to take the possessions of another are truly the sons of gods, or at least no less noble than myself, then simply take the Golden Fleece away with you. I begrudge men of courage nothing. But first you must prove yourselves by carrying out a highly dangerous task which I am wont to do myself. Two bulls of mine, beasts with hooves of brass and breath of fire, graze in Ares's fields. I use them to plow the rough ground before sowing it, not with Demeter's golden corn but with the hideous teeth of a dragon. These produce a crop of men who attack me from all sides, but I slaughter them with my lance. In the early morning I harness the bulls to the yoke, in late evening I rest after the harvest. Now, oh leader, when you have done the same, that very day you may take the Golden Fleece with you and deliver it to your king in his house. But not before! For it is only right that the less courageous man should give way to he who is braver." Jason listened in silence, for he dared not promise to undertake such a terrifying endeavor in haste. Then he composed himself and answered, "Your Majesty, this is so arduous a task that I shall be the one

> "WHEN YOU HAVE DONE SO, THAT VERY DAY YOU MAY TAKE THE GOLDEN FLEECE WITH YOU AND DELIVER IT TO YOUR KING. BUT NOT BEFORE!"

The chariot was ready.

to do it, even though I may lose my life. Mortal man cannot meet with a fate worse than death. I shall bow to the necessity that brought me here."

From behind her veil, Medea's eyes strayed towards Jason, following his every movement as if in a dream. All alone back in her chamber she began to weep, asking herself, "Why am I yearning like this? Why am I troubled by this hero? Whether he be the most glorious or the least admirable among the demigods, if he is fated to die, so be it! And yet – if only he could escape destruction! Oh Hecate, hallowed goddess, let him return home! But if he is destined to be defeated by the bulls, please let him know beforehand that I at least do not rejoice in his sad demise."

While Medea tortured herself and the heroes were on their way to the ship, Argus said to Jason, "Perhaps you will not heed my advice, but I shall still tell you what I think. I know of a young woman who understands the brewing of magic potions, an art she learned from Hecate, goddess of the underworld. If we could win her over to our side, I am convinced that you would emerge victorious from this task. If you wish, I shall go and try to persuade her to help us."

Medea slept restlessly on her couch, disturbed by a distressing dream. In it, she saw Jason preparing to fight the bulls, but it seemed that he had not taken up this challenge for the sake of the Golden Fleece, but to carry her back to his homeland as his wife. In her dream she was the one who survived the bull-fight, but her parents refused to keep their word and did not award Jason the prize they had promised, because it was he, not she, who had been commanded to yoke the beasts. This led to a bitter quarrel between her father and the strangers, with both sides choosing her as arbiter. In her dream, she judged in favor of the stranger and her parents cried out in pain and grief. And at that moment Medea awoke.

The dream led her to her sister's chamber, but shame and indecision caused her to linger in the courtyard. Thrice she stepped forward and thrice she turned back before finally scurrying back to her own chamber, where she threw herself weeping on to her own couch. She was discovered there by one of her faithful young handmaidens who, out of sympathy with her mistress, sent word to Medea's sister Chalciope, describing what she had seen. Chalciope received the message while she was advising her sons on how the young woman might be won over. She hurried to her sister's chamber where she found the young woman clawing at her cheeks, her face bathed in tears. "What has happened to you, my poor sister?" she asked most anxiously. "What pain is torturing your soul? Have the gods afflicted you with a sudden malady? Has our father told you hateful things about me and my sons? Oh, if only I were far away from our parents' home, in a place where the name of Colchis is never heard!"

Medea blushed at her sister's questions, her shyness rendering her too timid to answer them. One moment, the words were on the tip of her tongue, the next they flowed back to the very heart of her being. Finally, emboldened by her love for her sister, she subtly distorted the truth and replied, "Chalciope, my heart grieves for your sons, for I fear that our father, when he kills the strangers, will immediately turn and slaughter them too. This came to me in a bad dream and I pray that some god

THE ARGONAUTS:
MEDEA PROMISES TO HELP THE ARGONAUTS

"The following morning, anoint yourself with this magic balm I have brought for you, which will bestow upon you immeasurable power and colossal strength."

might prevent it becoming reality." Her sister was seized with unbearable fear. "This is why I have come to you. I beg of you to support me against our father," Chalciope said. "If you refuse, my murdered sons and I will pursue you like Furies from the underworld!" She clasped Medea's knee with both hands and buried her head in her lap while the sisters wept bitterly together. Then Medea spoke. "Dear sister, why speak of Furies? I swear to you by heaven and earth that I shall gladly do whatever I can to save your sons." "So," her sister continued, "for the sake of my sons, you must agree to provide the stranger with some form of trickery with which he can survive the terrible ordeal he must face. He has sent my son Argus to plead for your help."

Medea's heart leapt with joy, her beautiful face glowing, her shining eyes veiled by a moment of giddiness. Then suddenly she said, "Chalciope, may my eyes never again see the sunrise if I do not hold the lives of you and your sons dearer to me than my own! Did you not tell me, as our mother often did, that you both suckled me when I was a tiny child? This means that I not only love you as a sister but also as a daughter. Early tomorrow morning I shall go the temple of Hecate, from where I shall bring for the stranger the magic balm with which he can pacify the bulls."

The chariot was ready. Two handmaids climbed on board with their mistress. She held the reins and the whip herself as she drove through the city, with the rest of her maidservants accompanying them on foot. Along the way, the citizens stepped back respectfully to make way for the king's daughter.

Not long afterwards, Jason, a young man as tall and fair as Sirius when he rose from the sea, entered the temple with his companions. Medea felt as though her heart was about to leap from her body. Both cast their eyes bashfully down at the ground before looking again at each other and exchanging amorous glances from under their eyelashes. After a long pause and with considerable effort, Medea was the first to speak. "Please listen to me. I want to help you. When my father has given you the deadly dragon's teeth to sow, you must bathe alone in in the river and afterwards dress yourself in black. Dig a circular pit and in it build a funeral pyre, slaughter a female lamb, which you must burn to ashes. Then offer the goddess Hecate a libation of honey and move away from the pyre. If you hear footsteps, or a barking dog, do not turn around or your offering will be worthless. The following morning, anoint yourself with this magic balm I have brought for you, which will bestow upon you immeasurable power and colossal strength. You will feel equal not to men, but to the immortal gods. You must also smear your lance, sword, and shield with the salve, so that neither metal in the grip of human hands nor flames breathed by mythical bulls can injure or kill you. Do not delay, for its power will last no more than one day, and do not withdraw from the fight, since I shall give you another weapon. When you have yoked the huge beasts together and plowed the fallow field where the dragon seeds have sprouted into men, hurl a huge stone among them. These earthborn creatures will fight over it like dogs over a crust of bread. While they are busy fighting each other you can swoop in and slaughter them. You can then seize the Golden Fleece from Colchis without a struggle and take it with you. Then you can go. Yes, go wherever you please!"

THE ARGONAUTS

JASON MEETS THE DEMANDS OF KING AEETES

A king deceived:
Medea gives Jason a magical ointment that makes him invulnerable so he can
perform the tasks that King Aeetes, Medea's father, has demanded. The king refuses to give
the Golden Fleece to the Argonauts unless Jason completes these tasks. Realizing that
Medea has helped Jason with her magic, Aeetes weaves a plot against Jason.

Illustrations by Edmund Dulac and Merlyn Mann

THE ARGONAUTS:
JASON MEETS THE DEMANDS OF KING AEETES

The beasts broke out from their underground stable and came at him from an unexpected direction. Both animals breathed fire, engulfing their bodies in dense clouds of smoke.

And so Jason and Medea parted. He was happy to return to the ship and his comrades. Medea went back to join her handmaidens, barely noticing how they ran towards her, for her mind was up in the clouds. She softly sprang into the wagon and drove the mules, which instinctively knew their way back to the palace. There Chalciope had long awaited her, full of fear for her sons. She was sitting on a low stool, her head in her hands, eyes wet with tears beneath the eyelids as she thought of the evil entanglement in which she was now caught up.

Meanwhile, Jason explained to his friends how the girl had given him a fine and effective magical balm, which he showed to them as he spoke. They were delighted – apart from Idas, the hero who sat to one side, grinding his teeth with rage. The next morning two men were sent to ask Aeetes for the dragon's teeth. The king did not refuse. In fact, he presented them with the teeth of the very same dragon that Cadmus killed at Thebes.

The king did this willingly, for he believed it impossible that Jason would survive the battle, even if he was capable of yoking the bulls. The following night, Jason bathed and made an offering to Hecate, exactly as Medea had directed him. The goddess herself emerged from deep inside her cavern, a terrifying figure wrapped with hideous snakes and the blazing branches of oak. A pack of dogs came scurrying from the underworld, barking at her heels. The ground beneath trembled as she moved and the nymphs of the River Phasis howled with fear. Jason shared their fear as he prepared to make his way back to the ship but, obeying his beloved, he did not look back until he was side by side with his comrades again, while the snowy peaks of the Caucasus shimmered in the red light of dawn.

Then Aeetes donned the armor which Ares had stolen from the giant Mimas on the field of Phlegra. On his head he placed his four-crested gold helmet, while in his hand he took up his shield, so heavy that no hero other than Heracles could have lifted it. His son was keeping hold of the most powerful horses chosen to draw the chariot. The king mounted and, taking up the reins, flew away from the city watched by vast crowds. Fully armed, he wished to give the impression that he himself was about to go into battle. However, Jason had followed Medea's instructions and smeared his lance, sword, and shield with the magic balm. Gathering in a circle around him, one by one the heroes tried their own weapons against the lance, which held firm and refused to bend even after the fiercest blow. It was as though it had turned to stone in Jason's steady hand. This angered Idas, son of Aphareus, who aimed his blow at the shaft just beneath the point. But the blade sprang back like a hammer from an anvil and the heroes cheerfully hailed the prospect of victory. At last Jason anointed his body and began to feel extraordinary power spreading to his every limb, his hands swelling with strength, as well as a longing to go into action. As a war horse whinnies and stamps the ground before the slaughter, then raises its head high and pricks up its ears, so the son of Aeson prepared his body and mind for the combat, raising his feet and swinging shield and lance in his hands. The heroes rowed their leader to the field of Ares, where they were await-ed by King Aeetes and a host of Colchians, some on the shore, others on the jutting ledges of the Caucasian cliffs.

When the ship was moored, Jason leapt ashore armed with lance and shield and was immediately hand-ed a glittering helmet full of pointed dragons' teeth. He then strapped his sword to his shoulder and moved forward as majestically as Ares or Apollo. Looking across the open field, he quickly caught sight of the bulls' yokes lying on the ground close to the plow and plowshare, all forged from hammered iron. Having examined all these implements more closely, he fastened the iron point to the sturdy shaft of the lance and laid down his helmet. Then, protected by his shield, he stepped forward in an attempt to follow the tracks of the bulls, but the beasts broke out from their underground stable and came at him from an unexpected direction. Both animals breathed fire, engulfing their bodies in dense clouds of smoke. On seeing the two monsters, Jason's companions recoiled in fear, while their leader stood firm behind his shield with legs wide apart, like a cliff awaiting the crash of the waves. When they rushed straight at him, horns at the ready, he did not move a muscle. As if in a blacksmith's forge, where the bellows roar and turn the fire into a prodigious shower of sparks before holding their mighty breath, the bulls roared and repeated their thrusts, the fiery glow playing around the hero like streaks of lightning. Still protected by Medea's balm, he grabbed the outer horn of the bull on the right, yanking it with all his might until he dragged him to the place where the iron yoke lay. There, he kicked the beast's brazen hooves and pushed it to the ground on bent knees. Likewise, he overpowered the second bull as it charged towards him. Then he threw away his broad shield and, despite being surrounded by flames, he held down the kneeling animals with both hands. Aeetes could not but admire the young man's incredible strength. Then as previous-ly agreed, Castor and Pollux handed him the yokes which, with confidence and skill, he attached to the bulls' necks. Finally, he picked up the iron shaft which he inserted into the ring of the yoke. The twin brothers quickly took their leave as, unlike Jason, they were not protected from fire. The latter took up his shield again and strapped it across his shoulder. Then he grabbed the helmet with the dragon's teeth and once more reached for his lance which he used as a goad to force the angry, fire-spitting bulls to pull the plow. Their strength and that of their mighty plowman made deep cuts into the earth with huge clods crashing into the furrows. Jason walked behind at a steady pace, sowing dragons' teeth into the turned soil while carefully looking back to see whether the sprout-ing seeds were germinating into dragon men threatening to rise against him, while the bulls trudged forward on their brazen hooves.

THE BULLS ROARED AND REPEATED THEIR THRUSTS, THE FIERY GLOW PLAYING AROUND THE HERO LIKE STREAKS OF LIGHTNING.

THE ARGONAUTS:
JASON MEETS THE DEMANDS OF KING AEETES

The entire Grove of Ares was overrun with lances and shields.

When only one third of the day still remained, the bright afternoon sunlight revealed that the whole four-acre field had been plowed over by the tireless plowman. The latter now unharnessed the bulls, threatening them with his weapons and scaring them so much that they fled across the open field. Jason then returned to his ship, for there was no sign of the furrows being overrun by earthborn warriors. Surrounding him on all sides, his comrades met him with enthusiastic cries of welcome. He, meanwhile, did not say a word. Instead, he filled his helmet with river water to quench his desperate thirst. As he rubbed his knee joints, his heart filled with a longing for yet more conflict, like a boar that foams at the mouth and grinds its teeth as the hunters approach. The whole field had now been harvested and the entire Grove of Ares was overrun with lances and shields and glistening helmets whose gleam rose up into the sky. Then Jason recalled Medea's scheming words. He picked up a round stone, so heavy that four strong men could not lift it from the ground. Jason, however, easily grasped it with one hand and threw it so that it landed in among the warriors who had sprung up from the soil. Cautious but unafraid, he crouched on one knee and covered himself with his shield. The

Colchians roared, like waves breaking against a rugged cliff face, while Aeetes stood dumbfounded by the ease with which Jason had thrown the gigantic stone. The earthborn warriors, however, fell upon one another like hounds in pursuit of their prey, killing their comrades amid muffled gasps and groans. Struck by spears, they fell to Mother Earth, like pine trees or oaks uprooted by a whirlwind. At the height of battle, Jason plunged into them like a falling star, a miraculous omen sent to earth in the darkness of night. Then he unsheathed his sword, wounding those on either side of him, striking down any still standing, mowing down those who had only grown to shoulder height like grass, and beheading any others running to join in the battle. The furrows became rivers of blood. Dead and wounded fell on all sides while many, their heads drenched in blood, sank back into the earth as deeply as they were once sown.

Seething anger gnawed at the soul of King Aeetes. Without a word he turned on his heel and made for the city, thinking only of the most effective way to rid himself of Jason. And so the day ended for the king. Meanwhile, the hero rested from his labors, surrounded by his comrades celebrating his return.

THE ARGONAUTS
THE GOLDEN FLEECE

Mission accomplished:
When Jason promises to marry her in return for her help, Medea puts
the dragon that guards the Golden Fleece to sleep with a magic potion. This
enables Jason to remove the treasure from the oak to which it is fastened
with impunity. The Argo sets a course back to the Greek homeland.

Illustrations by Virginia Frances Sterrett

*There they sought the tall oak tree
on which the Golden Fleece hung.*

At the palace, King Aeetes assembled the elders of his people and throughout the night sought guidance as to how the Argonauts could be outwitted, for he knew only too well that all that had happened the day before could not have occurred without the help of his daughter. The goddess Hera saw the danger that threatened Jason. It filled Medea's heart with such foreboding that she trembled like a deer in the forest, terrified by the baying of the hounds. Medea soon guessed that the truth had not been hidden from her father, while also fearing that her handmaidens were aware of the situation. Tears burned beneath her eyelids and she heard a strange rushing sound in her ears. Her hair hung down bedraggled as if she were in mourning and, had fate not intervened, she would have immediately taken poison to put an end to her suffering. The brimming cup was already in her hand

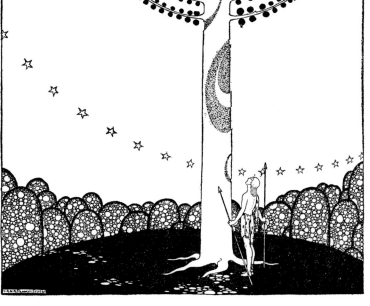

when Hera inspired her with renewed courage. With a change of heart, she poured the poison back into the flask. Her composure now regained, she decided to flee, first covering her couch and the doorposts with kisses and touching the walls of her room for the very last time, before snipping a lock of hair from her head and placing it on the bed as a token of remembrance for her mother. "Farewell, beloved mother," she said through her sobs. "Farewell, sister Chalciope and all those dwelling in the house! Oh, stranger. Would that you had drowned in the sea before coming to Colchis." And so she left her beloved home, like a prisoner escaping the unforgiving slavery of incarceration. The palace gates opened as she softly uttered the magic spells. Then she ran barefoot along narrow paths and, with her left hand, drew her veil across her cheeks while, with her right, she raised the hem of her garment to keep it clear of the ground. Unrecognized by the gatekeepers, she left the city behind and came upon a little-known footpath leading to the temple. As a sorceress and poisoner who gathered roots and herbs, she was familiar with all the trails through the woods and across the fields. Selene the moon goddess saw Medea approaching and murmured to herself with a smile, "So other women are tormented by love as I am for my beautiful Endymion! You have often used your magic to drive me from the sky. Now you are the one who suffers intolerable pain because of Jason. So go if you must, but be aware that you are not as clever as you think, so do not imagine that your cunning will save you from the worst anguish of all!" Selene talked to herself only to see the young woman hurrying away, then turning towards the seashore. There the bonfire built by the heroes in Jason's honor burned throughout the night, serving Medea as a guiding star. As she drew close to the ship she called out three times to Phrontis, her sister's youngest son who, along with Jason, recognized her voice and responded thrice. The heroes, at first astonished at what they heard, rowed to meet her. Before the ship was moored on the opposite bank Jason jumped ashore, followed by Phrontis and Argus. "Save me!" pleaded the girl, clasping them around

THE ARGONAUTS: THE GOLDEN FLEECE

their knees. "Save me and yourselves from my father! All have been betrayed and there is no longer any help. Let us flee on the ship before he even mounts his charger. I shall bring you the Golden Fleece by putting the dragon to sleep. But you, oh stranger, in the presence of your friends, swear by your gods that you will not disgrace me when I am all alone in a foreign land." She spoke these words sadly, but they gladdened Jason's heart. He raised her gently from her knees, embraced her and said, "Beloved, let Zeus and Hera, goddess of marriage, be my witnesses. I swear that I shall take you back to Greece where I shall lead you into my house as my lawful wife." Thus he swore and took her hand in his. Then Medea bade the heroes to row to the sacred grove that very night and take the Golden Fleece. Eagerly, the Greek oarsmen propelled the ship at top speed. Before dawn broke, Jason and Medea disembarked and made their way across the

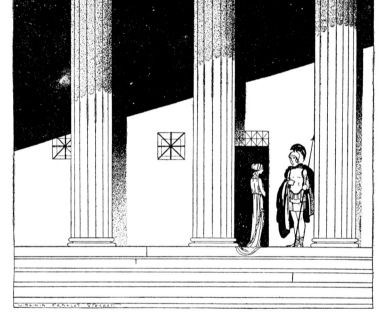

meadow to the grove. There they sought the tall oak tree on which the Golden Fleece hung, gleaming through the night air like an early morning cloud bathed by the beams of the rising sun. Facing the tree, however, was the dragon that never slept, its sharp eyes staring into the distance. Its long neck stretched towards them as they approached, and it hissed so viciously that the sound echoed along the river bank and through the woodlands. The monster slithered forward in an endless series of coils like flames rolling through a burning forest, its scales shimmering. But the young woman impishly stepped towards the beast and in a soft, sweet voice, sang it a lullaby. As she sang she called upon Sleep, the most powerful of the gods, to make the dragon drowsy and to bless her own intentions. Now Jason followed her fearlessly, but already Medea's magical song was making the dragon drowsy. It lowered the arch of its back and stretched the coils of its huge body. Only its hideous head remained upright, its open jaws ready to devour them both. Then Medea took a sprig of juniper and, softly murmuring a mysterious supplication, sprinkled the dragon's eyes with a magic potion. The sweet perfume of the liquid caused drowsiness to overtake every part of the creature, closing its eyes and its jaws and spreading the length of its body into the woods, where it fell into a deep sleep.

At her bidding, Jason pulled the Golden Fleece from the oak while she continued to sprinkle the dragon's head with magic oil. Then together they sped away from the shady grove and from afar Jason held high the broad fleece of a ram, whose reflected light caused his forehead and his blond hair to glow. It lit up the path still shrouded in darkness. He walked on, carrying the precious burden over his left shoulder so that it hung from his neck to his feet. But then he rolled it up, for fear that he might be met by a god or mortal eager to rob him of his treasure. At dawn they boarded the ship where the Argonauts surrounded their leader while gazing in awe at the Golden Fleece, which glittered like Zeus's lightning. Each of them wanted to touch it with his hands but Jason refused to let them and, instead, covered it with

The fleece gleamed in the night air like an early morning cloud bathed in the beams of the rising sun.

a newly made cloak. He seated Medea at the stern of the ship and addressed his friends, "Dear comrades, let us now sail swiftly back to our homeland. It is on this maiden's advice that we have made this journey and, in return, I shall take her to my house as my lawfully wedded wife. You, my friends, must help me protect her, for she is the savior of all Greece. For I do not doubt that soon Aeetes and his people will appear and attempt to prevent us heading from the river to the sea! Therefore, half of our number must row, while the other half hold our mighty shields of ox hide in the direction of the enemy, thus protecting us on our homeward voyage. Now we must return to our own people, for the honor or the humiliation of Greece rests in our hands!" With these words, he cut the ropes that held the ship, donned full armor, and lined up with Medea, alongside Ancaeus the helmsman. The oarsmen then rowed the ship at full speed towards the mouth of the river.

THE ARGONAUTS CONTINUE HOME

A dangerous voyage home:
Storms and waves wash the Argo onto foreign shores. Jason and Medea briefly
enjoy Circe's hospitality, but she refuses help them. Orpheus succeeds in drowning out
the treacherously sweet singing of the Sirens with his lyre. Divine intervention keeps
the Argonauts from being engulfed by the sea between Scylla and Charybdis.

Illustration by William Russell Flint

THE ARGONAUTS: THE ARGONAUTS CONTINUE HOME

The Argonauts sailed past many coasts and islands, even calling at the island that was home to Atlas's daughter, Queen Calypso. Already they thought that the highest mountaintops they saw rising in the distance belonged to their homeland, but Hera, fearing what the wrathful Zeus might be plotting, raised a violent storm that drove the ship towards the inhospitable Amber Island. Then the plank of wood with the gift of prophesy, which Athena had inserted into the middle of the ship's prow, began to speak, filling the listeners with dread. "You will escape neither the wrath of Zeus, nor your meanderings at sea," said the voice of the plank, "until Circe, sorceress and goddess of the sea, proves you innocent of the brutal murder of Absyrtus. Let Castor and Pollux pray to the gods to lead you to Circe, daughter of the sun god and the ocean nymph Perse." Such words flowed from the wooden mouth of the Argo's prow as dusk fell. On hearing such a strange prophet foretelling such hardship, the heroes were seized with fear and trembling. Only the twins, Castor and Pollux, were courageous enough to stand up and pray for protection from the immortal gods. But the ship sped onwards and into the inner reaches of the River Eridanus, into which Phaethon, burnt by the chariot of the sun, had once plunged. And even now his agonizing wounds continued to pour forth flames and smoke from the riverbed. No ship without sturdy sails could navigate these waters, for it would sail into the midst of the flames. All along the shore, Phaethon's sisters, the Heliades, now changed into poplar trees, stood in the wind sighing and weeping. Their amber tears that dropped to the ground were hardened by the sun and then swept away by the tide of the Eridanus. Although their mighty ship survived this peril, none of the Argonauts had any appetite for food or drink. By day they were nauseated by the intolerable stench of burnt flesh rising from Phaethon's remains, and by night they could clearly hear the Heliades wailing while their gold-like tears were seeped into the sea like droplets of oil. Rowing along the shores of Eridanus, they came upon the mouth of the Rhodanus. They would have entered if Hera had not suddenly appeared on a clifftop and, in her earsplitting goddess's voice, ordered them to leave. She cloaked the ship in black fog and for endless days and nights they sailed past many Celtic settlements, until they caught sight of the Tyrrhenian Sea. Soon afterwards, they safely entered the harbor of Circe's island.

There they found the sorceress standing on the seashore washing her hair and face in the waves. She had dreamed that her chamber and her entire house were streaming with blood, while a flame devoured all the magic herbal remedies that she used to bewitch strangers. Then she scooped up the blood in her cupped hands and extinguished the fire with it. Awakened at dawn by such a nightmare, she rose from her couch and hurried to the shore, where she washed her garments and her hair as if they were truly flecked with blood. Flocks of huge beasts unlike any other, their body parts borrowed from various creatures, trooped after her as cattle follow the shepherd out of the stalls. The heroes stood horror-struck, for they only had to look at Circe to know that she was the sister of the ruthless Aeetes. When the goddess had overcome the terrors of the night, she turned homewards, beckoning to the beasts and stroking them as others might stroke dogs.

Jason ordered his entire crew to remain on board, while he hurried ashore with Medea, who reluctantly followed him to Circe's palace. The sorceress did not know what had brought the strangers to her home. She invited them to sit in magnificent chairs, but softly and mournfully they approached the hearth where they both sat down. Medea bowed her head into her hands and Jason plunged the sword with which he had killed Absyrtus into the ground. He laid his hand upon it and rested his chin on the hilt without raising his eyes. At once, Circe realized that they were supplicants, brought to her by the despair of exile and their need to atone for the murder they had committed. To appease Zeus, defender of supplicants, and to produce the obligatory offering, she slaughtered a piglet whose mother was still alive, calling upon Zeus for purification. Her servants, the Naiads, were instructed to collect everything in the house that could serve in a ceremony of atonement. Meanwhile, she herself stood by the hearth, burning sacrificial cakes and at the same time offering up solemn prayers to pacify the Furies and beg the gods to forgive those whose hands were stained with murder. When all this was done, she again bade the strangers to sit on the magnificent chairs while she sat across from them.

The ship sped forth and soon there came into view a beautiful island laden with flowers. Here dwelled the perfidious sirens.

Then she asked them about their voyage and its intended purpose. She questioned why they had chosen to land on her island and why they had begged for her protection. All this because she recalled her own blood-soaked dream. When Medea raised her head to reply to Circe and looked her in the face, the sorceress was struck by the young woman's eyes, for Medea and Circe herself were descended from the sun god and all his descendants had eyes that sparkled like gold. Then she demanded to hear the native tongue of the land from which they had fled. So, in the language spoken in Colchis, the girl began to tell her, quite truthfully, all that had happened between Aeetes and the heroes. However, she failed to mention anything to do with the murder of her brother Absyrtus. But nothing could be hidden from the sorceress. She felt pity for her niece and said, "My poor child, you have fled from home under ignominious circumstances, thereby committing a grave transgression. Your father will surely come to Greece to wreak revenge on you for killing his son. You need not fear that I will harm you, for you are both a supplicant and my kinswoman. But do not expect me to help you. You must also abandon this stranger, whoever he may be. I cannot approve of your plans or of your dishonorable flight!" At these words, Medea was gripped by indescribable anguish. She threw her veil over her head and wept bitterly until the hero took her by the hand. She let him lead her out of Circe's palace with faltering steps.

But Hera felt a certain sympathy for her protégée. She sent her messenger Iris to travel along the rainbow path to summon Thetis, goddess of the sea, to whom Hera entrusted the safety of the heroes and their ship. As soon as Jason and Medea came on board, gentle breezes rose. In a more cheerful mood, the heroes weighed anchor and hoisted sail. Driven by a light wind, the ship sped forth and soon there came into view a beautiful island laden with flowers. Here dwelled the perfidious sirens, who lured passing ships with their melodious singing and then promptly sank them. Half bird and half maiden, they sat in wait and no stranger who approached them could possibly escape. As the Argonauts prepared to cast their ropes ashore and moor the ship, they were serenaded by the sirens. For the Argonauts they chose their sweetest songs, but then the Thracian singer Orpheus rose from his seat and began to pluck his divine lyre with such exuberance that it drowned out the sirens' voices. At the same moment a howling wind, sent by the gods, blasted into the ship's stern, completely silencing the sirens' song. Only one of the heroes, Butes, son of Teleon, failed to resist their melodious voices. He leapt from his rowing bench and into the sea, then swam towards the beguiling sounds. He would have drowned, had it not been for Aphrodite, ruler of Mount Eryx in Sicily. She hauled him from a whirlpool and threw him onto one of her island's headlands, where he would make his home from that time onwards. Then they came upon a strait where on one side lay Scylla, a steep rock which jutted out of the sea and could easily tear the ship apart. On the other side, the whirlpool Charybdis sucked water into the deep, threatening to swallow the vessel. Floating between Scylla and Charybdis were rocks torn from the seabed, where the forge of Hephaestus, god of war, once stood. Now only smoke rose through the water and darkened the air. As the Argo approached, suddenly the sea nymphs, daughters of Nereus, came from all sides to greet them, while Queen Thetis herself took hold of the ship's rudder. Together they swam around the ship and whenever it approached a floating rock, one nymph would pass it to another, like girls playing ball. At one moment, the stone rose to the sky on the crest of a wave, at the next, it sank back into the brine. Standing on a clifftop, his hammer on his shoulder, Hephaestus watched the game while Hera gripped Athena's hand, for observing all that was happening made her feel giddy. At last, they left all the danger behind and sailed across the open sea to the island where the Phaeacians lived under the rule of virtuous King Alcinous.

THE ARGONAUTS
THE HEROES' LAST ADVENTURE
MEDEA'S REVENGE AND JASON'S DEATH

*Instead of a happy ending, jealousy and murderous revenge
round off the last adventure:
Medea's magic helps the heroes to succeed in defeating the robotic adversary
Talos. Jason and Medea go on to Corinth and have three sons. What might have
been a blissful outcome to the myth of the Argonauts turns out rather differently.*

Illustrations by Henry Matthew Brock, Sybil Tawse, and Virginia Frances Sterrett

THE ARGONAUTS: THE HEROES' LAST ADVENTURE

Long had the heroes tried in vain to leave Lake Tritonis and head for the open sea, but the wind was against them. The ship slithered back and forth like a snake struggling to escape from its hiding place in vain, its head darting left and right with eyes sparkling and tongue hissing. On the advice of Orpheus the prophet, they returned ashore and presented the biggest sacrificial tripod they had aboard the Argo to the local gods. On their way back to the ship they met Triton, god of the sea, in the guise of a youth. He lifted a clod of earth from the ground and handed it to the hero Euphemus as a token of hospitality and friendship, which Euphemus hid close to his breast. The sea god said, "My father has appointed me protector of these coasts. Look, do you see where the water is still, deep and dark? That is a narrow outlet from the lake to the open sea. Row towards there and I shall offer you a fair wind, which will carry you as far as the Peloponnese." They boarded the ship, overjoyed. Triton hoisted the tripod on to his shoulder and disappeared into the water. After a few pleasant days at sea, they arrived at the rocky island of

Karpathos. From there they intended to cross to another island, beautiful Crete, which was guarded by Talos, a terrifying giant. He was the only survivor of the Men of Bronze generation, who had once sprung from beech trees. Zeus gave him the post of Europe's guardian and bade him to circle the island three times a day on his bronze feet. His whole body was made of bronze and therefore indestructible, although he had a small place on one ankle made of flesh, sinew, and a vein through which blood

flowed. This meant he was not immortal. Anyone who knew of this spot and could hit it could be certain of killing him. When the heroes rowed towards the island, Talos was keeping watch from a cliff close to the water's edge. As soon as he caught sight of them, he broke off blocks of stone and hurled them at the ship. They rowed backwards, terrified. Although plagued by thirst yet again, the Argonauts would have given up their plan to land on Crete, had Medea not stood up and told them there was nothing to fear. "Listen," she said. "I know how to tame this monster. Keep the ship out of throwing range!" Then she lifted the folds of her crimson gown and, guided by Jason, walked the length of the ship. Then she thrice repeated a menacing magic formula, directed to the Fates whose task is to cut the thread of life, and to the hounds of the underworld that hurtle through the air in pursuit of the living. Next, she cast a spell on Talos's eyelids and sent dark visions to trouble his soul. Confused and bewildered, he stooped to pick up a stone to defend the harbor, hitting his unprotected ankle against the sharp edge of a boulder. Blood gushed from the wound like molten lead. Like a partly chopped pine tree which crashes to the ground at the first gust of wind, Talos staggered around before plunging to the bottom of the sea with a mighty roar.

Now that the Argonauts could safely land, they decided to rest until morning on the hallowed island. Soon afterwards they reached the island of Aegina. From there they headed homewards. With no further misfortunes, the Argo and its heroes arrived safely in the harbor of Iolcus. Jason consecrated

THE ARGONAUTS: THE HEROES' LAST ADVENTURE

Page 91
*Next, she cast a spell on Talos's eyelids and
sent dark visions to trouble his soul.*

Page 92
*Talos staggered around before plunging to
the bottom of the sea with a mighty roar.*

the ship to Poseidon on the Isthmus of Corinth. When it finally crumbled to dust, the gods raised it to heaven, where it glittered as a shining constellation in the southern skies.

Jason did not succeed to the throne of Iolcus, which he had attempted to achieve after undertaking a perilous journey, stealing Medea from her father, and infamously murdering her brother Absyrtus. He was obliged to surrender the kingdom to Acastus, son of Pelias, and escape to Corinth with his young wife. He lived there with her for ten years and she bore him three sons. The two eldest, Thessalus and Alcimenes, were twins; the third son, Tisander, was much younger. During that time, Jason had loved and honored Medea, not only for her beauty but also for her fine mind and her quick-witted response to so many situations. However, as her looks began to fade with time, Jason became bewitched and infatuated by a beautiful young woman, Glauce, daughter of Creon, king of Corinth. Without a word to his wife, he courted the maiden and it was not until her father had consented to their union and their wedding had been arranged that Jason told Medea and exhorted her to give her willing consent to dissolve their marriage. He assured her that he had not tired of their relationship, but he believed their children would benefit from their father's close relationship to the royal court. But Medea was affronted by his demand and angrily called upon the gods to testify as witnesses to the oaths he had sworn to her. Jason paid no heed and decided to go ahead with his marriage to the king's daughter. In utter despair, Medea wandered through her husband's palace. "Woe is me!" she cried. "Would that a thunderbolt from heaven might strike me down. What more shall I live for? If only death would take me. Oh father! Oh country that I left in disgrace! Oh my brother, whom I murdered and whose blood has stained me! Yet it was not my husband Jason's place to punish me! It was for his sake that I sinned! Goddess of justice, I beg you to destroy him and his little concubine."

She was still wailing her way through the palace when Creon, Jason's new father-in-law, came upon her. "What a dismal-looking creature you are, whining about your husband," he cried. "Take your sons by the hand and leave my country this instant. I shall not return home until I have driven you across the border."

She then begged him to allow her to postpone her departure for just one day, so that she could find a means of escape and a refuge for her sons. The king responded, "I am not a tyrant by nature. My own feigned compassion has often led me to be foolishly indulgent. Even now, I feel I am not acting wisely. Nevertheless, you shall have your way."

When Medea had been granted the respite for which she begged, she was again seized by madness and prepared herself to carry out a deed which hovered at the back of her mind but she had never truly considered doing. First, however, she made a final attempt to convince her husband of his unscrupulous and unfair behavior. But Jason's heart had hardened. He promised to arrange for her and the children to be supplied with plenty of gold, and to send messages to friends who might offer them hospitality. But she treated all his promises with disdain. "Go, get married," she said. "Go and celebrate a wedding that will end in pain." After Jason had left her, she regretted her final words, not because she had changed her mind, but because she feared he might have her spied on and prevent her carrying out her malicious plan. So she asked him to agree to a second meeting, where she spoke to him in a kindlier manner. "Jason, forgive me. I was blinded by rage," she said. "I see now that all you have done is for our own good. We came here as poor exiles. By this marriage of yours, you are providing for yourself, your children, and even for me. When your sons have been away from you for a while, you will call them back so that they can share in the good fortune of the sisters and brothers they may have by that time. Come hither, my sons. Come and embrace your father. Make your peace with him as I have made mine!" Jason believed in this change of heart and was delighted. He promised to do more for her and the children. Medea went further to assure him, begging him to take the children while she moved away on her own. So as to be certain that his new wife and her father would agree to her plan, she ordered exquisite robes of gold to be brought from her stores and given to Jason as a wedding gift for his bride. After some misgivings, he allowed himself to be persuaded and sent a servant to take the gifts to the bride. But these fine garments were made from cloth that had been magically drenched with poison and, after Medea had bidden

Looking upwards, he caught sight of the vile murderess flying through the air on her dragon-drawn chariot as she fled the scene of her revenge.

her husband a duplicitously sweet farewell, she waited hour after hour for the messenger to report how her gifts had been received. Finally he appeared, crying out, "Get on board your ship, Medea, and flee! Your enemy and her father are dead. When your sons entered the palace with their father, we servants were overjoyed to see that everyone was reconciled and the feud was over. The King's young daughter greeted your husband with a serene smile, but on seeing the children she covered her eyes, as if she were revolted by their presence. But Jason tried to soothe her while speaking kind words about you, and he arranged the gifts before her. Charmed by the splendor of these beautiful garments, her heart softened and she agreed to abide by her husband's wishes. When her husband and children had left her, she eagerly grabbed the golden regalia. She threw the exquisite cloak around her shoulders, set the gold wreath in her hair, and eagerly admired herself in the mirror. Then she wandered through the royal apartments, parading her new clothes proudly, just like a little girl. But suddenly the scene changed. Her face turned pale, every limb trembling as she staggered backwards and, before she could reach a seat, she fell to the floor, her eyes rolling upwards until the pupils disappeared, while she lay frothing from the mouth. Her screams of pain echoed through the palace, sending some servants scurrying to find her father, while others ran in search of her future husband. Meanwhile, the magic wreath on her head had burst into flames. Poison and fire competed in their attacks on her body and, when her father arrived weeping and wailing, all that remained of his daughter was her disfigured corpse. In utter despair, he threw himself down on to her body and, as he inhaled poison from her deadly cloak, he also lost his life. I know nothing of Jason."

Hearing the story of these horrendous events did nothing to appease her anger; indeed it enflamed her even further, filling her with a furious thirst for revenge and she ran to deal her husband and herself the fatal blow. She hurried to the room where her sons lay asleep, for night had fallen. "Steel yourself, my heart," she told herself as she ran. "Why have qualms about doing a deed that is both gruesome and necessary? Forget that these are your children, to whom you have given birth. Forget for just one single hour! Then you can mourn them for the rest of your life. You are doing them an act of kindness. If you do not kill them, their enemies will."

When Jason sped towards his house to seek out the woman who had murdered his young bride and take his revenge upon her, he could hear his children's screams as they bled to death. Running through the open door of their chamber, he came upon his sons, stabbed as if they were guilt offerings. Medea, however, was nowhere to be seen. When he left the house in desperation, he heard a rushing sound overhead. Looking upwards he caught sight of the vile murderess flying through the air on her dragon-drawn chariot, summoned by magic, as she abandoned the scene of her vengeance. Jason lost hope of ever punishing her for her crimes. Overwhelmed by despair, he recalled the slaying of Absyrtus. Now, he fell on his sword and died on the threshold of his house.

MELEAGER AND THE BOAR

Tragedy strikes the royal family of Calydon:
Jealousy and pride break out among those blinded by love, and even a
mother is torn between grief and an overwhelming desire for revenge. The disaster
is recounted in the myth of the celebrated hunt for the Calydonian Boar.

Illustrations by Henry Justice Ford

It was a year of plenty and Oeneus, king of Calydon, made offerings of the first fruits to the gods. As a gift to Demeter he presented grain, to Dionysus wine, to Athena oil, and to other deities the crop over which they each presided. Only Artemis was forgotten, and no sweet aroma of incense arose from her altar. The goddess was enraged at being overlooked and resolved to avenge such negligence. She set a foul-tempered boar loose across Oeneus's kingdom. With eyes ablaze and neck bristling, lightning-like flashes bursting from its foaming jaws, and tusks as big as an elephant's, the porcine beast went on the attack. It trampled fields still sown with corn and other crops, thus barns and threshing floors were forced to wait in vain for the promised harvest. It gobbled up both grapes and vine branches and it wolfed down the olives and most of the trees. Neither shepherds nor sheepdogs could shield their flocks from the monster, and even the most intrepid bulls could not defend their herds. At last the king's son, the splendid hero Meleager, gathered hunters and hounds together to destroy the ferocious boar. Greece's most famous heroes were invited to the join the hunt, among them the equally heroic young woman, Atalanta of Arcadia, daughter of Iasus. Abandoned in a forest and suckled by a bear, she was found and raised by a huntsman. She grew up to be a fair maiden, but she loathed men and spent her days hunting in the woods. She snubbed any male who made advances on her and even killed two centaurs who refused to leave her in peace with bow and arrow. This time, however, her passion for hunting was enough to oblige her to tolerate the company of these heroes. She appeared with her hair tied in a simple knot, her ivory quiver hanging across her shoulder and her bow held in her left hand. Her face seemed to be androgynous – girlish for a boy, and boyish for a girl. When Meleager was first captivated by her beauty he said to himself, "How fortunate the man she considers worthy to be her husband." But the perilous hunt could be delayed no longer, and so time did not allow for him to take matters further.

The hunters walked together towards a wood of ancient trees extending from the plain to the mountain slope. When they arrived, some laid out nets to snare their prey, others unleashed the hounds, while still others set off to track the boar. Soon they reached a sloping valley carved out by swollen mountain streams. Reeds, marsh grass, willows, and rushes grew down in the gorge where the boar had made its hiding place. Now, trapped by the approaching hounds, it crashed at lightning speed through the wood and charged furiously into the midst of its foes. The youngest among the hunters shrieked and bellowed as they aimed their iron-pointed spears, which the beast avoided as it charged into the very center of the pack. Spear after spear, arrow after arrow flew at it, but none did any more than graze it and infuriate the beast even more. Short of breath, with eyes flashing, the boar rushed headlong into the hunters' right flank, like a stone shot from a sling, killing three of them outright. A fourth, Nestor, who would later become one of the most famous among heroes, saved himself by scrambling into the branches of an oak tree, on whose trunk the boar was ferociously sharpening its tusks. At this moment, the twin brothers Castor and Pollux, high astride their snow-white horses, would have pierced it with their spears

IT TRAMPLED FIELDS STILL SOWN WITH CORN AND OTHER CROPS, THUS BARNS AND THRESHING FLOORS WERE FORCED TO WAIT IN VAIN FOR THE PROMISED HARVEST.

MELEAGER AND THE BOAR

The first landed on the ground, the second in the middle of the boar's back.

had the bristly beast not fled into the tangled thickets. Then Atalanta fitted an arrow to her bow and shot at it through the bushes, striking it under the ear and, for the first time, staining its bristles with blood. Meleager was the first to see the wound and triumphantly announced in the presence of his comrades, "Beyond doubt, brave young woman, you deserve the prize for valor!" Mortified that a female should have deprived them of victory, the men all threw their spears at the same time. But among such a deluge of weapons not a single shot reached the monster. Then Ancaeus of Arcadia proudly raised his double-edged battle-axe in both hands and stood on the balls of his feet, ready to strike the blow. But before he could deliver it, the boar drove its tusks into the weak spot on the side of Ancaeus's body and he fell, bathed in blood, his entrails spilling on the ground. Then Jason, leader of the Argonauts, threw his spear, which by chance missed the mark and sank into the body of Celadon. Finally, Meleager cast two spears one after the other. The first landed on the ground, the second in the middle of the boar's back. The beast fumed with rage and began scurrying around in circles, blood and foam gushing from its mouth. With a hunting spear, Meleager delivered a fresh blow to its neck, then lances struck it from all sides. The boar now lay stretched out, writhing in its own blood. Meleager pressed his foot against the slain animal's head and, with the aid of his sword, stripped the bristly hide from its back. This he presented to the fearless Atalanta, as well as the boar's severed head and glimmering tusks. "Accept these spoils of the hunt," he said. "By rights they are mine, but you deserve to share the honor!" The hunters resented the award of such an honor to a mere woman and there was much angry muttering among their ranks. So, with clenched fists raised, the sons of Thestius, Meleager's uncles from his mother's side, stood before at Atalanta, yelling loudly. "Put those trophies down immediately, woman, and do not imagine that you can cheat us out of what is rightfully ours. Your beauty will not help you, neither will your besotted lover who dares to waste such tributes." With these words, they snatched the head and hide, while disputing Meleager's right to give them to another. This Meleager could not tolerate. Seething with rage he shouted, "Listen, you bandits! You men

HOW ATALANTA A

98

AGER SLEW THE WILD BOAR OF CALEDON

MELEAGER AND THE BOAR

Below
When Meleager was only a few days old and Althaea lay in the bed where she had borne him, the Fates appeared beside her.

Right
Her son's pain increased with the flames.

who would steal what others have rightfully earned, allow me to teach you this. Threatening is one thing, carrying out a threat is another!" And then he thrust his sword into one of his uncles then, before both men realized what was happening, he stabbed the other.

Meleager's mother Althaea was on her way to the temple of the gods to make a thank offering for her son's victory when her brothers' corpses were carried past. She beat her breast in anguish, hurried back to the palace and changed from her festive golden robe to the black of mourning. Her cries of grief echoed across the city. But when she heard that their murderer was her own son, she dried her tears as her sadness turned into a desire to kill. Then she suddenly recalled a memory long since forgotten. When Meleager was only a few days old and Althaea lay in the bed where she had borne him, the Fates appeared beside her. "Your son will become a brave hero," the first Fate predicted. "Your son will be a great man," the second one forecast. "Your son will live until the log lying on the hearth is consumed by fire," prophesied the third. No sooner had the Fates departed than the young mother took the still-glowing fragment of wood from the hearth, quenched it with water and, driven by the desire that her child should live a long life, hid it away in the most secret corner of her chamber. Fueled by revenge, she thought again of the log and hurried to the secret hiding place where she had carefully locked it away. She called a servant to lay kindling and brushwood on the hearth and set them ablaze. Then she seized the piece of wood she had hidden for so long.

THE·VISIT·FROM·THE·FATES

But in her heart she struggled with her role as both mother and sister, her face paling with fear then flushing with anger. Four times she attempted to lay the fragment among the flames, and four times she drew back. In the end, sisterly love triumphed. "Oh gods of retribution! Turn your gaze towards me and witness my offering to the Furies." she said. "And you, my newly departed brothers, recognize what I am doing for you and accept as my memorial gift the ill-starred fruit of my own body! My motherly heart is broken and soon I shall follow the one I am sending to you as consolation." She then turned away and with a trembling hand threw the log onto the fire.

Meanwhile, Meleager had also returned to the city and was now tormenting himself with mixed emotions over his victory, his love, and his act of murder. Then suddenly, his innermost being was invaded by an inexplicable agony. Where it came from, he did not know. He threw himself on his couch. He bore the pain as a hero should, but was deeply distressed at having to die an ignominious and bloodless death, envious of those comrades killed by the stampeding boar. He called for his brother, his sisters, his aged father, and his mother who stood by, staring pitilessly as the flames consumed the wood. Her son's pain increased with the flames, but as the fire gradually turned everything into colorless ash, his pain lessened and with the last spark his spirit left his body. His father and sisters mourned over his remains, but his mother was nowhere to be seen. She was found, hanged by the neck in front of the hearth where the fragile cinders of the log still lay.

QUEEN ALTHEA WATCHES THE BURNING LOG
while Meleager is dying outside

NIOBE

Cruel punishment for overbearing maternal pride:
Niobe, wife of Amphion, king of Thebes, is the mother of seven sons
and seven daughters. In a fit of hubris, she forbids her people from
worshipping Leto because she has only two children, Apollo and Artemis.
The wrathful divine siblings slay Niobe's fourteen children.

Illustrations by Gustaf Tenggren, John Flaxman, and Artuš Scheiner

Niobe, queen of Thebes, had much to be proud of. The Muses had given her husband, Amphion, a splendid lyre with a sound so sumptuous that, on hearing it, the stones destined to build the palace of Thebes had joined themselves together of their own accord. Her father was Tantalus, a guest of the immortals. Niobe ruled a powerful realm and was famed for her sense of duty and regal beauty. But nothing brought her so much happiness as her fourteen children, seven sons and seven daughters. Niobe was also regarded as the most fortunate of mothers. This she would have been, had she not flaunted her qualities so vigorously. Indeed, her awareness of her fortunes would prove to be her downfall.

One day, the seer Manto, daughter of the prophet Tiresias, was inspired by the gods to go into the streets and urge the women of Thebes to honor Leto, goddess of motherhood, and her twin children, Apollo and Artemis. This they would do by weaving laurel leaves to adorn their hair, then make a solemn prayer and offerings of incense. While the women gathered around to listen, Niobe suddenly appeared.

"WHO CAN DOUBT MY HAPPINESS? AND WHO CAN DOUBT IT WILL LAST?"

Accompanied by a regal entourage, she strutted around in a robe worked with gold thread. She looked dazzlingly beautiful, as much as rage would allow, and her glossy hair fell down to her shoulders from her lovely head. She stood among the women as they prepared to make a sacrifice under the open sky. Casting a disdainful eye over the attentive crowd, she said, "Are you not insane to honor the gods, who are no more than story-book creatures, when people even more favored by heaven are here, living among you? If you set up altars to Leto, why do you not burn incense in my name? And is not my father Tantalus the only mortal ever to have dined at Zeus's table? And my mother Dione is sister to the Pleiades, those stars who light up the sky. One of my forebears, the mighty Atlas, carried the vault of heaven on his shoulders. My father's father is Zeus, father of the gods.

Even the peoples of Phrygia obey me, while the city of Cadmea, whose walls arose of their own accord to the music of Amphion, defers to me and my spouse. In every chamber in my palace I can admire priceless treasures. What is more, I have the face worthy of a goddess and a brood of children the likes of which no other mother can boast. I have seven sturdy sons and just as many flourishing daughters, and soon I shall have an equal number of sons- and daughters-in-law. Is it any wonder that I am so proud? And yet you dare to pay more respect to Leto than to me? She, the daughter of some unknown Titan, for whom the wide earth could not find even the smallest space in which to bear her children to Zeus. That was until the floating island of Delos took pity on the poor wandering creature and offered her a makeshift refuge. There the poor soul gave birth to only two children. That's merely one seventh of my own joys of motherhood. Who can doubt my happiness? And who can doubt it will last? The goddess of fortune would have much to do if she wished to do serious harm to my possessions. Even if she took one or more of those I have borne, when would their number sink to only two like poor Leto's meager offspring? So away with your offerings! Away with the wreaths on your heads! Disperse! Return to your houses and never let me catch you behaving together in such a ridiculous manner!"

Shocked and horrified, the women tore the wreaths from their heads, left the ceremony unfinished and slunk homewards, silently praying to honor the goddess.

Meanwhile, Leto and her twins stood on the peak of Mount Cynthus, gazing through their divine eyes at what was happening in distant Thebes. "See, children, how proud I am to have given birth to you. But also see how this insolent mortal insults me, one who yields to no goddess but Hera. If you do not help me, I shall be banished from my ancient holy altars! And yes, Niobe is maligning you too, by placing you second to her own

Page 103
The twanging of the bow sounded again.

Below
*He was struck by the cold steel of Phoebus
Apollo's arrow.*

vast herd!" She was about to protest even further, but Phoebus interrupted her. "That is enough protesting, mother. You are only delaying punishment!" His sister, who was standing beside him, agreed. Veiling themselves in a cloud, the two raced through the air to the city of Cadmea, outside whose ramparts lay a spacious area of open country that was devoted not to crop cultivation, but to races and competitions between horses and chariots. There, Amphion's seven sons were amusing themselves, some by riding on fine steeds, the rest cheerfully spectating. Ismenus, the eldest, was driving his mount in a circle at a trot, guiding the horse firmly with his hand close to the bit in its foaming mouth, when he suddenly howled in pain. The rein slipped from his flagging grasp and, struck through the heart by an arrow, he slowly sank to earth at the animal's right flank. His brother Sipylus was riding his horse next to him. He heard the rattling of the quiver in the air

and fled at full speed, like a helmsman catching the wind in his sails so as to enter port before the weather breaks. Even so, an arrow hummed through the air and caught him in the nape of the neck, its iron point protruding from his throat. Over the mane of his galloping horse he slid to the ground, spattering the earth with his blood. Two other brothers, one named Tantalus after his grandfather, the other Phaedimus, were facing off in a wrestling match, each wrapped around the other. The twanging of the bow sounded again and an arrow skewered the brothers together. Both whimpered, their limbs in excruciating pain as they writhed on the ground, their eyes dimming as they died

together in the dust, their souls departed in a single death. A fifth son, Alphenor, saw them fall. Beating his breast, he tore towards them and tried to revive them by wrapping their cold bodies in his embrace. But, as he fulfilled this brotherly act of mercy, he was struck by the cold steel of Phoebus Apollo's arrow and as he pulled it from his heart, his blood and breath flowed away. Damasichthon, the sixth brother, a charming, long-haired youth, was struck in the knee joint by an arrow. When he bent backwards to extract the projectile, a second arrow flew into his open mouth, sending blood leaping up from his throat, as if from a fountain. Ilioneus, the last and youngest son, had watched it all and fell to his knees, arms outspread, and began to plead, "Oh all gods of heaven, I beg you spare me!" Even the most fearsome of bowmen was moved with compassion, but his flying arrow could not be called back. The boy fell, but died of a painless wound as the arrow barely grazed his heart.

Word of the tragedy soon reached the city. When Amphion, father of all the dead, heard the terrible news, he fell on his sword, piercing his own breast. The weeping of the servants and the citizens soon reached the women in their chambers. It took a long time for Niobe to grasp that such terrible things could happen. She refused to believe that the immortals were so powerful and could not accept how much they dared, and succeeded, to do. Soon, however, she could no longer doubt the truth. How different was this version of Niobe from the woman who drove worshippers away from the altars of the mighty goddess and

Nothing survived but the tears flowing endlessly from her lifeless eyes.

then haughtily strutted her way across the city! Then she was the envy of her dearest friends. Now even her enemies pitied her! She hurried out of the city and to the field where she threw herself on the cold bodies of her sons, kissing one after the other. Then, lifting her weary arms skywards, she cried, "Now you can gloat over my suffering. Now with your vicious heart, merciless Leto, revel in the knowledge that the death of my seven sons will speed me to my grave! The triumph is yours, victorious enemy!"

Then her seven daughters, already dressed in mourning, with hair unbound, came and stood beside their fallen brothers. A gleam of malicious glee passed rapidly across Niobe's ashen face. Forgetting herself, she looked up to heaven with a smirk and said, "You? Victorious? No! Anguished as I am, I still have more than you in your triumph. Even with so many dead, I remain the conqueror." She had barely finished speaking when there came through the air the sound of a string tightening on a bow. All those present trembled, apart from Niobe, a woman left hardhearted by such grave misfortunes. Suddenly one of the sisters put her hand to her heart and pulled out an arrow. She fell senseless to the ground, turning her dying gaze towards

SHE SAT STIFFENED BY SORROW; THE HAIR ON HER HEAD LAY UNRUFFLED BY THE BREEZE.

the brother lying closest to her. Another sister hurried to comfort her unfortunate mother, but her words were cut short by an unseen arrow. A third fell as she turned to flee, others stumbled as they bowed over their dying siblings. The only one remaining was the youngest, who fled to her mother, burying her face in her lap and hiding under her robe. "Leave me this one!" Niobe cried out in deep distress. "Only the youngest of so many!" But even as she begged, the child fell from her lap and now Niobe sat alone, surrounded by the bodies of her sons and daughters. She sat stiffened by sorrow; the hair on her head lay unruffled by the breeze; the color drained from her cheeks; her eyes stayed motionless in her cadaverous face; no life seemed to remain in her entire being. Blood ceased to flow through her veins; her neck turned to one side; her arm barely stirred; her feet ceased to move; even her insides had turned to stone. Nothing survived but the tears flowing endlessly from her lifeless eyes. Now a tempest arose and swept her through the air and across the sea to her old home among the barren mountains of Lydia, then set her down among the stony crags of Sipylus. Here she still stands, a block of marble which even now is bathed in her tears.

HERACLES
AND·THE·HYDRA

Deeds worthy of a hero:
Eurystheus, king of Argos, gives Heracles the task of flaying
the invincible Nemean Lion and bringing back its skin, subduing the
nine-headed Hydra, and pursuing a fleet-footed hind for a year.

Illustration by Arthur Rackham

The first labor commissioned by the king was that Heracles should bring him the skin of the Nemean lion. The monster lived in the Peloponnese, in a forest between Cleonae and Nemea in the region of Argolis. The lion could not be harmed by the weapons brandished by humans. Some have claimed that he is the son of the giant Typhon and the serpent Echidna, while others assert that he dropped down to earth from the moon. Thus Heracles set out to deal with the lion. He carried his quiver on his back, in one hand his bow, and in the other a club made from the trunk of a wild olive tree he had found on the Helicon and torn up by the roots. When he reached the woods of Nemea, he looked warily in every direction to find the ravenous beast before it spotted him. It was noon and he found no trace of the lion nor could he inquire about the path leading to his lair, for he met no one, either with cattle in the meadows or felling trees in the forest. All of them had fled to their homes, well away from where the lion prowled, and fearfully locked themselves in. Determined to prove his strength as soon as he found the monster, Heracles spent the entire afternoon wandering through the dense woodlands. Towards evening, the lion, bloated with flesh and blood, was running along a forest path in search of a place to rest after the hunt. His head, mane, and chest dripped with blood from his kills while his tongue licked away the drops trickling from its jaws. The hero spotted him from afar and hid behind a dense wall of bushes, waiting for the animal to approach as he pointed an arrow at the lion's flank between the ribs and haunch. But the shot failed to penetrate the flesh, instead bouncing off like a stone and landing on the moss-covered ground. The lion raised his bloodstained head, eyes rolling in all directions, and bared his terrifying teeth. He stretched his neck towards the demigod, who quickly shot an arrow at his chest, aiming for the

SHE REARED HER NINE HEADS, WHICH SWAYED LIKE THE BOUGHS OF A TREE IN A STORM.

place where the lion drew his breath. Again, the missile did not even pierce the skin but bounced off and fell at the monster's feet. Heracles was preparing to load a third arrow when the lion turned and saw him. The lion's long tail dragged between his hind legs, his neck inflated with rage and his mane bristled as a roar rumbled in his throat, his back bent like a bow. Ready to attack, he leapt at his enemy. Heracles threw down his arrows, cast off his lion's skin and with his right hand swung the club over the animal's head, striking his neck so hard that he dropped from midair to the ground, then staggered on to his feet with his head spinning. Before the lion could catch his breath, Heracles rushed at him. This time, to ensure his freedom of movement, the hero flung aside his bow and quiver. He rushed the lion from behind, curled his arms around the lion's neck and strangled him to death, sending his vile soul back to Hades. For a long time, Heracles attempted to skin his dead enemy, but the hide resisted both iron and stone. Finally, it suddenly occurred to him to peel off the creature's hide using his own claws. This time he was successful. Later, he would turn the splendid lion skin into a cuirass, while out of the jaws he would make a new helmet. However, for the time being he picked up the hide and the weapons with which he had come, slung the hide of the Nemean lion over his shoulder, and headed back to Tiryns. When King Eurystheus saw him approach, carrying the skin of the monstrous beast, he was so petrified by the hero's prodigious strength that he crawled into an iron cauldron. Henceforth, he refused to set eyes on Heracles and instructed his herald Copreus, son of Pelops, to meet him beyond the city walls to transmit his regal orders.

The hero's second labor was to slay the Hydra, also a child of Typhon and Echidna. She had grown up in the swamps of Lerna and had the habit of slithering on to dry land, tearing the

*She then curled herself around one of
his feet, at first evading direct conflict.*

cattle limb from limb and destroying the crops. She was an ab-
normally large snake with nine heads, eight of them mortal, but
the ninth, set in the middle, was born to live forever. Heracles
approached this encounter with trepidation. He immediately
climbed on board a chariot with his nephew Iolaus as his charioteer. Son of his stepbrother Iphicles, Iolaus had long been
Heracles's inseparable companion. Now they sped side by side
to Lerna, where the Hydra eventually came into view on a hill
near her lair, close to the springs of Amymone. Here Iolaus
reined in the horses as Heracles leapt from the chariot. He began shooting flaming arrows at the nine-headed serpent to
force her from her hiding place. She came out hissing and lash-
ing out at them, rearing her nine heads which swayed like the
boughs of a tree in a storm.

Heracles moved fearlessly towards her, seized her in his
powerful grip and held her fast. She then curled herself around
one of his feet, at first evading direct conflict. He began to smash
her heads with his club, but to no avail. Whenever he shattered
one head, two more sprouted in its place. Suddenly a giant
crab came to the Hydra's aid, wounding the hero by clawing at
his feet. Nevertheless, Heracles clubbed the creature to death
before calling to Iolaus for help. The boy was already equipped
with a torch, which he used to set part of the nearby forest ablaze.
He took the burning branches to scorch the snake's newly
sprouting heads, thus preventing them growing to their full size.
Now the threat of the Hydra's ever-growing heads was gone, and
the hero was able to cut off the immortal one and bury it by the

wayside, covering the grave with a heavy stone. He split the
snake's body in two and dipped his arrows in her poisonous
blood. Thereafter, the wounds he dealt to other beings would
never heal.

The third labor to be carried out on Eurystheus's instructions was to capture the hind of Mount Cerynea and bring her
home alive. She was a beautiful creature with golden horns
and brazen feet, living on a hill in Arcadia. She had been one of
the five hinds with which Artemis had first proved her hunting
skills and the only one allowed to return to the woods and run
free, since Fate had ruled that Heracles should be exhausted
by his long pursuit of that fine animal. He hunted her for a
whole year during which time he found his way to the land of
the Hyperboreans and the source of the River Ister. He finally
caught up with the hind on the bank of the River Ladon, not
far from the city of Oenoe, near the mountain where Artemis
dwelt. Even so, he recognized that the only way to capture the
animal was to wound her with an arrow and carry her across
Arcadia on his shoulders. Here he met the goddess Artemis,
accompanied by her brother Apollo. She berated him for even
thinking about killing a creature she regarded as sacred. Indeed,
the look on her face hinted that she was about to seize his quarry.
"Mighty goddess, I did not consider doing such a thing for my
own amusement," he replied in his defense. "It was a matter of
sheer necessity. How else could I satisfy Eurystheus's demands?"
With these words he appeased her anger and brought the hind
alive to Mycenae.

HERACLES AND THE THREE GOLDEN APPLES

A sly trick:
Heracles persuades Atlas, who holds up the vault of heaven, to procure the
Golden Apples of the Hesperides while the hero bears this burden on his shoulders.
When Atlas wants to leave Heracles trapped there so he can enjoy his new-found
freedom, Heracles can only resort to a cunning ruse.

Illustrations by Milo Winter

A long time ago, the magnificent wedding of Zeus and Hera was held, and all the gods arrived bearing gifts for the supreme bridal pair. But Gaia, goddess of the earth, had no wish to be outdone by her fellow guests. On the western shore of the ocean she planted a fine tree whose many branches were weighed down with golden apples. The Hesperides, four virgin daughters of Night, were tasked with guarding the sacred gardens in which the tree stood. They had the help of Ladon, a hundred-headed dragon, the offspring of Phorcys, famed as the father of a multitude of different monsters, and Gaea's daughter Ceto. The dragon never slept, and its presence was heralded by horrendous hissing noises emanating from its hundred throats, each one producing a different sound. On Eurystheus's orders, Heracles was to seize the golden apples of the Hesperides from this monstrosity. The demigod set forth on his long and perilous journey, following a haphazard path as he did not know how or where to find the Hesperides. First, he reached Thessaly, home of the giant Termerus, who slaughtered all the travelers he met by hurtling towards them and striking

them dead with his huge, hard-as-a-rock forehead. But when his head collided with the skull of the divine Heracles, his own was smashed to pieces. Then, as the hero approached the River Echedorus, another monster, Cycnus, son of Ares and Pyrene, crossed his path. When Heracles asked him the way to the Garden of the Hesperides, instead of answering politely, he challenged him to single combat and was slain by the demigod. At that, Ares appeared, determined to avenge his dead son and Heracles had no choice but to fight him. But Zeus did not wish to see his children spill each other's blood, so to separate them, he hurled a bolt of lightning between the two would-be combatants. Heracles strode on still further through Illyria and hurried across the River Eridanus where he came upon the nymphs, daughters of Zeus and Themis, who lived on the riverbanks. When the hero asked them the way, they replied, "Go to Nereus, the old river god. He is a seer and knows everything there is to know. Catch him while he is asleep and then bind him, so that he will be forced to point you in the right direction." Heracles followed their advice and subdued Nereus, even though the river god changed himself into all kinds of

HERACLES AND THE THREE GOLDEN APPLES

Page 113
Heracles hurried across the River Eridanus where he came upon the nymphs who lived on the riverbanks.

Page 114
"Go to Nereus, the old river god. He is a seer and knows everything there is to know."

Below
Heracles picked up the apples and walked away.

shapes, as was his custom. The hero refused to let him go before he revealed where the Hesperides and their golden apples could be found. He then continued through Libya into Egypt, the realm of Busiris, son of Poseidon and Lysianassa. After nine years of famine, a seer from Cyprus had grimly prophesied that the fertility of the land would only return if a stranger were sacrificed to Zeus every year. Busiris showed his gratitude by making the Cypriot oracle the first stranger to be sacrificed. Increasingly, the barbarous king found this custom so exhilarating that he took to slaughtering every stranger who set foot in Egypt. Heracles was also seized and dragged to the altar of Zeus, but he broke free and killed Busiris, his son, and the priest who served as the king's herald. As he journeyed onwards, the hero had more adventures. As recounted in an earlier chapter, it was in the Caucasus that Heracles freed Prometheus from his shackles and, in return, the unfettered Titan gave him directions to the place where Atlas stood bearing the weight of the heavens on his shoulders. According to Prometheus, this was not far from where the golden apple tree stood safeguarded by the Hesperides. He also advised the demigod not to undertake the robbery himself, but to send Atlas to carry it out. Atlas agreed, while Heracles slid the vault of heaven onto his own massive shoulders. Meanwhile, Atlas went about his business, lulling the dragon curled around the tree to sleep before killing it. Having caught the watchful Hesperides off guard, he now returned to Heracles, proudly bearing three apples. "Let me tell you," said Atlas, "My shoulders have just discovered how good they feel when they do not have to carry the burden of the heavens. I shall never make them do it again!" Then he threw the apples on to the grass at the demigod's feet, leaving him weighed down by an unaccustomed and unbearable load. Heracles was obliged to devise a ploy to free himself. So he asked the bearer of the skies if he would allow him to wind a woven rope around his head. "Otherwise, my brain will explode from bearing so much weight!" Atlas found this a reasonable request and took over the burden for what he believed would be just a few moments. And so the trickster got tricked: Atlas would have to wait a very long time for Heracles to relieve him. Heracles picked up the apples and walked away. He delivered them to Eurystheus, whose aim had been to rid himself of the hero, but not having succeeded, he gave the apples back to the hero as a gift. The latter laid them on the altar of Athena, but the goddess, knowing that the destiny of these divine fruit was that they should not be moved from the Garden of the Hesperides, carried them back to where they belonged.

HERACLES AND CERBERUS

Journey to the underworld:
The last task on the list is arduous, even for the likes of Heracles.
The hero is ordered to bring Cerberus, the hound of hell, into the light of day.
Eurystheus, his harsh taskmaster, believes Heracles is sure to fail; but far
from it. With the permission of the Lord of the underworld, Heracles briefly
subdues the monster and brings it to Eurystheus.

Illustration by Arthur Rackham

Far from annihilating his detested rival, Eurystheus had so far only commissioned Heracles to carry out labors well suited to the skills Fate had bestowed on him. This had resulted in even greater glorification of the hero as the true champion of ordinary mortals, whose mission was to eradicate every form of atrocity committed on earth. However, according to the devious monarch's plan, his final assignment would be carried out in a place where heroic strength would be of no use. He was to be confronted by the sinister powers of the underworld as he attempted to capture and carry away Cerberus, the watchdog at the gates of Hell. This monstrous creature had three dogs' heads with cavernous jaws that ceaselessly slobbered venom, a dragon's tail and, instead of hair, his head and back were covered with hissing, writhing snakes.

AS SOON AS CERBERUS SAW THE LIGHT OF DAY, HE WAS OVERCOME BY TERROR AND BEGAN SPEWING VENOM IN EVERY DIRECTION.

To prepare himself for this horrifying mission, Heracles went to the city of Eleusis in Attica, where learned priests directed a secret cult devoted to the study of divine matters, both on earth and in the underworld. There, the priest named Eumolpus introduced him to mystic teachings, having first absolved him of the guilt of murdering the centaurs. Thus equipped with newly-acquired knowledge of all things mystical, Heracles traveled to the Peloponnese, to the city of Taenarum in Laconia, where there was an entrance to Hades. There he was met by Hermes, guide of souls, who led him down the deep cleft in the earth until they reached the city of King Pluto. The spirits drifting mournfully around the gates took flight the moment they saw flesh-and-blood humans, for life in the underworld has no joy as it does in the sunlight. The only ones to linger were the Gorgon Medusa and the spirit of Meleager. Heracles attempted to draw his sword, but Hermes rested his hand on the hero's arm and explained that the departed souls of the dead were no more than shadows and could not be harmed, even by the sharpest of weapons. By contrast, the demigod engaged in friendly conversation with Meleager's soul and readily agreed to carry his most affectionate greeting to his beloved sister Deianira, still living on earth.

As he came close to the gates of Hades, he saw his friends Pirithous, who came to the underworld as a suitor of Persephone, and Theseus, who accompanied him. Condemning their behavior as rude and disrespectful, Pluto chained both of them to the rock on which they had sat to rest. When they caught sight of the demigod, they stretched their hands pleadingly towards him, trembling with the hope he would have the power to help them find their way back to earth. Indeed, Heracles caught Theseus by the hand, freed him from his bonds and helped him to remain standing. His second attempt, this time to free Pirithous, was a failure, for the earth began to shake under his feet. Moving forward, Heracles also recognized Ascalaphus, who had once betrayed Persephone by telling her that she had eaten pomegranates produced in the underworld which would hinder her return to earth. He rolled back the stone that Demeter, distraught at the loss of her daughter, had used in an attempt to crush him. Then he tore into Pluto's herds of cattle and slaughtered one of the oxen so that the souls might quench their thirst with the blood. But the herdsman, Menoetius, refused to allow this and instead challenged the hero to a wrestling match. Heracles clutched him around the body, broke his ribs and only set him free when Persephone, queen of the underworld, commanded him to do so. King Pluto stood at the gates of the city of the dead and refused to let him past. But the hero's arrow pierced the shoulder of the god, who had to suffer the same torments as mortals. When the demigod calmly asked his

Heracles led the shackled monster back to Tiryns.

permission to take away Cerberus, the hound of hell, Pluto no longer refused. However, he set one condition: Heracles must control the creature without using any of the weapons he had brought with him. So, clad only in his breastplate, with the lion's skin around his shoulders, the hero set out to find the monster. He found him crouched at the mouth of the Acheron and, ignoring the hound's triple bark, which sounded like dull rumbles of thunder but a hundred times louder, Heracles clamped the heads between his knees and wound his arms around the necks without loosening his hold. Then the beast's tail, a dragon in its own right, struck out at him and bit him in the thigh. Even so, he held onto the creature's throats and the monster held fast until Heracles finally mastered the hound of hell in all its frenzy. He then picked it up and found his way out of Hades, returning safely to the upper world through another gate close to Troezen in Argolis. As soon as Cerberus saw the light of day, he was overcome by terror and began spewing venom in every direction, causing deadly aconite to spring from the ground. Heracles led the shackled monster back to Tiryns and showed it to a dumbfounded Eurystheus, who could barely believe what he saw. Now the king despaired of ever divesting himself of this odious son of Zeus. At last he resigned himself to his fate and released the hero, who took the three-headed dog back to the underworld.

BELLEROPHON

The gods give and the gods take away:
Bellerophon is tasked with hunting down the Chimaera, a horror with a lion's head,
a goat's body, and the hindquarters of a dragon. The gods give him Pegasus, a winged
horse, to the monster from the air. Bellerophon arrogantly wants Pegasus to fly him up
to the summit of Mount Olympus, but he is thrown off and falls back to Earth.

Illustrations by Gustaf Tenggren

BELLEROPHON

He honored his guest in various ways, with a fresh feast daily and the sacrifice of a bullock to the gods every morning.

Sisyphus was the son of Aeolus, the most devious of all mortals. He built and governed the city of Corinth, which stood on a peninsula between two seas and two countries. Because he was proven guilty of many cases of deceit and dishonesty, his punishment in the underworld was to forever roll a heavy piece of marble from the plain to the top of a steep hill, relying only on his hands and feet. However, just as he was sure he was about to reach the top, his burden broke loose and the mischief-making stone hurtled back down the hillside. Again and again, the tormented lawbreaker had to roll the lump of rock back uphill, the sweat of fear streaming from his limbs.

His grandson was Bellerophon, son of Glaucus, king of Corinth. Forced to flee because of an unforeseen murder, the youth headed for Tiryns, where King Proteus ruled. The monarch made him welcome and absolved him of his crime. However, the immortals had endowed Bellerophon with physical beauty and masculine virtues, so much so that Anteia, the king's wife, fostered a guilty infatuation for him and tried to seduce him into wicked ways. But Bellerophon, a virtuous young man, rejected her passionate advances. Her love turned to hate and she conjured up lies that would result in his downfall. She then appeared before her spouse and said, "Dear husband, you must slay Bellerophon, if you yourself are to avoid an ignoble death! Your adulterous guest has told me of his disgraceful intent to persuade me to deceive you." Although beside himself with rage on hearing her words, the king dreaded the thought of killing the intelligent young man of whom he had become so fond. Nevertheless, he considered other means of destroying him. He sent the blameless Bellerophon to his father-in-law, Iobates, king of Lycia, and gave him a sealed tablet addressed to the king. On arrival, he was to present it to the monarch as an introduction. The tablet contained certain engraved signs decreeing that the bearer should be slain. Bellerophon set off on his journey, knowing neither the contents of the tablet, nor that he had the protection of the invincible gods. After crossing the sea to Asia and arriving in Lycia with its beautiful River Xanthus, he went in search of King Iobates. The king was a kind and hospitable man who, in accordance with ancient tradition, believed in receiving a stranger without asking who he was or where he had come from. Bellerophon's handsome appearance and gracious manner were enough to convince the host that he was not about to entertain a common ruffian. He honored his guest in various ways, with a fresh feast daily and the sacrifice of a bullock to the gods every morning. Nine days had passed and the tenth morning sky was veined with rose red before the king asked his guest his name and what his plans might be. Bellerophon replied that he had come from Proteus, the monarch's son-in-law. To prove it, he showed the tablet as his credentials. When King Iobates realized that the signs were commands to kill, he was deeply disturbed, for he had become genuinely fond of the youth. Even so, he found it hard to imagine that his son-in-law would have condemned Bellerophon to death without a very sound reason, which in turn led him to believe that the young man had committed a crime worthy of the death penalty. But he could not kill someone who had been his guest for so long and whose entire nature had won his affection in cold blood. Therefore, he decided only to assign him to missions on which he would be bound to perish. His first task

BELLEROPHON

would be to slay the Chimaera, which was laying waste to Lycia. This monster was no human, but a creature of divine origin, the offspring of the hideous Typhon and the giant snake Echidna. It had the head, chest, and front paws of a lion, the back legs and tail of a dragon, and the torso of a goat. From its mouth it breathed fire and blasted sweltering heat. The gods themselves took pity on the innocent youth dispatched on such a dangerous mission, so they sent to his rescue the winged horse Pegasus, fruit of the union of Poseidon and the Medusa, an animal that could neither be caught nor tamed. Exhausted by having struggled in vain, Bellerophon had fallen asleep where he had found the horse, near the fountain of Pirene. It was there in a dream that he saw Athena, his patron goddess, standing before him with an exquisite golden bridle. She said, "So, descendent of Aeolus, why are you sleeping? Take these reins. They will help you handle a troublesome steed. Offer up a fine bullock to Poseidon and then use the bridle." These were the words she addressed to the hero as she appeared in his dream. Then, shaking her dark shield, she disappeared. He awoke from his sleep and leapt to his feet. He reached out and, miracle of miracles, the very bridle he had held in his sleep was really and truly there in his hand.

Bellerophon now went to the seer Polyidus and told him about his dream and the miracle that took place at the same time. Polyidus bade him to do as the goddess commanded with no further delay, namely slaughter a bullock for Poseidon and build an altar for his patron goddess. Once all of this was done, Bellerophon effortlessly caught and tamed Pegasus with the greatest of ease and fitted him with the golden bridle. Then, having donned his armor, the hero climbed on the winged horse's back. Then he shot an arrow through the air and killed the Chimaera. Thereupon Iobates sent him to the borders of Lycia, territory of the Solymi, a belligerent people. When the youth

was unexpectedly victorious in his battle with them, Iobates dispatched him to deal with the Amazons, women warriors who fought like men. Again, he returned triumphant and unscathed. Now the king thought it was time for him to do as his son-in-law had asked, so he laid an ambush for Bellerophon as he made his way back. Even though he had deployed the bravest and strongest men in the kingdom, the youth had slaughtered his attackers down to the last man. The king now recognized that his guest was no criminal, but a favorite of the gods. Far from persecuting him, he allowed him to stay in the kingdom and share the throne. He even gave him his beautiful daughter Philonoe in marriage. The Lycians presented him with the finest fields and orchards to cultivate. His wife bore him three children, two sons and a daughter.

But now Bellerophon's good fortune had come to an end. Although his eldest son Isander had indeed grown up to be a great hero, he died in battle against the Solymi. His daughter, Laodamia, bore Zeus a son, Sarpedon, and was killed by an arrow from the bow shot by Artemis. Only his youngest son, Hippolochus, lived to a ripe old age and sent his own heroic son, Glaucus, to take part in the war against Troy. His cousin Sarpedon was his comrade in arms and together they went to the aid of the Trojans, at the head of an army of gallant Lycians.

As for Bellerophon, because he had mastered the immortal winged horse, he became conceited and arrogant. He wanted to ride it up to Mount Olympus so that he, a mortal, could mingle among the gods when they assembled. But the divine horse protested at his mortal rider's insolent bravado and reared up, throwing him to the ground. Bellerophon recovered from his fall but from then on, the immortals hated him. Too ashamed to appear among his kind, he wandered alone through many lands, avoiding paths trodden by his fellow humans, thus spending an inglorious and sorrowful old age alone.

THESEUS

What begins in hope, ends in tragedy:
Theseus's most famous adventure has reverberated through literature and art as
the story of the prince of Athens who travels to Crete to slay the Minotaur in
the labyrinth. Ariadne, daughter of the king of Crete, helps him accomplish this task.
On the voyage back Theseus loses Ariadne and then his father, who casts himself
into the sea at Athens in an act of tragic misunderstanding.

Illustrations by Virginia Frances Sterrett and William Russell Flint

THESEUS

Theseus drew the sword that his father had left under the rock for him.

I n Athens, the young hero failed to find the peace and friendship he had hoped for. Confusion and discord reigned among the citizens and he found the house of his own father, Aegeus, in a sorry state. Medea, who had boarded her dragon-drawn chariot and left Corinth – and a heartbroken Jason – was already in Athens, having curried favor with old Aegeus by promising him that her magical charms could restore to him the strength of his younger days. Now she and the king were living in wedlock. Through her skills as a sorceress, the vile woman had learned of Theseus's arrival in Athens before the news had reached the palace. The political strife in the city had rendered Aegeus suspicious of any newcomer, and he did not recognize the stranger as his son. Medea persuaded the king that the young man was a dangerous spy, whom he should welcome as a guest and then promptly poison. Theseus came to the morning meal without having revealed his identity and relishing the thought of his father

discovering for himself whom he had before him. The cup of poison was at Theseus's place. Medea, fearing that the new arrival would drive her out of the palace, waited impatiently for the moment when he took the first sip, which should be enough to close his alert young eyes forever. But Theseus cared more about embracing his father than drinking from the cup. He drew his sword, the one left under the rock for him by his father, ostensibly to cut his meat, but in truth so that Aegeus might see it and know that the man to whom it belonged was his son. As soon as the king saw and instantly recognized the weapon, he threw the cup to the ground. He then posed a few questions, whose answers convinced him that this was indeed the son he had implored Destiny to grant him, and then threw his arms around the young man. The father immediately presented his son to the assembled Athenians and Theseus told them about

the adventures he had had while traveling. In return he was joyously hailed as one who had proved his bravery and fortitude at so young an age. Now King Aegeus felt nothing but hatred towards the duplicitous Medea and the venomous sorceress was banished from the land.

Living at his father's side as prince and heir to the throne of Attica, the first endeavor Theseus undertook was to annihilate the fifty sons of his uncle Pallas, all of whom had hoped to succeed to throne if Aegeus were to die childless. Now they were outraged, not only at the thought that Aegeus was an adopted son of Pandion, king of Athens, but also by the knowledge that they and the whole country would be ruled by a wandering vagabond who had recently strayed into the city. So they seized their weapons and set up an ambush for the interloper. However, the herald accompanying them, himself a stranger, revealed the plan to Theseus, who launched a sudden attack on their hiding place and massacred all fifty. For fear that this violent, but necessary, attack would turn the people away from him, Theseus set forth on a series of exploits that would benefit them all. He captured the bull of Marathon, which had beleaguered the inhabitants of four provinces on the Attic Peninsula, then led the beast through the streets of Athens for all to see before sacrificing him to Apollo.

At around this time, King Minos of Crete sent messengers to demand, for the third time, the tribute now due to him for the following reason. It was said that Minos's son Androgeos was perfidiously slain in Attica. In revenge, his father had waged a destructive war on that country's people, while the gods themselves had devastated the land with drought and plague. Then the oracle of Apollo made known that the wrath of the gods and the sufferings of the people of Athens would cease if they could

The cup of poison was at Theseus's place.

appease Minos and earn his forgiveness. Thereupon, the
Athenians appealed to the king and peace was agreed on condition that, every nine years, they would send a tribute in the form
of fourteen young people, seven youths and seven maidens, to
Crete. There were rumors that Minos locked these young people
in his famous labyrinth where they were killed by the Minotaur,
a hideous monster, half man half bull, or simply left to waste
away. Now that the time had come for the third tribute to be
delivered and for the fathers of unmarried sons or daughters
to submit to this terrible fate, the citizens once more turned
against Aegeus. They began complaining that he, as the one
responsible for this catastrophe and the only one who did not
have to face its consequences, had made a bastard son, a complete stranger, heir to the throne. At the same time, they claimed
he was entirely unmoved by the plight of parents forced to have
their legitimate children torn away from them. Theseus, now
accustomed to sharing the fate of his fellow citizens, shared
their grief. Rising to speak at the public assembly, he declared
that he would go to Crete of his own free will, without being
chosen by lot. All the listeners were full of admiration for his
heroism and selfless public spirit, while he remained resolute,
despite his father's desperate pleas not to deprive an old man
of his newly-found son and heir, who had so recently brought
him such unforeseen happiness. Theseus comforted his father
by assuring him that he did not intend to die, nor to abandon
the young people to their fate. His simple aim was to vanquish
the Minotaur. So far, the ship carrying the unfortunate victims
to Crete had been rigged with a black sail, as a symbol of their
hopeless situation. How, having heard his son speak with such
intrepid confidence, Aegeus ordered that the ship be equipped
in the traditional way, but also gave the helmsman a white sail
to be hoisted to signal that Theseus had returned safely. If not,
the black sail would remain, thus announcing disaster from
afar. When lots had been drawn, young Theseus led the boys
and girls whose names had been chosen to the temple of Apollo
where, on their behalf, he offered an olive branch wrapped
with white woolen thread, the votive offering of those seeking
protection. When the ceremonial prayer had been said, he
and the children, accompanied by a great crowd of people,

THESEUS

Theseus killed the Minotaur with his magic weapon.

walked down to the seashore, where they boarded the ship of mourning.

The oracle of Delphi had advised him to choose the goddess of love as his guide and plead for her patronage. Theseus did not at first understand the oracle's advice, but nonetheless made an offering to Aphrodite. The success that was to follow would reveal its meaning. For when Theseus landed in Crete and appeared before King Minos, his beauty combined with the majestic demeanor of a young hero caught the eye of Ariadne, the king's enchanting daughter. In a clandestine conversation, she confessed her feelings for him, then handed him a ball of thread. He was to fasten one end to the entrance to the labyrinth and unroll the ball as he progressed through the bewildering maze until he reached the place where the repugnant beast lay in wait. She then handed him a magic sword with which to kill the monster. Minos ordered that all his victims be sent to the labyrinth, but Theseus led his young companions to the Minotaur, which he killed with the magic weapon Ariadne had given him and then, following the thread, led them back through the tortuous passages. Their safe escape was helped by Ariadne, the wonderful and unforeseen prize the young hero had won for his victory. On her advice, he had also slashed the keels of the Cretan ships, so preventing the king from pursuing them. Believing that his new-found treasure was safe with him, he steered the ship towards the island of Dia, later known as Naxos. There the god Dionysus appeared to him in a dream, claiming that Ariadne was the bride Fate had destined for him, and threatening to cause harm to Theseus if he did not renounce his beloved. Theseus's grandfather had brought him up to fear the gods, so now he submitted to the wrath of Dionysus and sailed onwards, leaving the princess on the lonely island, weeping in despair. During the night, Ariadne's rightful bridegroom appeared and

carried her away to Mount Drios, where the god disappeared and, soon after, Ariadne was also lost from sight. Theseus and his young friends were so disheartened by the loss of Ariadne that they forgot that the ship was still riding under the black sail, raised before they left the coast of Attica. Having failed to remember the king's command to hoist the white sail to signal that they were safely home, their ship approached their native coast as though in mourning. Aegeus was waiting on the shore, looking out to sea from a high, rocky promontory. On seeing the black sail, he assumed that his son was dead. Overwhelmed by unendurable grief, he threw himself into the waters below. It was in his memory that those waters were named the Aegean Sea. Meanwhile, Theseus had landed and, after making the offerings he had promised, he dispatched a herald to the city to proclaim the safe return of himself, the seven boys and seven girls. The messenger did not know how to interpret the reception he received from the citizens. While some were full of joy and placed wreaths on his head as the bearer of good tidings, others were so deep in mourning that they paid no attention to his words. He remained puzzled until he heard the news of the king's death slowly spreading throughout the city. While he continued to accept the wreaths presented to him, he simply wove them around his herald's staff before returning to the shore. There he found that Theseus was still in the temple attending to the offerings of thanks, so decided to stand at the entrance to the temple to avoid disturbing the sacred rites with a message of grief. As soon as the burnt offering was poured away, the herald announced the death of King Aegeus. Struck with sorrow as if by a thunderbolt, Theseus flung himself to the ground. When he recovered and got to his feet, they all hurried to the city, not to celebrate as they had planned, but lamenting and weeping for the dead.

OEDIPUS

The ultimate in tragedy, crime, and atonement:
The story of Oedipus, son of the king of Thebes, still stirs emotions. Three tragic events
determine his life. He murders his father, marries his mother, and blinds himself
when he realizes what he has done. He once saved his native city from the menacing
Sphinx, but this heroic deed is all but forgotten as he leaves Thebes.

Illustrations by Artuš Scheiner and Alexander Zick

Laius was king of Thebes, son of Labdacus, and member of the House of Cadmus. He had been married for many years to Jocasta, daughter of the Theban noble, Menoeceus, but their marriage was childless. Deeply longing for an heir, he consulted the oracle of Apollo at Delphi, who advised him as follows: "Laius, son of Labdacus! You long to be blessed with a child. Well, your wish for a son shall be granted. But be aware that you are destined to lose your life at the hands of your own male child. This is the will of Zeus, son of Cronos. He heard the curse of Pelops, whose son you once stole."

It was true that in his youth Laius had fled from his homeland to the Peloponnese where the king offered him refuge at the royal palace. However, he had repaid this act of kindness with one of gross ingratitude by abducting the monarch's beautiful son at the Nemean games. Conscious of his guilt, Laius believed the words of the oracle and for a long time kept his distance from his wife. In the end, their great love for each other caused them to ignore the warning they had received. They came back together and, in due course, Jocasta gave birth to a son. When their child was born, his parents remembered the oracle's words and how they needed to escape the will of the gods. When he was three days old, they had the newborn's feet pierced and bound together, then had him thrown out into the wild Cithaeron Mountains. But the shepherd they had chosen to carry out this cruel deed felt sorry for the innocent child. He handed him over to a fellow shepherd who, in those same mountains, tended the sheep of King Polybus of Corinth. Then he returned home and announced to the king and his wife Jocasta that he had obeyed their orders. They were sure that the child would starve to death or be torn apart by wild beasts so that the oracle's predictions could never be fulfilled. They soothed their consciences with the thought that, in sacrificing the child themselves, they had saved him from slaying his father and they could now live with lighter hearts.

Meanwhile, the shepherd who cared for King Polybus's flocks had untied the bonds of the child he had simply accepted without knowing who he was or where he came from. On noticing the damage to the infant's feet, he named him after his wounds, calling him Oedipus, or Swollen Foot. Then he took the foundling to his master, King Polybus, who took pity on the tiny outcast, entrusted him to his wife, Merope, and bade her to raise him as if he were her own son. Indeed, the court and the whole country came to recognize him as such. As he grew into young manhood, he was always regarded as one of the city's noblest citizens and was happily convinced that, since the king had no other descendants, he was Polybus's son and heir. But then, by coincidence, his self-confidence was suddenly plunged into doubt. At a banquet, there was a citizen of Corinth who had always been jealous of Oedipus. He partook of too much wine and told Oedipus he was not really the king's son. Deeply affronted by such a reproach, the young man was anxious for the feast to end. Even so, he kept his doubts to himself that day, but the following morning he confronted his parents – who were, in fact, his foster parents – and demanded an explanation. Polybus and his wife were infuriated to find that his misgivings were provoked by the babblings of a drunken troublemaker and tried to allay them with ambiguous replies. He was comforted by the love that was clear to see from their faces, but was still tormented by mistrust, for the words of his enemy had penetrated too deep. Without a word to his parents, he set off on a journey.

OEDIPUS WAS COMFORTED BY THE LOVE THAT WAS CLEAR TO SEE FROM THEIR FACES, BUT WAS STILL TORMENTED BY MISTRUST.

OEDIPUS

A winged beast with the front half in the shape of a maiden and the rear half of a lion.

His undisclosed destination was the oracle of Delphi, whom he hoped would refute what he had been told. But Phoebus Apollo did not see his question as worthy of an answer. Instead, he revealed a new, far more terrible misfortune awaiting Oedipus. "You will murder your father," said the oracle. "You will marry your mother and leave descendants of reprehensible origin for the world to see." When Oedipus heard this, he was gripped by indescribable fear. While his heart told him that Polybus and Merope were his loving parents, he did not dare return home for fear he might be driven by madness to physically attack his beloved father Polybus, and that the gods would strike him with such overpowering insanity that he would brutishly enter into wedlock with his mother. Leaving Delphi, he followed the road to Boeotia. While still between Delphi and the city of Daulia, he came to a crossroad, along which he saw a chariot heading towards him. In it sat an old man whom he had never seen, with a herald, a charioteer, and two servants. On seeing the wayfarer approaching, the charioteer and the old man boorishly shoved him out of their way. Oedipus, naturally quick-tempered, dealt a mighty blow to the uncouth charioteer. But when the old man saw the youth yelling loutishly at his charioteer, he grabbed his spiked goad and struck him hard on the top of the head. Now Oedipus was beside himself. For the first time he applied the heroic strength the gods had bestowed on him and raised the staff he had carried throughout his journey and struck the old man, who immediately toppled backwards out of the chariot. A hand-to-hand brawl ensued. Oedipus had to defend himself against three assailants. Nevertheless, his young man's strength prevailed. He killed all but one, who escaped and ran away.

He had no idea that he had done anything other than take revenge against some common Phocian or Boeotian and his servants who had tried to harm him, but there was nothing to suggest that old man was in any way his superior. In fact, the dead man was King Laius of Thebes, Oedipus's own father, on his way to the Pythian oracle. Thus the prophesy dealt by Fate to both father and son was now fulfilled, even though both men had done their utmost to evade their destiny.

Not long after this event, there appeared before the gates of the Boeotian city of Thebes a sphinx, a winged beast with the front half in the shape of a maiden and the rear half of a lion. She was the daughter of Typhon and Echidna, the serpent nymph, fertile mother to many such monsters and also sister of Cerberus, the hound of Hell, the hydra of Lerna, and the fire-spitting Chimaera. The monster had made its home on a cliff, from where she asked citizens of Thebes to solve a whole assortment of riddles, which the Muses had taught her. She would tear to shreds and devour anyone who could not answer correctly. Such tribulation came at a time when the citizens were mourning their king who was slain while on a journey, and no one knew by whom. Jocasta's brother Creon seized the reins of power and became king. It then came to pass that Creon's own son had failed to unravel one of the sphinx's conundrums, had been seized and gobbled up by the beast. This latest blow persuaded King Creon to issue a proclamation that anyone who freed the city from the vile creature would be rewarded with the kingdom and the hand in marriage of his sister Jocasta. Just as the proclamation was being made, Oedipus entered the city of Thebes. Both the danger and the reward attracted him, and besides he felt that a life overshadowed by such a pessimistic prophesy was hardly worth defending. He headed for the cliff where the sphinx had settled and asked for a riddle to solve. The monster intended to offer this audacious stranger a riddle impossible to disentangle. She began, "In the morning, it is on four feet. At midday, it is on two, then in the evening on three. Among all living creatures, only one changes the number of its feet; yet when it moves on the greater number of feet, its strength and speed are at their lowest." Oedipus smiled as he listened to the riddle, which to him seemed far from difficult. "The answer to your riddle is Man," he replied. "For it is in the morning of his life, when as a weak and helpless child, he crawls on his two feet and two hands. At the noon of his life he has grown stronger and now only walks on two feet. In the evening of his life when he is old, he needs something to support him, so he uses his staff as his third foot." The riddle was so easily solved that, out of shame and despair at her failure, the sphinx threw herself from the cliff to her death. Oedipus accepted his reward of the kingdom of Thebes and the hand of the widow Jocasta, who was, in fact, his own mother. In the course of time, she bore him

He headed for the cliff where the sphinx had settled and asked for a riddle to solve.

four children, first the twin boys Eteocles and Polynices and then two daughters, the elder Antigone, the younger Ismene. But the four siblings were not only his children but also his brothers and sisters. For many years, the terrible secret remained unknown, while Oedipus, with Jocasta by his side, became a good and fair-minded ruler of Thebes who, despite the occasional error, was loved and respected by his subjects.

Then one day the gods sent upon the land a plague, for which there was no known cure, thus wreaking havoc among the people. Against this vicious disease, which the Thebans regarded as a scourge by the gods, they sought protection from their king whom they believed to be a favorite of the immortals. When Oedipus heard the clamor of a large crowd, he stepped out of the royal place and asked why crowds were gathered there and why the city air was laden with sacrificial smoke and filled with the sound of weeping and wailing. The eldest among the priests replied, "Once before you saved us from the tyranny of the sphinx and her riddles. Surely this was not possible without the aid of the gods. This is why we trust you again to find help for us."

"My poor children," Oedipus replied. "I know all too well why you are praying. I know you are tormented by disease and no other heart is more saddened than my own. For I have sent Creon, my own brother-in-law, to Delphi to consult the Pythian oracle Apollo and ask by what deed or what other means our city can be set free."

Even as the king spoke, Creon appeared among the crowd and, in the presence of all the people, reported to the king the words of the oracle, which were hardly consoling. "We are commanded to rid ourselves of an evil our country is concealing and not to set store by that for which no kind of purification can atone. For the blood guilt for King Laius's murder weighs heavy upon the land." Oedipus had no idea that the old man he had slain was the very same one whose death had provoked the wrath of the gods, which led to the punishment of his people. He believed the people should be told what was known of the killing and then kept informed. Before dispersing them, he told those gathered there to take care of the dead. Then he ordered that a proclamation be issued throughout the land stating that anyone who knew of King Laius's murderer should report all that he had learned. In addition, he sent two messengers to the blind seer Tiresias, whose powers of insight and ability to probe the unknown were almost equal to Apollo's. The aged seer soon appeared, a boy leading him by the hand, ready to appear before the king and the people's assembly. Oedipus described to him the hardship besetting himself and the whole country, begging him to exercise his gift of prophesy to help track down the murderer of King Laius.

But Tiresias broke into a lament and spoke, his hands stretched towards the king, "How terrible is the knowledge which only brings sadness to him who knows! Let me go home, oh King! Bear your own burden and leave me to bear mine!" Oedipus pressed the seer even further and the people surrounding him fell to their knees, entreating him to speak. When the soothsayer was still unwilling to give any further information, King Oedipus's rage was kindled. He taunted Tiresias, accusing him of being a confidante or even an accomplice of Laius's killer. Indeed, he claimed, only the old man's blindness kept him from thinking that he himself had committed the crime. This accusation loosened the blind prophet's tongue. "Oedipus," he cried. "obey your own orders. Do not speak to me, do not speak to any one of your subjects. For the abomination defiling the city is you! Yes, it is you who murdered the king. It is you who lives in degenerate union with those dearest to you!"

> "OEDIPUS, OBEY YOUR OWN ORDERS. DO NOT SPEAK TO ME OR TO ANY OF YOUR SUBJECTS. FOR THE ABOMINATION DEFILING THE CITY IS YOU!"

Oedipus was deluded and wholly unable to accept the truth. He accused the soothsayer of being a trickster, a scheming charlatan. He also cast suspicion on his brother-in-law, accusing both men of conspiring against the throne and spinning a pack of lies against him in their attempt to overthrow him, the savior of the city. But Tiresias's responded by explicitly accusing him of murdering his father, husband of his mother, and predicting his own imminent catastrophe. The seer then hurried away seething with rage, clutching the hand of his little guide. On hearing the accusation launched against him, Creon did not wait to confront Oedipus. A violent quarrel erupted between them, while Jocasta tried in vain to separate them. Creon walked away from his brother-in-law, infuriated and unreconciled. Jocasta

was even blinder than the king himself. Hardly had she heard Tiresias naming her husband as Laius's murderer than she broke out with cursed maledictions against the seer and the powers for which he was renowned. "Don't you see, husband," she exclaimed, "how little these seers know? Here is one example! It was an oracle that told my first husband Laius that he would die at the hands of his son. In fact, he was killed at a crossroad by a band of thieves, while our only son was bound by the feet and abandoned on wasteland in the mountains when he was only three days old. That is how true seer's prophesies are!"

Such words disdainfully spoken by the queen affected Oedipus in a completely unexpected way. "Did you say Laius died at a crossroad? Tell me, how old was he? What did he look like?" Failing to understand her husband's alarm Jocasta replied, "He was tall, with a few gray hairs. He looked very much like you, dear husband. Not at all dissimilar." "Tiresias is not blind, Tiresias can see!" Oedipus exclaimed in increasing terror. It was as if the dark night of his soul had been lit up by a flash of lightning. But it was dread that drove him to keep asking question upon question, in the hope that the answers might prove the terrible discovery to be a mistake. But in fact, they proved it to be true, and he discovered that a servant who survived the attack had reported the murder in full. As soon as Oedipus came to the throne, this fellow begged to be sent as far as possible from the city to tend the monarch's pastures. Oedipus summoned the servant, who was brought in from the countryside. However, just as the man reached the palace, a messenger from Corinth arrived with the news that Oedipus's father Polybus had died and Oedipus was to ascend to the nation's throne.

When she heard this message, the queen responded triumphantly, "Oh divine oracle, what kind of truth are you telling? The father, whom Oedipus was alleged to have slain has just died of old age!" But King Oedipus, although he was still inclined to regard Polybus as his father, did not dare believe that an oracle might be untrue. Nor did he wish to go to Corinth, for a different reason. There was another part of the oracular message to consider. His mother Merope was still living there and Fate might force him into marrying her. His doubts were soon dispelled by the messenger. He told how, many years ago when he was a herdsman on Mount Cithaeron, a servant of Laius entrusted him with a newborn child. He then told how he had loosened the bonds tied around the infant's injured heels. He could easily prove that Oedipus was only the foster child of King Polybus of Corinth.

A more sinister urge to find the truth obliged Oedipus to ask about the servant of Laius who had handed over the newborn to the herdsman. From his own servants, he discovered that it was the man who escaped death when Laius was murdered, and had since tended the king's cattle in meadows close to the border. On hearing this, Jocasta left her husband and the people surrounding him, wailing bitterly in despair. Oedipus, deliberately attempting to hide the look in his eyes under the cover of darkness, made an excuse for her leaving. "Of course she is afraid," he told his entourage. "She is a very proud woman, afraid to discover that I may be of low birth. I see myself as the son of good fortune and am not ashamed of my origin!"

There then appeared the elderly herdsman, who had been brought there from afar, and was immediately recognized by the messenger from Corinth as the one who handed the child over to him on Mount Cithaeron. The old shepherd, white-faced with fear, tried to deny everything. Only when Oedipus angrily fettered and threatened him did he finally tell the truth, namely that Oedipus was the child of Laius and Jocasta, that the oracle predicted he would kill his father, but that he was the one who, out of pity, had saved his life.

Now, all doubt was lifted and the terrible truth remained. With an anguished, panic-stricken scream, Oedipus charged out of the main hall then hurtled around the palace demanding a sword to wipe the monster who was both his mother and his wife from the face of the earth. Petrified by his furious rampaging, the entire household had scurried away and there was no one to answer him. Howling like a wounded animal, he made for his bedchamber, smashed down the gate and broke into the room. An unspeakable sight met his eyes, leaving him paralyzed. Strung up high above the bed was the body of Jocasta, hair flying and disheveled; tight around her throat was the rope with which she had hanged herself. For a long time Oedipus could only stare silently at the dead woman. He then approached, mournfully wailing, and lowered the rope until the body touched the floor. Now she lay prone before him, he tore the golden clasps from her robe, lifted them high in the air, aligning them with his eyes, bidding them never to see what he did and how he suffered, then pierced his eyeballs with sharp pieces of gold, until blood streamed from the sockets. Blind as he now was, he called to the servants to open the gate and lead him out, so that the people of Thebes might behold him as the man who slew his father and married his mother – a monster on earth, cursed by the gods in heaven. The servants did as he asked, but his subjects received their so beloved and so respected ruler, not with revulsion but with heartfelt compassion. Even Creon, the brother-in-law whom he had so unjustly accused, did not choose to mock the man in torment, but to move him out of the sunlight and entrust him to the care his family. Oedipus was deeply moved by such kind interventions. He appointed Creon keeper of the throne to guard it for his young sons. He demanded that his ill-fated mother be fittingly buried and that his orphaned daughters be protected by the new ruler. For himself, however, he asked to be banished

NOW, ALL DOUBT WAS LIFTED AND THE TERRIBLE TRUTH REMAINED.

OEDIPUS

Only his daughters felt true compassion for the outcast.

from the country he had defiled by his two-fold misdeed and pleaded to be exiled to Mount Cithaeron where his parents had once left him to die so long ago, there to live or die according to the will of the gods. He then called for his daughters, whose voices he hungered to hear for the last time and to lay his hands on their innocent heads. He blessed Creon for all the love he had shown to a man who had never deserved it, and prayed that he and all the people be better than he himself had been.

Creon then led Oedipus back to the palace. Oedipus, he who had been honored as the liberator of Thebes, the mighty ruler obeyed by many thousands, the man who solved an extraordinarily difficult riddle and also unlocked the mystery of his own life, although all too late, was no more than a blind beggar.

Only his daughters felt true compassion for the outcast. Ismene, the youngest, remained behind in her brothers' house so as to deal more effectively with her father's affairs. The elder daughter, Antigone, joined her blind father in exile. Barefooted, she accompanied him on a seemingly meaningless journey, which took them wandering aimlessly through the wild woods. Both had to suffer

hunger, the burning sun, and heavy rain, but despite having been reared in comfort and even though her brother's house might have been more luxurious, the gentle maiden was content with privation as long as her father had enough to eat. At the beginning, his intention was to live a life of misery or to seek death in the wilderness of Mount Cithaeron. But because he was a devout man, he did not wish to take such a step without the blessing of the gods and so made a pilgrimage to the oracle of Pythian Apollo. Here he received some reassurance.

The gods recognized that Oedipus had severely sinned, albeit unknowingly, against the laws of nature and the most sacred conventions of human society. Punishment was deserved, but it did not need to last for all eternity. As the oracle foretold, "In the fullness of time, you will finally be absolved once you have reached the land chosen by Fate, where venerable goddesses, the formidable Eumenides, will offer you sanctuary." The name "Eumenides," which means "the benevolent ones," was a kindly title which mortals had conferred on the Erinyes, the goddesses of vengeance otherwise known as the Furies, to honor and appease them. The oracle's words were strange and sinister. As Oedipus understood it, the Furies were to offer him peace and redemption for his sins against nature! Even so, as he wandered across Greece, he trusted the promise of the gods and left it to Fate to decide when fulfilment should occur. He was accompanied by his pious daughter who took care of him. Both of them lived on the charity of the compassionate. He only ever asked for little and received little, but it was enough for him. For his long exile and his own principled way of thinking had taught him to be content with a life of frugality.

TALES OF TROY
PRIAM, HECUBA, AND PARIS

The most celebrated cycle of ancient Greek myths:
The stories of Troy encompass the panoply of human life and show how far the Olympian
gods can go when they assume too many human qualities. It starts with the famous
Judgement of Paris. Paris, the son of the king of Troy, selects Aphrodite, goddess of love and
beauty, as the winner of the beauty contest over competitors Hera and Athena. Aphrodite
promises him the most beautiful woman in the world as his reward.

Illustration by Charles Edmund Brock

We have already recounted elsewhere the further fate of King Laomedon and his daughter Hesione. He was succeeded to the throne by his son Priam, who took as his second wife Hecuba (or Hecabe), daughter of Dymas, king of Phrygia. Hecuba had one son, Hector. But while expecting her second child, one dark night she had a horrifying dream. In it, she gave birth to a flaming torch which set ablaze the whole city of Troy, reducing it to ashes. Still full of fear, she told her husband Priam, whherao immediately summoned Aesacus, the son from his first marriage. He was an oracle whose maternal grandfather, Merops, had trained him in the art of interpreting dreams. Aesacus explained that his stepmother was about to give birth to a son who would bring disaster upon his native city. He therefore advised that the child she was expecting should be given away. In fact, the queen bore a son, and her loyalty to her fatherland outweighed any maternal feelings. She allowed Priam to hand the newborn to a slave, who carried him up Mount Ida and abandoned him there. The slave, whose name was Agelaus, did as he was told. Meanwhile, a mother bear gathered the child up and nursed him. Five days later, Agelaus returned to where he had left the child and found him curled up safe and sound on the forest floor. He gathered the infant in his arms, carried him home, then raised him as his own son on his little strip of land, and named him Paris.

Brought up and cared for by the shepherd, the king's son grew into a strong and handsome youth. He became the protector of all the herdsmen on Mount Ida, against the robbers lurking around there. For this reason, they called him Alexander, helper of men.

One day he happened to find himself in a valley whose rough terrain led through a mountain gorge, heavily shaded by pines and holm oaks. He was a long way from his herd, which could not find its way into this secluded spot on Mount Ida. He was leaning against a tree, arms folded, looking down through a gap in the mountains to the palaces of Troy and the distant sea, when he heard the footsteps of a god shaking the earth. Before he had time to think he saw Hermes, messenger of the gods, moving towards him. Hermes was carried half by his wings and half by his feet, his hands holding his golden herald's staff. Yet he was doing no more than lead three goddesses from Mount Olympus who landed on their dainty feet on grass never sheared nor grazed upon. Trembling with wonder, his hair standing up on his head, the youth heard the voice of the winged messenger. "Have no fear. The goddesses have come to you so that you may judge them. They have chosen you as the one to decide which of them is the fairest. Zeus requests you accept the office to which he has appointed you. In return, he will not deny you his help and protection!" So said Hermes, who then rose on his wings high above the narrow valley until he was lost from view. His words had given the simple shepherd the courage to look up at the beautiful immortals who stood before him, awaiting his decision. At first glance, he was tempted to say that any one of them could be judged the most beautiful. The longer he spent looking at one and then another, the more he hesitated. But there was one who gradually captivated him. She was the youngest, the most graceful, the sweetest, most refined, and most enchanting of the three. To him, it felt as though her shining eyes were turned straight towards him, enfolding him in love. Then the proudest of the three women, who was taller and more imposing than the others, chose to enlighten the young man. "I am Hera, sister and wife of Zeus," she said. "This is the golden apple which Eris, goddess of discord, threw among the guests at the wedding feast of Thetis and Peleus, upon which the words 'To the Most Beautiful' are imprinted. If you, who were once cast out of a palace and are now a paltry shepherd, were to present me with this apple, you shall rule the greatest empire on earth."

"I am Pallas Athena, goddess of wisdom," said the second, whose smooth forehead was pleasingly curved and whose deep blue eyes matched the maidenly seriousness of her beautiful face. "If you award me the victory, you shall be reputed as the wisest and most virtuous among all men!" The third, who thus far had only spoken with her eyes, looked at the shepherd with a sweet but serious smile and said, "Paris, surely you do not wish to be persuaded by the promise of gifts which may well put you in danger without any promise of success. I shall present you with a gift that can only bring you joy, something you only have

The charms of the other goddesses paled against her loveliness and the shimmer of hope she offered.

to love to achieve happiness. I shall lead into your arms the most beautiful woman on earth who will become your wife! For I am Aphrodite, goddess of love!"

While she stood before Paris, giving him her word, Aphrodite was adorned with a golden sash which lent her even more magical beauty. The charms of the other goddesses paled against her loveliness and the shimmer of hope she offered. Enchanted by the love goddess's beauty, Paris summoned up the courage to hand her the golden apple he had received from Hera. Hera and Athena angrily turned their backs on him, swearing to take their revenge for what they saw as his bad behavior, as well as on his father Priam and on the Trojan people, rich and poor. Hera swore to be the Trojans' most remorseless enemy from that moment onwards. Nevertheless, Aphrodite bade the enraptured shepherd a sweet farewell, solemnly repeating her promise, affirming it with a divine oath.

SHE STOOD BEFORE HIM, ADORNED WITH A GOLDEN SASH WHICH LENT HER EVEN MORE MAGICAL BEAUTY.

For a long time, Paris continued to live in hope as a nameless herdsman on the slopes of Mount Ida herdsman. But when the wishes which the goddess had promised to grant him failed to materialize, he married Oenone, a delightful girl born and bred in the region who was rumored to be the daughter of a river god and a nymph. Together they spent many happy days tending his herds in the seclusion of the mountains. Finally,

he was lured to the city, where he had never previously set foot, to attend the funeral games held by King Priam in honor of a deceased kinsman. There were to be contests for which the prize would be a bullock, which Priam had ordered to be fetched from his herds on Mount Ida. It so happened that this very bullock was Paris's favorite and, since he could hardly refuse to give it to his master, he decided at least to enter the competitions and try to win the animal back. And indeed, he defeated all his brothers, even the great Hector, the bravest and strongest of them all. Deiphobus, another of King Priam's more daring sons, was so overcome with anger and shame at his defeat that he was about to strike down the young herdsman. But Paris fled to the altar of Zeus and Priam's daughter, Cassandra, to whom the gods had granted the gift of prophesy, recognized him as the brother who had been given away. Amid the joy of reunion, his parents embraced him, forgetting the soothsayer's ominous prophesy at the time of his birth, and welcomed him as their son.

For the time being, Paris returned to his wife and his herd, but now he lived in a stately residence as befitted the son of a king. Soon, however, he was given the opportunity to conduct business on the king's behalf, without knowing that he would be travelling towards the prize his friend, the goddess Aphrodite, had promised him.

141

TALES OF TROY
THE ABDUCTION OF HELEN

The abduction of a queen sparks a war:
While enjoying the hospitality provided by Menelaus, king of Sparta, Paris is taken
by the beauty of his host's wife. She seems to reciprocate, so he soon whisks her away to his
ship and sets sail for Troy. This monstrous abuse of the time-honored hospitality provokes the
great Greek campaign against Troy, and the massing of Greek troops before its walls.

Illustrations by Henry Justice Ford and Clément Gontier

TALES OF TROY: THE ABDUCTION OF HELEN

Then Priam commissioned ships to be built on Mount Ida, equipped them for the voyage and sent his son Hector to Phrygia, and Paris and Deiphobus to neighboring Paeonia to enlist allied peoples from those neighboring countries. Every Trojan capable of bearing arms prepared for war and soon a mighty army was assembled, which the king placed under the command of his son Paris. As his aides, the king assigned his brother Deiphobus, Polydamas, son of Panthous, and Prince Aeneas. The powerful fleet was put to sea, heading for the Greek island of Cythera, where they planned to make their first landing. On the way, they crossed paths with the Greek prince and king of Sparta, Menelaus, bound for Pylos to visit Prince Nestor, renowned for his wisdom. Menelaus was astounded by the great convoy, while the Trojans were intrigued by the fine Greek vessel, festively decorated in honor of one of the foremost princes of Greece, who seemed to be on board. However, as the ships passed each other as they glided over the waves, neither side knew the other and each side wondered where the other might be heading. The Trojan fleet landed safely on the island of Cythera, from where Paris was to continue to Sparta, there to negotiate with Zeus's twin sons, Castor and Pollux, for the return of his father's sister Hesione. Should the Greek heroes refuse to surrender her, his father had ordered him to take the fleet to Salamis and seize the princess by force.

Before departing on his mission to Sparta, Paris wished to make an offering in a temple devoted to both Aphrodite and Artemis. Meanwhile, the inhabitants of the island had reported the approach of the great fleet to Sparta where, in the absence of her husband Menelaus, Queen Helen was holding court alone. This daughter of Zeus and Leda, and sister of Castor and Pollux, was the most beautiful woman of her era who, when little more than a child, was abducted by Theseus, but was seized and taken home again by her brothers. As she blossomed into young womanhood while living in the palace of her stepfather, King Tyndareus of Sparta, her beauty attracted legions of suitors, so many that the king feared that if he chose a son-in-law from among them, he would make enemies of the others. Then the shrewd Greek hero, Odysseus of Ithaca, suggested he would be well advised to demand that each suitor take an oath that, with his own weapons, he would defend the chosen bridegroom against anyone whose hostility the king might provoke through his daughter's marriage. Tyndareus accepted this wise recommendation and obliged all the suitors to swear such an oath, eventually choosing Menelaus, king of the Argives, son of Atreus, brother of Agamemnon, giving him the hand of his daughter and making him ruler of Sparta. Helen bore him a daughter, Hermione, who was a mere infant when Paris reached Greece.

For the lovely Helen, days at the palace were joyless and tedious when her husband was away, so she was interested to learn of the arrival of a foreign prince and his splendid fleet on the island of Cythera. Her feminine curiosity was sufficiently aroused to make her want to receive the stranger and his martial entourage. To ensure that her desire might come to fruition, she also arranged a ceremonial offering in the temple of Artemis on Cythera, making her entrance to the holy place just at the moment when Paris was concluding his own sacrifice. When he saw the queen arrive, he lowered the hands he had raised in prayer as he became lost in wonder, for he believed that he once more beheld the goddess Aphrodite, who had appeared to him at his shepherd's smallholding. He had long since heard of Helen's reputation as a beauty and now that he was on Sparta, he was curious to see her with his own eyes, although he had always believed that the woman promised to him by the goddess of love would be much fairer than the descriptions of Helen suggested. He also assumed that she would be a virgin, rather than another man's wife. But now that he saw the queen of Sparta face to face, it became clear that her beauty outshone that of the goddess herself and that she alone could be the woman Aphrodite had promised him as a reward for his judgment. His task set by his father and the whole reason for preparing for war and putting to sea completely slipped his mind. He firmly believed that he and his thousand men-at-arms had set sail only to capture Helen. While he stood entranced by her beauty, Queen Helen was looking with instantly recognizable pleasure at a handsome, long-haired, Asiatic prince, clad in oriental splendor in gold and purple. The image of her spouse faded from her memory and in his place stood the beguiling young stranger.

Below
*His artistry on the lyre, his engaging con-
versation, and the intensity of his passion
overwhelmed the queen's defenseless heart.*

Right
*The fair Helen, who resisted but without
great enthusiasm.*

Nevertheless, Helen returned to her palace in Sparta, striv-
ing to erase the vision of the beautiful young man from her
heart and to reawaken her longing for her husband Menelaus,
who was still in Pylos. But it was Paris who, surrounded by
select Spartan allies, appeared in Sparta, bearing a message
deemed important enough to give him access to the royal
court, even though Menelaus was absent. The queen greeted
him with the hospitality due to strangers and the decorum
befitting sons of kings. His artistry on
the lyre, his engaging conversation
and the intensity of his passion overwhelmed the queen's defenseless
heart. When Paris saw her faltering
in her role as a faithful wife, he forgot
his obligation to his father and his
people. Indeed, he remembered
nothing but the love goddess's captivating promise. He assembled the
loyal followers who had accompanied
him to Sparta bearing arms, and
tempted them with the prospect of
rich pickings to persuade them to
help him carry out his dubious plan.
He then stormed the palace, seized
the Greek prince's treasures together
with his wife, the fair Helen, who resisted but without great enthusiasm.

While crossing the Aegean with
his delightful plunder, the wind suddenly died down and the speeding
ships were becalmed. Ahead of the
ship bearing the robber and his princess, the waves parted and
there emerged Nereus, the ancient sea god, his aged head
crowned with seaweed, drops trickling out of his hair and beard.

He called to the ship, so still that it might have been nailed to the
surface of the water, which seemed like an iron wall surrounding the ribs of the vessel. Then Nereus called to the seafarers,
uncouthly tormenting them with his loathsome prophesies.
"Birds of evil omen are flying ahead of you, you filthy robber!
The Greeks will come with their mighty army, sworn to destroy
you and your criminal gang and tear asunder the ancient kingdom of Priam. Alas, how many horses, how many men are
doomed to die! How many corpses
will the descendants of Dardanus
blame on you! Already Pallas is don-
ning her helmet and taking up her
shield and her weapons of anger!
This war with all its bloodshed will
last for many years and only the anger
of a hero will delay the destruction
of your city. But when the appointed
time is come, it will be firebrand
Greeks who devour the homes of
Troy like beasts!"

Thus prophesied the elderly god
before sinking back into the sea.
Paris listened in horror and dismay.
But a fair wind began to blow and,
locked in the arms of the kidnapped
queen, he soon forgot the forewarn-
ings. The fleet dropped anchor in the
harbor of Cranae, and now the wife
of Menelaus freely offered him her
hand and their solemn vows were
exchanged. Both forgot their homes
and their native lands, and they lived for many years on the
spoils they had brought with them. Years passed before they set
off again for Troy.

TALES OF TROY
PARIS AND MENELAUS

A goddess rescues her favorite:
The Trojan War is to be decided by single combat between Paris and the
man he has wronged. But just as Menelaus is closing in on his hated adversary,
Aphrodite spirits Paris away from the battlefield in a cloud. She leads the
beautiful young man to a bedchamber and sends Helen to him.

Illustration by Fortunino Matania

TALES OF TROY: PARIS AND MENELAUS

The charioteers on both sides reined in their horses, the heroes leapt down from their chariots, cast off their armor and laid it on the ground not far from that of their adversaries. Hector quickly sent two heralds to Troy to bring back the sacrificial lambs and summon King Priam to the battlefield. Likewise, King Agamemnon sent his herald Talthybius to the ship to bring another beast to be slaughtered and sacrificed. Iris, messenger of the gods, assumed the shape of Priam's daughter Laodice to go into the city to inform Helen what was happening. Iris found her seated at the loom weaving a sumptuous garment interwoven with scenes of battle between the Trojans and the Greeks, her eyes fixed on her work. "Do come out, my precious one," she called to her. "There is something extraordinary happening which you must see. Only a short while ago the Trojans and the Greeks were full of hatred and trying to kill each other. Now they are standing there, face to face, calm and still, leaning on their shields, their spears thrust into the ground. The war is over, only leaving your husband Paris and Menelaus to fight over you. He who wins will reclaim you as his wife!"

So said the goddess, filling Helen's heart with longing for Menelaus, husband of her youth, and for her home and friends. Quickly she drew a silvery-white veil across her face to hide the tears dripping onto her eyelashes. Then, attended by two of her servants, Aethra and Clymene, she hastened towards the Scaean Gates. There, seated on the ramparts, was King Priam. Beside him sat the oldest and wisest of the Trojans: Panthous, Thymoetes, Lampus, Clytius, Hicetaon, Antenor and Ucalegon. The latter two were Troy's most learned men. Because of their great age, none of them had gone to war, but in council, their words were judiciously chosen. When they saw Helen approaching from the top of the tower, the elders were struck by her beauty and, whispering among themselves, they spoke of their surprise. "In truth, no one should blame the Trojans or the Greeks for allowing such a woman, one as beautiful and resplendent as an immortal goddess, to endure such misery for so long. Even so, her wish to return home aboard a Grecian ship should be granted, so that we and our sons are not left to carry the blame!"

But then Priam gently beckoned Helen to his side. "Come closer, sweet daughter," he said. "Come and sit beside me so that I may show you your first husband, your friends, and your kinsfolk. As far as I am concerned, you are not to blame for this deplorable war. It is the fault of the gods. Now tell me the name of that remarkable man whose stature and splendor shine out among the Greeks. Among the ranks there are men taller than him, but none cut the same kingly figure."

Respectfully Helen replied to the king, "Dear father-in-law, when I approach you I succumb to timidity and trepidation. Better if I had died a bitter death than leave my home, my daughter, and my friends to follow your son here. I could weep rivers of tears for having done so! But hear me now. The man whose name you asked me is Agamemnon, the finest of kings and a brave warrior. And alas, he was once my brother-in-law!" "Oh, blessed son of Atreus!" exclaimed Priam, contemplating the hero. "Oh, glorious leader, whose scepter is honored by countless Greeks! As a young man, I too commanded a huge army, keeping hordes of Amazons away from Phrygia. Although my army was not quite as huge as yours!" Then the old man asked Helen another question. "Now, dear daughter, what is the name of the one over there? He is not as tall as the son of Atreus, but his chest is broader, his shoulders more solid. His weapon is left lying on the ground while he saunters around rows of men like a ram among sheep." "That is Odysseus, the shrewd son of Laertes," Helen replied. "The rocky island of Ithaca is his home." At this point, another elder, Antenor, joined the conversation. "You are right, princess," he declared. "I know him well," he continued. "I am well acquainted with him and Menelaus. Once, I invited them to stay at my house when they were both emissaries. When standing up, Menelaus towered above Odysseus but, when seated, Odysseus was the more striking. Menelaus did not say much, but when he did his words were full of meaning. When Odysseus was about to speak, he would cast his eyes down to the ground, his staff held stock-still in his hand. He seemed so ill at ease that it was hard to tell whether he was a devil or a dimwit. But once he began, his mighty voice blasted from his chest and his words flowed out, cascading down like snowflakes in winter. No mortal could hope to compete with the eloquence of Odysseus."

Pages 148/49
"Now tell me the name of that remarkable man whose stature and splendor shine out among the Greeks."

Meanwhile, Priam had been looking further afield. "Who is that giant over there?" he asked. "So tall and muscular he stands out amongst the rest." Helen replied, "That is the hero Ajax, whom the Greeks look upon as a tower of strength. Then further over there, standing like a god among his Cretans, is Idomeneus. I know him well. Menelaus often invited him to our house. Oh, how well I recognize, one after another, my country's jovial warriors. If we had the time, I would delight in naming them all! The only ones I cannot see are my dear brothers, Castor and Pollux. Have they not come? Or do they hesitate to join in battle because they are ashamed of their sister?" With this thought, Helen fell silent. She did not know that her brothers had departed from the earth a long time ago.

Meanwhile, as these conversations continued, the heralds carried through the city the offerings of two lambs and a goatskin filled with wine grown in the region for the libation. The herald Idaeus followed with a glittering bowl and a golden cup. As they passed through the Scaean Gates, he approached King Priam and said to him, "Arise, oh King! The Trojan and Greek princes each summon you to the battlefield to swear a solemn oath. In their fight for Helen, your son Paris and Menelaus are to engage with lances in single combat. He who wins will carry her off with all her treasures. Thereafter the Greeks will return home." The king was taken aback but commanded that the horses be harnessed, and then he and Antenor climbed into the chariot. Priam took hold of the reins and soon the horses flew through the gates and out into open country. When the king reached the two armies, he and his companion stepped down from the chariot and stood between them. Agamemnon and Odysseus hurried from the Greek side towards them. The heralds brought forth the sacrificial lambs, mixed the wine in the bowl and sprinkled the two kings with holy water. Then the son of Atreus drew the sacrificial knife which he always carried with him beside the great scabbard of his sword. He cut the forelock from the lambs as the rite of sacrifice demanded, calling upon the father of the gods to witness the taking of the pledge. He then slit the lambs' throats and laid their bodies in the dust. The heralds prayed and poured the wine from the golden cup and all the people from Greece and Troy made a loud supplication: "Zeus and all your immortal gods. May the brains of the first to break this solemn oath, theirs and those of their children, be poured over the earth like this wine."

Priam then spoke, "Now, Trojans and Greeks, permit me to return to my fortress on the mountain ridge of Ilium, for I cannot bear to watch with my own eyes as my son fights King Menelaus in mortal combat. Only Zeus knows which of them is doomed!" Thus spoke the old man, who then laid the sacrificial lamb in the chariot, climbed aboard with his companion, and drove the horses back to Troy.

Hector and Odysseus now measured the space for the combat and in a brazen helmet shuffled two lots to decide who would be the first the throw his lance at his opponent. Hector turned away and shook the helmet and out fell Paris's lot. The two heroes donned breastplates and helmets and took up arms. Then, with their mighty lances in their hands and threatening looks on their faces, they passed between Trojans and Greeks, who stood there awestruck. They finally met in in the measured space, their spears raised in defiance. As decided by lot, Paris was the first to throw his weapon, which struck Menelaus's shield, but the spearhead bent as it struck the metal. In turn, Menelaus lifted his spear and prayed aloud, "Zeus, let me punish the one who has first offended me,

> "BETTER IF I HAD DIED A BITTER DEATH THAN LEAVE MY HOME, MY DAUGHTER, AND MY FRIENDS TO FOLLOW YOUR SON HERE."

so that our descendants will know it is wrong to harm one who has shown them kindness!" He then threw his own spear, piercing Paris's shield, penetrating his breastplate and ripping his tunic. Then the son of Atreus snatched his sword from its scabbard and struck out at his rival's helmet, but his blade splintered with a loud jangling sound. "Cruel Zeus, why do you begrudge me victory?" yelled Menelaus, charging into his enemy and gripping him by the helmet. Then he turned and dragged him towards the Greeks as they stood in battle order. He would have hauled Paris along the ground and throttled him with his chinstrap had not the goddess Aphrodite witnessed his plight, seen the hero was in danger, and broken the strap. Now the hero Menelaus stood there, in his hand an empty helmet, which he then hurled at the Greeks and prepared to launch a new attack on his rival. But all in vain, for Aphrodite had wrapped Paris in a sheltering mist and spirited him back to Troy. There, she laid him in a sweet-scented chamber and then, disguised as an old woman, a spinner from Sparta, she found Helen, seated among other Trojan women on one of the city's towers. The goddess gently tugged at her robe and told her, "Come, Paris is asking for you. He awaits you in the chamber, dressed as if for a feast and ready to dance rather than emerging from single combat." As she looked up, Helen saw the divinely beautiful Aphrodite disappear from sight. Unnoticed by the

other women, she slipped away and hurried to the palace. There she found her husband reposing on a couch, tastefully adorned by Aphrodite. Seating herself facing him, she turned her eyes from him and rebuked him. "This is how you return from the battle? I would sooner have seen you killed by the fine man who was my first husband. It is not long since you bragged that you could annihilate him with your spear or by fighting him hand-to-hand! Go back and challenge him for a second time. But perhaps that is unwise. Stay away, for this time he might do you worse harm!" Paris retorted, "Do not enrage me with your mockery, woman. If Menelaus defeated me, he did so with Athena's help. Another time I shall conquer him, for the gods have never abandoned us." At this, Helen's heart was moved by Aphrodite. She looked again at her husband, this time with greater affection, offering him her lips for a kiss of reconciliation.

On the battlefield, Menelaus was still storming around, trying to track Paris down, like a predator hunting its prey. But neither Trojan nor Greek could show him where the prince could be found. Indeed, they would certainly not have hidden him, for they hated him more than death. At last, Agamemnon raised his voice and said, "Hear my words, Trojans and Greeks! Menelaus is clearly the winner. Hand Helen over to us with all her treasures, then pay us tribute for all time to come." The Greeks greeted his proposal with jubilation. The Trojans remained silent.

TALES OF TROY
HECTOR IN TROY

Farewell to his loved ones:
Hector, commander of the Trojan forces and son of King Priam,
brushes aside his wife's despairing pleas for him to stay off the battlefield.
In a touching scene the hero bids a tender farewell to Andromache and their
little boy, Astyanax, probably aware that he will not see them again.

Illustration by Clément Gontier

Meanwhile, Hector had arrived at Paris's palace, which stood high on the mountain close to his own home, for both princes had their independent homes near Priam's regal residence. In his right hand he carried his spear, eleven cubits long with a brazen point joined to the shaft by a ring of gold. He found his brother in his room examining weapons and smoothing the curve of a bow, while his wife Helen sat among her women, busy weaving while also directing their work. On seeing his brother, Hector berated him. "You should not be lolling about here when, for your sake, men are fighting in the turmoil of battle outside the city walls! You should be out there, you who would be the first to rebuke anyone who behaved like this at such a time. Stand on your feet and help us defend our city before enemy firebrands burn it down!" Paris replied, "You are wrong to reproach me, brother. For it is out of grief, not resentment, that I sit idly by. But now my wife has gently persuaded me to return to battle. I ask you merely to wait while I don my armor, or go on ahead and I will quickly join you." Hector remained silent, but Helen meekly told him, "Oh brother-in-law, I am a loathsome creature who wreaks one disaster after another! If only the waves had engulfed me before I came ashore with Paris! Now that evil threatens, I only wish I were the spouse of a better man, one who has acknowledged the disapproval and scorn he has brought upon himself. This man does not have a heart in his body, and never will. Nor will it be long before the results of his cowardice become clear to see. But you, Hector, are welcome to come in and rest from your labors, most of which lie heavily on your shoulders." "No, Helen," replied Hector. "You are kind to invite me to sit, but I truly must refuse. My heart hungers to help the men of Troy. Your only duty is to provoke this man, so that he may soon join me within the city walls. Before this, I must go

home to see my wife, my small son, and my servants," Hector said this and hurried away. But his wife was not at home. The gatekeeper told him, "As soon as she heard that the Trojans were under attack and succumbing to the Greeks, she left the house, beside herself with anxiety, ready to climb one of the towers, with the nurse behind her carrying her child."

Quickly, Hector turned back and hurried through the streets of Troy. As he reached the Scaean Gates his wife, the beautiful, vivacious Andromache, daughter of Eetion, king of Cilician Thebe, came hurrying towards him. Behind her came a serving woman with Andromache's infant son Astyanax, as bright as a star, clutched to her breast. As his father smiled quietly at the little boy, Andromache rushed to his side, eyes filled with tears, and gently held his hand. "You dreadful man! One day your courage will surely be the death of you! Have you no compassion for either your little son or your inconsolable wife, who may soon become your widow? If I were to lose you, it would be better that I were simply to sink into the earth. Achilles killed my father, my mother was struck by the arrow of Artemis; my seven brothers were also slain by the son of Peleus. Without you, Hector, there is no one to comfort me. You are my father, my mother, and my brothers. So take pity on me. Stay here with me on the tower. Do not make your son an orphan or your wife a widow! Place your troops on the hill with all the fig trees. There the bravest warriors, the two Ajaxes, Idomeneus, the sons of Atreus and Diomedes, have led the attack three times, perhaps guided by the words of an oracle, perhaps by their own instinct."

Lovingly Hector replied, "This grieves me too, beloved. But were I to stay idling here like a coward, viewing the battle from afar, I would humiliate myself before the men and women of Troy. Nor does my own courage allow me to behave thus, for it has taught me to fight in the front ranks. True, in my heart

"IT IS THE MEN OF TROY, MYSELF INCLUDED, WHO MUST BEAR THE BRUNT OF WAR!"

The father smiled quietly at the little boy.

I predict that the day will come when sacred Troy shall fall, taking with it Priam and all his people. But neither the sufferings of the Trojans nor those of my own parents and my beloved brothers when they fall under the Grecian sword shall cause me the pain my heart shall feel for you when a Greek carries you away, weeping and lamenting, into servitude and then to Argos, where you are forced to sit at the loom or fetch water. Then one day a man will see your tears and say, 'That was Hector's wife!' Let me be buried in a grave rather than hear your cries when they carry you away!" Thus he spoke, holding out his arms to the child. But the little one screamed and snuggled up to the nurse's breast, for he was frightened by his father's display of affection and by his glittering helmet with its terrifying crest of fluttering horsehair. Hector smiled at the child and his mother, took the helmet from his head and placed it on the ground. Then he kissed his beloved infant son and rocked him in his arms. Looking heavenwards he prayed, "Zeus and all the gods! Let my little boy become a leader of men, like his father. Let him strive to raise the hopes and desires of the Trojan people. Let him become the powerful governor of the city and, when he returns to the city laden with the spoils of battle, let the people say, 'He is even braver than his father and will make his mother prouder still.'" With these words, he laid his son in the arms of his wife, who smiled through her tears as she held him to her. With profound sadness, Hector gently stroked her hand, saying, "My poor dear wife, do not grieve for me. I shall not be killed if I am not fated to die. But no mortal can escape his destiny. So return to your spindle and loom and attend to your women. It is the men of Troy, myself included, who must bear the brunt of war!" As he spoke, Hector set his helmet on his head and left. Andromache walked toward the palace, repeatedly glancing backwards while shedding tears of grief. On seeing her approach, her women shared her sorrow, and in his own palace Hector was mourned as if he were already dead.

Paris, too, had not delayed. Bearing his shining bronze weapons, he sped through the city like a superb stallion breaking loose from its halter and galloping towards the river. He reached his brother, just as he turned away from Andromache. Calling from afar, he said, "I have kept you waiting, have I not? I have obliged my elder brother to tarry because I have not arrived in good time!" But Hector responded benevolently, "My good brother, of course you are a fearless warrior, but it often seems that you prefer to pass the time doing nothing. You must understand how it breaks my heart when I hear the Trojans mocking you, those who have suffered so much for you. But we must deal with this matter some other time, when we have driven the Greeks from our country and can sit at ease in the palace, drinking from the cup of freedom!"

GONTIER

TALES OF TROY
ACHILLES REARMED

A visit to the god of the forge:
Achilles needs new weapons and armor for his battle with Hector.
His mother, Thetis, a sea deity, hastens to Hephaestus, the god of the art of forging,
who makes armor, a helmet, greaves, and the celebrated shield described in the
Iliad as decorated with motifs, from the mundane to the cosmological. Thetis takes
the new weapons and armor to Achilles' tent the following day.

Illustrations by Clément Gontier and John Flaxman

Both armies could now rest after the unrelenting battles. The Trojans released the horses from the chariots, but before they even considered eating, they quickly assembled in council. All stood upright in a circle, none daring to sit, for they still trembled in the presence of Achilles and feared that he might reappear. Finally, Polydamas, wise son of Panthous who was able to see both the future and the past, advised the troops not to wait until dawn but to return immediately to the city. "When Achilles is fully armed and finds us here in the morning," he declared, "those who escape to the city will be blessed by Fortune, but many others will become a good meal for dogs and vultures. I pray my ear will never hear such things! My advice to you is that you and all your soldiers spend the night in the marketplace of Troy, where, militarily speaking, you will be guarded on every side by high walls and solid gates. At the break of dawn we must man the ramparts and woe betide anyone who comes sprinting from the ships to start a fight."

Then Hector spoke, glaring at the speaker. "I heartily disagree with what you have said, Polydamas. At the very moment when Zeus has allowed me victory and I have driven the Greeks back into the sea, your so-called advice will sound downright ridiculous to our people, and not one single Trojan will follow it. I for my part order you all to eat, sharing your supplies between you, and remember to keep watch. Should any among you fear for his rations or his wealth let him spend it all on a feast to be enjoyed together. Better our own men, and not the Greeks, have that pleasure! In the morning we shall resume our attack on the ships. It is true that Achilles is back in action. He has returned to a far worse fate, for I shall not give up this terrible struggle until one of us wears the victor's crown!" The Trojans ignored the salubrious words of Polydamas in favor of Hector's somewhat less wholesome advice. They loudly applauded before ravenously throwing themselves on their food.

Meanwhile, throughout the night, the Greeks mourned the death of Patroclus. Achilles grieved more than his companions

"WE BOTH MUST COLOR THE EARTH WITH OUR BLOOD."

as he laid the hands that had slain so many on the breast of his departed friend. He said, "Oh, such empty words occurred to me as I attempted to comfort the old hero Menoetius at his palace. I promised I would bring his son back home to Opus, rich in fame and plunder after the destruction of Troy! Now both of us are destined to color the same alien earth with the red of our blood. It seems that I too shall never return to the palace of my gray-haired father Peleus and my mother Thetis, but shall lie beneath Trojan soil. But since I am destined to sink into the ground before you, I shall not hold your funeral until I have brought you the weapons and the head of Hector, your murderer. I shall also offer up twelve of Troy's most noble sons at your funeral pyre. Until this has come to pass, rest here by my ships, beloved friend!" Then Achilles ordered a great cauldron of water to be placed on the fire and washed and anointed the body of the fallen hero. He was then laid on a bier, spread with fine linen from head to foot and finally covered with a glistening white robe.

Thetis, meanwhile, had arrived at the beautiful palace, built to last for all eternity and shining like stars, which the lame blacksmith, Hephaestus had constructed for himself from bronze. She found the god working hard and sweating at the bellows. He had completed twenty tripods. At the base of each he had attached golden wheels which, without the touch of a human hand, could be made to roll into the great hall of Mount Olympus. After this he went straight back to his workshop. The technical marvels here were wonderful to behold, complete but for the handles, which he was in the process of adding, hammering them into their appropriate place. His comely wife, Charis, one of the Graces, took Thetis by the hand and led her to a silver chair, placed a footstool at her feet, then went to fetch her husband. On seeing the goddess of the sea, Hephaestus called out jubilantly, "How happy it makes me to welcome the noblest of the immortals to my house, for it was she who saved me, a newborn, from destruction. Because I was born lame, my mother immediately cast me out and I would

He began by constructing a gigantic shield, whose five layers made it remarkably strong, with a silver strap and a sparkling triple rim.

have perished miserably, had Eurynome and Thetis not taken me and raised me in the marine grotto until I was nine years old. There, with the vaulted grotto as my forge, I designed and made all sorts of jewelry – bracelets, rings, earrings, hairpins and chains of all kinds – while echoing around us was the sound of the foaming, surging stream of the ocean. And now, the one who rescued me is visiting me in my own house! Entertain her, my sweet Charis, while I clear away the tools of my trade." The god said this, covered in soot as he rose unsteadily from the anvil, wobbling back and forth, and removed the bellows from the fire. Then he locked his many different implements in a silver chest, and then wiped his hands, face, neck, and chest with a sponge. Then he wrapped himself in his tunic and, with the willing help of his maidservants, made his way out of his workplace. The maids, however, were not living creatures born of women, but only images, fashioned out of gold and endowed with the charms of youth, namely strength, intelligence, voice, and skill. Moving on swift feet, they hurried away from their master. Now refreshed, he sat beside Thetis, took her hand, and said, "Dear and honored goddess, what has led you to my home today, when you so seldom visit me? Tell me what you desire. Anything I can accomplish, I shall, with all my heart. I will do whatever you wish me to do."

Thetis then told him all her troubles and, clasping his knees, she spoke of her son Achilles who was destined soon to die. She begged Hephaestus to create armor for him, as long he still survived under Greek protection. It should consist of helmet, shield, cuirass, and greaves fitted with ankle pieces. The armor he once owned, a gift from the gods, had been lost when a comrade fell at Troy. "Be brave, noble goddess," Hephaestus replied. "Do not distress yourself. Would that I could save your son from

the violent death Fate may one day deal him, as surely as I can fashion for him armor so splendid and so strong that every mortal who sees it will be filled with wonder!" Thereupon he hobbled away from Thetis and made his way to his furnace, where he turned his bellows towards the fire. Of their own accord, twenty such bellows blasted upon the vast crucibles, in which he placed to melt bronze, tin, silver and gold. He then set his anvil on its block and with his right hand took up his mighty hammer, while in the left he held his tongs. He began by constructing a gigantic shield, whose five layers made it remarkably strong, with a silver strap and a sparkling triple rim. To adorn the surface he shaped images of the earth, the surging waves of the sea, the sunlit sky, the moon, and all the stars in heaven. Then he added two flourishing cities. The first was all aglow with wedding celebrations and feasts, a public gathering, argumentative citizens, heralds, and city bureaucrats. The second was besieged by two armies. Inside the walls were women, small children, and tottering elders;

WHEN HE FINISHED THE SHIELD, HEPHAESTUS FORGED A CUIRASS THAT GLOWED BRIGHTER THAN A BLAZING FIRE.

outside were men of the city, warriors lying in ambush, and shepherds tending their flocks. Another part of the shield portrayed the tumult of battle, with wounded men and survivors wrangling over the bodies of the dead and what remained of their armor. In yet another space he showed farmers and oxen drawing ploughs in a fallow field with soil tilled and ready to cultivate. He then added a field of waving grain harvested by reapers, with fellow workers preparing food under an oak tree on one side. Further on was a vineyard where maturing black grapes hung from stakes of pure silver from vines surrounded by a trench of bluish metal and a fence of tin. This was harvest time and along a single path, sturdy youths and pretty girls could be seen carrying the sweet fruit in finely woven baskets.

TALES OF TROY: ACHILLES REARMED

Left
To adorn the surface he shaped images of the earth, the surging waves of the sea, the sunlit sky, the moon, and all the stars in heaven.

Below
She laid the armor before him, a work of art that clanged proudly as it was moved.

In their midst was a boy with a lyre to which they danced. Furthermore, he created a herd of cattle from gold and tin, guarded by four golden shepherds and nine dogs. Cattle at the head of the herd had been set upon by two lions, which also seized a bullock. The shepherds had let their dogs loose, which stood barking loudly within jumping distance of the attackers, both of which now lay dead. He then created a gentle valley with grazing sheep scattered across the slopes, where there were houses, sheepfolds, and shepherds' huts. Finally, he introduced a band of brightly clad young dancers, the girls wearing wreaths and the boys with golden daggers hanging from silver straps. Two acrobats whirled about to the sound of a singer and his harp, and a large audience had gathered to enjoy the merrymaking. Around the outermost rim of the shield the River Oceanus wove like a serpent.

When he finished the shield, Hephaestus forged

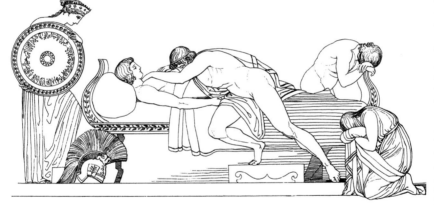

a cuirass that glowed brighter than a blazing fire. Then he turned his attention to a heavy shining helmet, fitting well to the temples and topped with a crest of gold, and finally greaves of the most flexible tin. When all was complete, he laid it before the mother of Achilles. She pounced upon the armor as a falcon would upon its prey, thanked him, and bore away the shimmering weaponry in her goddess's hands.

With the first glow of dawn she was back with her son who, surrounded by grieving comrades, was still weeping over body of his dear friend Patroclus. She laid before him the armor, a work of art that clanged proudly as it was moved. The faithful followers of Achilles trembled at the sight, but none dared to look the goddess straight in the face. But under their tear-soaked lashes, the eyes of the son of Peleus flickered with anger and joy. His heart relished the gifts of the god Hephaestus as he lifted them one by one for all to see. Then he donned his full armor. As he set forth, he commanded his friends, "For my sake, take care that no fly settles on the wounds of my fallen comrade-in-arms and disfigures his beautiful body." "Let me take care of him," said Thetis, as she poured ambrosia and nectar through the half-open lips of Patroclus. This balm of the gods was known to pervade flesh, making him look as though he were still alive.

Achilles walked down to the seashore and summoned the Greeks with a voice like thunder. Whoever could stand on his feet ran immediately to his call, even the helmsmen who had so far never left their ships. Although they were wounded, Diomedes and Odysseus hobbled up to him, leaning on their lances. They were followed by all the heroes, the last to appear being Agamemnon, still weak from the wound inflicted by the spear of Coon, son of Antenor.

TALES OF TROY

THE DEATH OF HECTOR

Unfettered lust for revenge:
Achilles gleams like Ares, god of war, when he meets Hector on the battlefield.
A frightened Hector is chased three times around the walled city before making
a stand to fight. But all his courage is futile against his adversary's wrath.
Hector falls, but before he dies, he prophesies Achilles' death, provoking the
successful combatant to despoil Hector's corpse.

Illustrations by Max Wulff, Charles Edmund Brock, and John Flaxman

Page 163
So Hector fled along the wall, along the wagon track, and past the bubbling hot and cold springs of the Scamander.

Left
His breathing already shallow, Hector began to beg: "Please, don't let the dogs near the Greek ships tear my flesh apart!"

Achilles came closer and closer, as terrifying and magnificent as the god of war himself. The lance of Pelian ash on his right shoulder quivered as he moved, while his brazen weapons glittered around him like a blazing fire or like the rising sun. When Hector saw him, he could not help but tremble, nor could he stand still any longer. He turned towards the gate and the son of Peleus flew behind him like a falcon relentlessly pursuing a dove that tries to dodge from side to side. So Hector fled along the wall, along the wagon track, and past the bubbling hot and cold springs of the Scamander River, moving further and further around the ramparts. Thus he and his pursuer circled the wall of Priam's city three times, as the immortal gods on Mount Olympus watched with rapt attention. "Consider carefully, oh gods," said Zeus, "for the moment of decision has come. The question is, should Hector once again escape death? Or, brave though he be, should he fall?" Pallas Athena answered, "Father, what are you thinking? Would you retrieve from death a mortal drawing his last breath, whose fate has long since been sealed? Do as you think best, but do not count on the approval of the gods!" Zeus nodded, a sign of his willingness to respect the opinion of his daughter, who then flew like a bird from the rock-strewn heights of Olympus to the battlefield below.

There, Hector was still fleeing from his pursuer, who raced like a hound that frightens a deer from its hiding place and allows its quarry neither shelter nor rest. At the same time, Achilles signaled to his men to hold their fire, for he himself sought the honor of being the first and only one to slay Greece's greatest enemy.

When they had rounded the ramparts and reached the springs of the Scamander for the fourth time, Zeus rose on Olympus, holding before him his golden scales in which he laid two death lots, one for the son of Peleus and one for Hector. He then held the scales in the middle to weigh them; Hector's lot plunged towards Hades, and instantly Phoebus Apollo abandoned him. But Pallas Athena came up close to Achilles and whispered in his ear, "Stay here and rest while I convince your enemy to come forward bravely and fight you." Obeying

the goddess, he stood still, resting on his spear of Pelian ash, while she, assuming the shape of Deiphobus, moved close to Hector and said, "Ah! My dear elder brother, the son of Peleus is no more than a bully! Why do we not stand up to him and fend him off!" With a smile, Hector looked up at his brother and replied, "You were always my favorite brother, Deiphobus, but I think even more highly of you now as I see that you have been brave enough to leave the city and encourage me, while all the others only sit there behind the walls!" Athena, alias Deiphobus, beckoned the hero and, lance raised, led him to the place where Achilles was resting. Hector was the first to speak. "No longer shall I try to escape you, son of Peleus," he said. "My heart commands that I confront you, knowing that I shall destroy you or be destroyed by you! But let us make a pledge before the gods: If Zeus grants me victory, I shall never mistreat you after death, until such time as I have stripped you of your armor and returned your dead body to your people. You shall do the same for me!"

"Pledges mean nothing to me!" replied Achilles morosely. "Friendship between us has as little chance as a dog encouraging friendship between lions and men, or attempting to create harmony between wolves and lambs. One of us shall shed his blood on the ground. Summon up all your skills, for you may need both to throw your spear and fence with your sword. You cannot escape me, for the time has come for you to atone for all the grief you have caused my warriors with your weapons of war!" At this, Achilles turned and hurled his lance, but Hector ducked quickly and the weapon flew over him and lodged in the earth. Athena took hold of it and, unseen by Hector, immediately handed it back to Achilles. Smoldering with rage, Hector cast his spear, which this time hit its target, striking the center of Achilles' shield but bouncing off again. In desperation, Hector looked back to see his brother Deiphobus, for he had no other lance to throw, but Deiphobus had disappeared. At that moment, Hector suddenly knew that Athena had deluded him. Indeed, he now saw that he was about to meet his fate. Now his only thought was to avoid sinking ignominiously into the dust. With his right hand drew his mighty sword from the scabbard on his hip and waved it in the air as he rushed forward, like an eagle swooping from the air to capture a hare or lamb cowering on the ground. The son of Peleus did not wait to be struck. He also advanced, covering himself with his shield, his helmet shaking, its plumes fluttering as he brandished a spear that shone as bright as a star in his right hand. His eyes scanned Hector's body, searching for a place where he could inflict a fatal wound, but finding it completely covered by the stolen armor. Only where the shoulder and neck joined at the collarbone was there a small patch of skin exposed. This was among the most vulnerable places on the surface of the body and it was here that Achilles calmly took aim and stabbed it so violently that the point emerged from the back of his opponent's neck. Nonetheless, the spear had not cut the windpipe, which meant the wounded hero could still speak, even though he lay in the dust as Achilles joyously proclaimed out loud that he would leave his body for dogs and birds to feast on. His breathing already shallow, Hector began to beg: "I beseech you, by your life and those of your parents and those of your children, do not let my flesh be torn apart by the dogs that wander near the Greek ships! Take bronze and gold, as much as you want, then send my body to Troy so that the men and women of the city may do me the honor of witnessing my funeral pyre."

But Achilles shook his head in anger and replied, "Do not implore me by my children or by my parents, you who have murdered my friend. Even if your compatriots were to pledge me a twentyfold ransom and then promise more. And even if Priam offered me his weight in gold, there will be no one chasing the dogs away from your head." "I know you well," groaned the dying Hector. "I presumed that you would do nothing to ease my fate. You have a heart of iron. But think of me when the gods avenge me and you fall from the height of the Scaean Gates, struck by the deadly shaft of Phoebus Apollo and, like me, finish in the dust!" With this prophesy, Hector's soul left his body and sped down to Hades. Achilles roared after the departing soul, "Die! I shall meet my fate when it is the will of Zeus and the other gods!" He then drew the spear from the corpse, laying it aside while he stripped the blood-drenched armor from the dead Hector's shoulders.

Then many warriors from the Greek army came out to admire Hector's fine physique and handsome face, some

speaking and touching him, saying, "Is it not wonderful how much gentler and softer to the touch he is now than when he was hurling firebrands among our ships?" Then Achilles stood up to address the people and said, "Friends and heroes! Now the gods have permitted me to rid ourselves of this man, who has done us more damage than all the others put together. Let us approach the city in full armor and find out whether they will surrender the citadel to us or whether they still dare to resist, even without Hector. But why do I waste time talking? Does not my dear friend Patroclus still lie unburied among the ships? Let us sing the victory song and, above all, present my friend with the man I have slain to atone for his murder."

With these words and a callous expression on his face, Achilles again bent down to the body and pierced the tendons of each foot between ankles and heels, threading thongs of ox hide through each opening and binding them tightly to his chariot. Then he leaped on board and urged his horses towards the ships, with the corpse dragging along the ground. Clouds of dust rose around the dead man's face, which not long before had been so handsome, while his matted and soiled hair plowed a furrow through the sand. Looking from the top of the tower and seeing this gruesome spectacle, his mother Hecuba tore off her veil as she wailed for her son. King Priam also wept in anguish. The whole city resounded to the howls of grief and cries of fear from the Trojans and their allies. In his anger and pain, the old king could scarcely be prevented from storming out of the Scaean Gates and chasing after his son's murderer. Throwing himself on the ground he cried, "Hector, Hector! In my sorrow for you, I forget all my sons whom the enemy has killed. Oh, had you but died in my arms!"

Andromache, Hector's wife, still knew nothing of the signs of mourning, since no messenger had come to tell her that her husband had not yet returned to Troy. She sat peacefully in her chamber in the palace, embroidering a fine purple robe with threads in bright colors. Moments ago, she had ordered one of the handmaids to place a large cauldron on the fire so that her spouse could take a warm bath whenever he returned from the battlefield. Then from the tower she heard pain-stricken cries of grief and distress. Her heart full of sinister foreboding, she

*Her heart throbbed painfully as she ran
through the palace, sped up the tower, then
looked down from the wall. She saw the horses
of the son of Peleas mercilessly dragging her
husband's body through the countryside.*

cried to her maids who stood close to her, "Alas, I fear Achilles alone has cut my courageous husband off from the city, for he is a man so brave he always attacks from the front ranks. Both of you, follow me. We must see what is happening!" Her heart throbbed painfully as she ran through the palace, sped up the tower, then looked down from the wall. She saw the horses of the son of Peleas mercilessly dragging her husband's body behind the victor's chariot as they made their way through the countryside. Andromache collapsed and sank backwards into the arms of her father- and mother-in-law. She tore the priceless adornments she wore in her hair from her head. The frontlet, the snood, the plaited band, and the beautiful veil that had been Aphrodite's wedding gift to her all fell to the floor. When she finally regained consciousness, the words she directed to the Trojan women were broken by her sobs. "Hector! Woe is me!

You, as wretched as I, born as humble as I! Now left in pain and misery, I shall sit at home, a widow with an infant child who must grow up bereft of his father, his eyes cast downwards, his lashes wet with tears. He will have to beg from his father's friends, pulling one by the cloak, another by the sleeve, hoping that they will give him a bowl of food and something to drink! And sometimes a child of prosperous parent will push him away from a feast saying, 'Go away! Your father is not at the feast!' Then he will run weeping to his mother, who has no husband. But the dogs will have devoured Hector, while the worms take what is left! What use to me now are his elegant tunics stored in my chest? I shall burn them, for they mean nothing to me anymore. Hector will no more wear them when he is at leisure or flaunt them when occasion demands!" She said this, weeping and lamenting, and the Trojan women joined her.

TALES OF TROY
THE DEATH OF PARIS

An inglorious end at the hand of a foe:
Paris's luck does not hold much longer – after all, his fate has already
been decided. Wounded by a poison-tipped arrow fired by Philoctetes, Paris
flees from the battlefield. As the toxin begins to take hold, and the man who
had abducted Helen from Sparta and taken her to Troy meets his end.

Illustrations by John Flaxman and Henry Justice Ford

TALES OF TROY: THE DEATH OF PARIS

Soon war broke out between the two armies.

The next day the Trojans were continuing to bury their dead outside the city walls when they saw the Greeks approaching, ready to fight again. Taking account of their weakness, Polydamas, wise friend of the fallen Hector, advised them to withdraw behind the walls, where they could defend themselves more easily. "Troy is the work of the gods," he said, "and their work is not easy to destroy. Nor do we lack food and drink, and in the halls of rich King Priam's palace are stores enough to feed three times as many people living in our city for years to come." But the Trojans did not listen, having eagerly accepted the advice of Aeneas, who urged them to conquer or die on the battlefield. Soon war broke out between the two armies. Neoptolemus struck down twelve Trojans with his father's spear, one after another. So, too, did Eurymenes, brother-in-arms of the brave Aeneas, while Aeneas himself tore blood-drenched gaps in the Greek ranks, and Paris killed Demoleon of Sparta, the friend of Menelaus. By contrast, like the war god himself, Philoctetes raged among the Trojans, like torrential rain flooding the surrounding fields. Any enemy who dared look at him was done for. Even the armor Philoctetes wore, the armor of Heracles, seemed to spell disaster for the Trojans. It was as if they saw the Medusa's head on his breastplate. Finally, though, Paris summoned up the courage to approach him, holding his bow and arrow. Quickly, he shot an arrow into the air, but it flew over Philoctetes, wounding Cleodorus, the man at his side. Cleodorus backed off, attempting to defend himself with his lance, but Paris's second arrow killed him. Then Philoctetes seized his bow and shouted with a voice like thunder, "You Trojan bandit! You, the cause of all our misfortunes! You shall atone for your barefaced attempt to measure your strength against mine. Once you are dead, destruction will speed at an alarming rate to your dynasty and your city!" Following these words, he drew his bow's twisted string towards his chest, inserting the arrow so that it jutted only a little beyond the curved bow. The twang of the string sent the arrow hissing through the air. The Greek hero's aim was true, but the arrow merely grazed Paris's beautiful skin, so he aimed again. A second arrow from the bow of Philoctetes hit him in the flank. Unwilling to continue fighting and trembling from head to foot, Paris fled like a dog from a lion.

TALES OF TROY: THE DEATH OF PARIS

But then he threw himself at the feet of the woman he had scorned.

The war and its bloodshed continued as physicians tended Paris's painful wound. But as night fell, the Trojans withdrew behind the city walls and the Greeks returned to their ships. Paris passed a sleepless night on his bed of pain. The arrow had pierced him to the marrow and the poison, in which the arrow of Heracles had been dipped, had left the wound black and putrid. The physicians could not help, even though they applied every possible means to soothe the pain. Then Paris remembered the words of an oracle telling him that when he was most in need, only Oenone, the wife he had abandoned, could help him. When he was still a humble shepherd on Mount Ida, they had enjoyed many happy days together, and when he left for Greece it was she who told him about the oracle's words. So, very reluctantly but driven by his agonizing physical distress, he asked that he might be carried up Mount Ida where his first wife still lived. All the way up to the summit, birds of ill omen croaked as the servants carried him past. Their cries filled him with terror but his desire to live was so strong, he attempted to ignore them. When he arrived at the home of Oenone, his former wife, she and her servants were astounded by what they saw. But then he threw himself at the feet of the woman he had scorned and cried, "Honorable lady, I beg you, do not hate me in my time of tribulation because I once unwillingly abandoned you, leaving you an unwilling widow. It was the implacable will of the Fates that I should go to Helen. Would that I had died before bringing her to my father's palace! But now I implore you by the gods and the love we once shared, pity me and free me from this excruciating pain and anoint my wound with balm, for it was you who predicted that you alone could save my life!"

But his words did nothing to change the embittered mind of the wife he had deserted. "How dare you come to me, the wife you left inconsolable so that you could take pleasure in Helen's eternal youth? Why not go and throw yourself at her feet to see whether she is willing to help you? Because for all your weeping and wailing, you leave my soul unmoved." Then she turned him away from her house, without ever thinking that her fate was bound up with his. Paris dragged himself away and then his servants carried him down from the wooded heights of Mount Ida, while Hera took pleasure in his distress as she watched from Mount Olympus. But he never reached the lower slopes, for he died from his poisoned wound, his spirit breathing its last on the summit of Mount Ida, knowing that Helen would never see him again.

Alone in her lonely house set high on Mount Ida and far away from the companionship of other Trojan women, Oenone was suddenly seized by deep remorse and only then did she remember sharing the joys of young love with Paris. Like the ice that forms in the forests on the high mountains and melts away in the shady gorges and begins to flow, driven by the soft west wind, the hardness in her heart melted with such anguish that she sprang from her couch, heaved the great door open and rushed through it like a tempest. From cliff to cliff, over ravines and mountain streams, she scurried through the night. Full of compassion, Selene looked down on Oenone from the dark blue night sky. At last she reached the place in the mountains where the body of her husband lay on a funeral pyre. The logs burst into flame, surrounded by the shepherds of the mountain region, who came to honor their friend, son of the king's last marriage. When Oenone saw him, she was speechless with grief and, veiling her beautiful face with her gown, threw herself on the pyre before the bystanders could save her. Now all they could do was bewail her fate as, beside the body of her husband, she was consumed by the flames.

TALES OF TROY
THE WOODEN HORSE

Deception wins in the end:
The fall of Troy is imminent. Odysseus, cunning as always, suggests building a
gigantic wooden horse with sinister contents. The Trojans fall for the ruse and pull the
horse into the city as the spoils of war. No sooner have the victory celebrations subsided
than the Greeks concealed in the wooden horse climb out and open the city gates.
The killing and looting do not stop until Priam's city is destroyed.

Illustrations by Charles Edmund Brock and Henry Justice Ford

TALES OF TROY: THE WOODEN HORSE

So far, the Greeks had made many unsuccessful attempts to capture the gates and walls of Troy, but had always been forced back on all sides. Then the soothsayer Calchas called an assembly of the most distinguished heroes and addressed them thus: "Do not submit further to the hardship of a violent struggle, because this is not the way to reach your goal. It makes more sense for you to devise a ruse that enables you and your ships to fulfil your purpose. Allow me to tell you about something I saw yesterday. A hawk was chasing a little dove, but the smaller bird slipped into a cleft in a rock to escape its pursuer, who sat for a while, menacingly waiting in front of the crack. But the little creature did not reappear. Then, curbing his frustration, the hawk hid behind a nearby bush. Then, lo and behold, the dove was foolish enough to flutter out, and the hawk swooped down on the poor bird and mercilessly throttled her. Let us take the bird as an example and cease fighting to take over Troy. Instead, let us see what can be achieved by subterfuge."

Having at least pondered the soothsayer's words, none of heroes were ready to consider any kind of plan that would put an end to the brutal war. Only Odysseus had the kind of mind able to offer any kind of solution. "How does this sound to you, my friends?" he asked, for the seer's advice appealed to him. "Let us build a gigantic wooden horse and hide as many of Greece's bravest heroes as it will hold in its belly. The rest shall retreat aboard the ships to the island of Tenedos, and before sailing they must burn everything left behind in the camp, so that when the Trojans see the fire and smoke from their walls they will deem it safe enough to scatter over the field. However, one among us, a man of courage who is unknown by sight to any Trojan, must remain outside the wooden horse. He must go to Troy, claiming to be a fugitive who fled the atrocious violence of the Greeks who were about to sacrifice him to the gods to guarantee them a safe journey home. He will tell them that he hid under the wooden horse, dedicated to the goddess Pallas Athena, the Trojans' enemy, and only crawled out from under it once the Greeks had set sail. He must have the self-assurance to repeat his story to any questioner, so that he eventually begins to conquer the interrogator's mistrust and the latter begins to believe his words. They will then regard him as an unfortunate stranger and allow him to enter the city. There, his task will be to ensure that the Trojans drag the wooden horse inside the gates. Then, while our foes are asleep, he shall send us a signal, whereupon we shall leave our hiding place. We shall then leap from the horse and raise a burning torch to signal to our comrades on Tenedos that we are about to devastate the city by fire and sword."

Together, they all returned to the ships, but before starting work, the heroes indulged in some deeply refreshing sleep. Then, at midnight, Athena appeared to the Greek hero Epeius in a dream, ordering him, a highly skilled craftsman, to build an enormous horse from wooden beams, and promised him her help so that the work would be rapidly completed. The hero recognized the goddess. He awoke and sprang cheerfully up from his couch. All that he could think of was the task he had been given and the pleasure he would feel as he applied his skill and artistry to achieve it. At daybreak, he stood surrounded by his comrades and told them about his dream. Immediately, the sons of Atreus sent men to the richly forested slopes of Mount Ida with the order to cut down the tallest pine trees. These were quickly carried down to the Hellespont where many young men were ready and willing to help Epeius. Some sawed the timbers, some chopped the branches from the tree trunks, while others assisted in different ways. Meanwhile, Epeius began shaping the horse's hooves, then the belly, and over all these he constructed the animal's back, with the loins at the rear and the neck at the front, giving it a mane so delicately carved that it appeared to flutter in the wind. The head and tail were generously covered with hair, the ears pointed upwards, and beneath the brows were eyes that sparkled like clear glass. Nothing was lacking from this depiction of a horse, which could seemingly move at will. With Athena's help, Epeius completed the work in three days and the entire army marveled at the artist's magnificently impressive creation of a living, breathing horse. The men expected that the giant horse would start whinnying at any minute. But Epeius raised his hands to heaven and prayed before the whole army: "Hear me, mighty Pallas Athena! I beg you, holy goddess, save your horse and save me!" And every Greek joined in his prayer.

Meanwhile, the Trojans had remained timidly within their walls since their last battle. And the division among the gods, who would seal their fate, had become even wider. The immortals had now split into two different factions, one in favor of the Greeks, the other hostile to them. They had descended to earth and now stood in battle array on either side of the city of Xanthus, invisible to mortals. The sea gods also elected to stand on either side. The Nereids, who were related to Achilles, sided with the Greeks, while others supported the Trojans, turning the tide against the Greek ships and against their devious horse, and would have destroyed both if had Fate allowed. Meanwhile, the battle had begun between the supreme gods, with Ares striking out against Athena, signaling the outbreak of war to the rest. Their movements set their golden armor rattling, while the sea sent its waves surging inland. The earth quaked beneath the feet of the immortals whose war cries were so loud that they reached the underworld and could even be heard by the Titans in Tartarus. However, the gods had chosen to wage war at a time when Zeus, father of gods and men, was required to visit Oceanus. Nevertheless, even at such a vast distance, his farsightedness meant that he knew what was happening. As soon as he was aware of the situation, he leapt aboard his winged four-horse chariot and, with Iris as charioteer, returned to Olympus. From the mountaintop, he threw thunderbolts down among the warring gods, who dropped their weapons and ceased fighting. Themis, the goddess of justice, sped down to the gods and broke up the fight, warning them that Zeus was committed to the destruction of all the gods if they refused to obey his command. Fearing the loss of their immortality, they suppressed their hostility and made their way homeward, some to Mount Olympus, others to the depths of the sea.

In the Greek camp, the wooden horse stood ready and Odysseus gathered the heroes together and announced, "The time has come for you, the leaders of the Greeks, to show who among you is truly strong and heroic. For this is the time to enter the horse's belly, in which we must live and face a highly uncertain future! Believe me, it requires much greater courage to crawl into a hiding place such as this than to face death on the battlefield! So, who among you is daring enough to take such a risk? For now, the rest can sail to Tenedos! One fearless young man must remain close to the horse and do as I have instructed. Who will volunteer for this?"

The heroes hesitated. Then a young man, Sinon by name, approached Odysseus and said, "I am ready to do whatever has to be done! Let the Trojans torment me! Let them throw me alive into the fire! My decision is made!" The men cheered him on, while many old heroes asked themselves, "Who is this young man? We have never heard his name, nor is he famous for any special deed. He must be possessed by a demon who wants to do away with either the Trojans or us." But Nestor stood up and encouraged the Greeks. "Now, dear children, what we need now is courage," he declared. "For the gods have laid the means to overcome ten years of hardship in our hands. So, as quickly as we can, let us get straight into the horse's belly. As for me, I can feel the same youthful strength in my old limbs as I did on the day I wanted to board Jason's ship and become an Argonaut, and would have done so had King Pelias not stopped me."

Thus having spoken, the old man attempted to be the first to pass through the side door into the wooden horse's belly, but Neoptolemus, son of Achilles, pleaded with him to confer this honor onto himself, a younger man. He then suggested that, mindful of his age, Nestor take over the leadership of the other Greeks on their journey to Tenedos. Nestor was difficult to convince, but finally Neoptolemus was able to climb, in full armor, into the horse's spacious inside. He was joined by Menelaus, Diomedes, Sthenelus and Odysseus. Then followed Philoctetes, Ajax, Idomeneus, Meriones, Podalirius, Eurymachus, Antimachus, Agapenor, and as many others as would fit into the horse's belly. The last to enter was Epeius, the man who built the wooden horse. He then drew up the ladders through the opening, shut himself inside, and then bolted the door from within. The others waited in deep silence and sat in the black of night, somewhere between victory and death.

The remaining Greeks, having reduced their tents and their equipment to ashes, boarded their ships and set sail for Tenedos under the command of Agamemnon, prince of nations, and King Nestor. The Greeks had appointed these two heroes as commanders since neither were permitted to enter the wooden horse, the former because of his noble reputation, the latter on account of his age. They weighed anchor off Tenedos and went ashore, longing to see the flames that were their agreed-upon signal.

The Trojans soon noticed smoke rising in the air along the Hellespont. Then from the city walls, where there was a clearer view, they also noticed that the Greek ships had disappeared. They thronged to the shore in high spirits, but not before they had donned their armor, for they were still fearful. When they caught sight of the smoothly polished wooden horse on the site of the enemy camp, they stood around it in amazement, for it was indeed a fine work of art.

While all this was happening, some shepherds were drawn close to the wooden horse by curiosity. There they noticed Sinon, who had craftily hidden himself under the animal's belly. They dragged him out as if he were a Greek prisoner and took him to King Priam. Sinon finally gave up on his imitation of fear and said, "I am a Greek and I do not deny it. Even if I am beset with despair, it is no excuse for me to lie. Perhaps you may have heard of Palamedes, prince of Euboea? At the instigation of Odysseus, he was stoned to death for condemning his countrymen for waging war against Troy. When, as a kinsman of his, I entered the war, I was a poor man. Then, after his death, I had no one to turn to. And because I threatened to avenge the murder of my cousin, I earned the hatred of the two-faced son of Laertes, who has persecuted me throughout the war. Nor did he rest until he and the lying soothsayer Calchas had plotted my death. For when my compatriots finally decided to carry out their plan – a plan so often agreed upon then so often postponed – they dispatched Eurypylus to the oracle of Apollo, because they had seen ill-omened signs in the sky. Apollo replied, 'When you went to war you appeased the anger of the winds with the blood of a virgin. Therefore, you must buy your safe return with blood, the blood of a fellow Greek.' On hearing this, a shudder ran down their Greek spines. But Odysseus summoned Calchas the soothsayer

to the people's assembly and, amid much commotion, bade him reveal the will of the gods. For five days, the underhanded mystic remained silent and cunningly refused to name any warrior to be sacrificed. Finally, forced by Odysseus's constant shouting, he named me. Everyone readily agreed because each was glad that he himself was not threatened with death. The terrible day dawned. As was the tradition, I, the victim, had a sacred band wrapped around my head, while the altar and the grain were fully prepared. But I tore off the bands, then ran away and hid among the reeds in a nearby swamp until they had set sail. Then I crept away and took shelter under the belly of their sacred horse. I cannot return to my homeland or to my compatriots. I am in your hands and it is for you to decide whether to be compassionate and spare my life, or to kill me as my fellow Greeks have threatened to do."

The Trojans were moved, and King Priam spoke kindly to Sinon, telling him to forget the evil Greeks and promised him a place of refuge in his city. Sinon had spun his web of lies so skillfully that Priam and all his warriors believed and trusted him. But Athena was watching over the fate of her friends as they sat in trepidation inside the horse and, since Laocoon's warning, were in constant fear of death. But the heroes were freed from danger by a blood-chilling miracle. Following the death of Poseidon's priest, Laocoon, who was a priest of Apollo, had been chosen by lot to succeed him, and so Laocoon was now priest of the sea god as well. Just as he was preparing to lay a fine bull on the sacrificial altar, lo and behold, two enormous snakes came swimming towards the shore from the direction of Tenedos through water as smooth as glass. Their heads topped with blood-red crests were held high above the surface while the rest of their bodies writhed swiftly beneath, the sea splashing as they moved. Then, once on land, they hissed, darted their tongues out and looked around with eyes like fire. The Trojans, many of whom were still standing around the wooden horse, turned deathly white and ran for their lives. But

"LET US SEE WHAT CAN BE ACHIEVED THROUGH SUBTERFUGE."

Some shepherds were drawn close to the wooden horse by curiosity. There they noticed Sinon, who had craftily hidden himself under the animal's belly. They dragged him out as if he were a Greek prisoner and took him to King Priam.

the snakes headed straight for the altar of the sea god where Laocoon and his two young sons were preparing the sacrifice. First, they wound themselves around the bodies of the two children and pierced their tender flesh with their venomous fangs. When they screamed and their father came rushing to their aid with his sword drawn, they wrapped their heavy coils twice around him, rearing their long necks and hissing violently. His priestly headband dripped with venom. With his bare hands he struggled in vain to loosen the coils from around the boys. Meanwhile the bull, already struck by Laocoon's axe, fled bleeding and bellowing from the altar, shaking the blade from its neck. Laocoon and his two sons died from the snakebites and now the creatures slithered their way to Athena's towering temple, where they hid at her feet under the goddess's shield.

The people of Troy saw this horrific event as punishment for the dishonorable doubts the priest had expressed. Some hurried back to the city and hacked an opening in the wall, large enough to admit the wooden horse; others attached wheels to the horse's hooves while others still twisted strong ropes to throw around the animal's towering wooden neck. Then they led the horse to the city in triumph. Boys and girls, their hands resting on the rope, chanted festive hymns together. The wooden construction caught on the raised threshold of the gates four times, and the rattle of metal against metal sounded from inside its belly. But the Trojans turned a blind eye and still failed to hear as they jubilantly led the wooden monster up towards their holy fortress. Amid the frenzy of public celebration, only the mind and spirit of Cassandra, King Priam's daughter, to whom the gods had bestowed the gift of prophesy, remained unconvinced. She had never made a prediction that did not come true, but she also had the curse of never being believed. This time she had already recognized warning signs in the sky and in the world of nature. Driven by the spirit of prophesy, she rushed from the royal palace, hair disheveled, eyes glazed, her slender neck swaying back and forth like a twig in the wind. Then, taking a deep breath, she began to run through the city streets, crying aloud, "You poor, wretched people. Do you not realize that we are travelling down the road to Hades? That we are standing on the brink of death? I see the city filled with blood and fire. I see death surging from the belly of the horse you have brought to our stronghold while you sing merrily. But you will not believe a single word I speak. You are victims of the Furies, who seek vengeance for Helen's ill-fated marriage."

Indeed, the listeners mocked and reviled the young woman and her prophetic words. Every now and then, someone would confront her, saying, "Have you abandoned your maidenly shame, Cassandra? Have you completely lost your mind, running around the streets for all to see, never realizing how people are ridiculing you and the nonsense you come out with, you silly little windbag? Go home, before something bad happens to you!"

For half the night, the Trojans abandoned themselves to feasting and carousing. There was the sound of flutes. There was dancing and singing. There were also boisterous and colorful exchanges between those concentrating on the feast. Again and again, cups were filled with wine, then seized with both hands and drained to the last drop, until the wine-lovers began to mumble and sank into a drunken stupor. As midnight approached, Sinon, who had been feasting out in the open with the rest and had feigned sleep, rose from his couch and crept through the gates. He then lit a torch, which he waved so that it was visible from the shores of Tenedos, using the agreed-upon signal so that the Greeks would cast their own fire into the air. Then he extinguished the torch before creeping up to the horse and knocking gently on the belly as Odysseus had instructed him. The heroes heard the sound but did no more than turn their heads silently towards Odysseus to hear his instructions. Speaking softly, he commanded them to leave quietly and with the greatest possible care. Holding back the more impatient among them before silently sliding back the bolts as Epeius had instructed, he put his head out and peered into the darkness to be sure that not a single Trojan was awake. Then, as a ravenous wolf sneaks softly towards the sheep pen between the shepherd and his dog, he quietly climbed down the rungs of the ladder which Epeius had made along with the horse and left it in position. One hero after another made his way down the ladder with a pounding heart. When the space inside the wooden horse was empty, they brandished their lances, drew their swords, and spread out among the city's streets and buildings. A grisly slaughter broke out among the Trojans who were half-asleep or drunk. Flaming torches were hurled into their houses and soon the roofs were ablaze above their heads. At the same time, the Greek fleet had set sail from Tenedos in response to Sinon's signal, and a favorable wind carried it into the harbor on the Hellespont. Soon the entire Greek army burst through the great breach in the city wall, through which the wooden horse had been dragged only days before, with much grunting from men all too eager to go to war. Now the city, already overthrown, was filled with rubble and corpses. The half-dead and maimed crawled around amid the bodies, while a survivor still standing would be hit in the back by a lance. The whimpering and howling of terrified dogs mingled with groans of the wounded and the wails of grieving mothers and tiny children.

But the war brought many casualties among the Greeks, even though most of their enemies were unarmed and defending themselves as best they could. Some threw cups at the foe, others hurled furniture, some grabbed firebrands straight from the hearth, others attacked with skewers, hatchets, and axes, or whatever else came to hand. Even though they had swarmed the city with fire and swords, many Greeks also lay dead or dying.

As the battle continued through the night, the city grew ever lighter as fire spread between houses and palaces, and the light of the many torches carried by the Greeks made Troy bright as day. Now that the Greeks no longer feared mistaking friend for foe, they became better prepared and increasingly vindictive as they decided on which of the noblest Trojan heroes they would take revenge. Diomedes killed Coroebus, son of the mighty Mygdon, driving his lance through the enemy's stomach. Then he slew Eurydamas, son-in-law of the Trojan elder Antenor, and expert wielder of the spear. Then he came upon Ilioneus, one of the oldest Trojans, who fell on his knees before the Greek hero's drawn sword and cried in a trembling voice, "Whichever Greek you may be, let go of your anger! For only victory over the young and strong will bring you fame! Therefore, spare an old man! You too will one day be old and plead for mercy." For a moment Diomedes hesitated and held back his sword, but then he pierced the elderly enemy's throat and said, "Indeed, I look

forward to a healthy old age, but for now I need my youthful strength to send all my foes to Hades!" Then he tore ahead, killing Trojans one after the other. Ajax the Locrian was doing likewise, while Neoptolemus singled out Priam's sons and slaughtered all three before turning on Agenor, who was once heroic enough to fight the young man's father, Achilles. Finally, he found King Priam himself, praying to Zeus at an altar he had built in the open air. Eagerly, Neoptolemus drew his sword while Priam looked him in the eyes without fear. "Kill me, oh son of brave Achilles," he ordered. "Now I have endured so much and seen nearly all my children die, how much longer do I need to see the light of the sun? If only your father had killed me! But now you can satisfy your own intrepid heart and release me from all my misfortunes!" "Old man," Neoptolemus replied. "You exhort me to do what my own heart intends!" Then he separated the old king's head from his body.

Soon, Death crept from one house to another. He spared only one. It was the home of the old Trojan, Antenor, who had once been a hospitable host to Menelaus and Odysseus and even saved their lives when they came to Troy as envoys. For this, the Greeks now spared him and all his possessions.

In other places, Death ruled. Just outside of the chamber of his unfaithful wife Helen, Menelaus came upon Deiphobus, son of Priam, who since Hector's death had supported his house and his family. Then, following the death of Paris, he had become husband to Helen. Deiphobus had come straight from his usual evening's drinking bout and was still drowsy and disoriented as he staggered to his feet and careened along the corridors of the palace. But Menelaus overtook him and killed him with his sword. "Die here, outside my wife's door!" He roared in a voice like thunder. "If only I could have killed the scoundrel Paris right here with my lance. But now he is long since dead. So, can I assume that is it now your duty to pleasure my wife, you degenerate good-for-nothing? You will soon discover that no malefactor can escape the hands of Themis, goddess of justice!" Menelaus then kicked the corpse aside and began his search through the palace, for his heart was torn by conflicting emotions. He yearned for Helen, his wife. She had rushed trembling to a dark corner of the house where she hid in fear of her husband's wrath.

*Upon seeing her, his jealous feelings
incited him to kill her.*

On first seeing her, his jealous feelings incited him to kill her, but Aphrodite had made her even fairer than before and now the goddess struck the sword from his hand, soothed his anger, and filled his heart with the love of before. On seeing her otherworldly beauty, again and again he found it impossible to raise the sword and in one moment he forgot all the wrong she had done him. Then he heard the battle cry of the Greeks and was gripped by a feeling of shame for standing before his unfaithful wife, not as an avenger but as a slave. Unwillingly, he picked up the sword which he had thrown to the ground, fought his natural instinct and aimed a blow at his wife. But in his heart he had no real desire to harm her so he welcomed the sudden arrival of his brother Agamemnon, who stood behind him with a hand on his shoulder, and said, "Wait, Menelaus. It does not seem right that you should kill your lawful wife for whose sake we have had to endure so much suffering. It seems to me that she is far less guilty than Paris, who so disdainfully broke the rules of hospitality. But now he and all his kinsfolk and his people have been punished and have paid with their lives!" So said Agamemnon. Menelaus obeyed, reluctantly but gladly.

While these events happened on earth, the immortals cloaked themselves in dark clouds and mourned the fall of Troy. Only the hearts of Hera, deadly enemy of the Trojans, and Thetis, mother of Achilles who had died far too soon, were filled with joy at the news. Pallas Athena, who had been working for the Trojan downfall, could not hold back her tears when she saw Ajax, the brutish son of Oileus, enter her temple. He approached Cassandra, her priestess, who had sought shelter there and was clutching the goddess's own image. Ajax then seized her and dragged her away by her hair. The goddess did nothing to help the daughter of her enemies, but her cheeks reddened with shame and anger and her image gave out a sound that shook the temple floor. As she turned her eyes away from the scene of the crime, she vowed to avenge the wrong done to Cassandra.

The conflagrations and the slaughter continued for a long time. The pillar of flames soared heavenwards from Troy to announce the overthrow of the city to those living on the neighboring islands and to the ships sailing back and forth across the sea.

ODYSSEUS

TELEMACHUS AND THE SUITORS

The father of the gods decides Odysseus may return home:
After years of wandering, the king of Ithaca is permitted to return, where
a pack of rivals are courting his wife Penelope and squandering his wealth.
Athena advises his son, Telemachus, to go out and look for his father. Odysseus
meanwhile is held captive by the nymph Calypso on Ogygia, her island.

Illustrations by William Russell Flint

ODYSSEUS: TELEMACHUS AND THE SUITORS

Page 181
Athena herself bound the divine golden sandals to her feet, took her powerful lance in her hand, and descended from the rocky summit of Olympus in a fury.

The Trojan War was over and all the Greek heroes who had escaped death on the battlefield and survived the stormy homeward voyage were now back on their native soil. Some were happy, others were not. Only Odysseus, son of King Laertes of Ithaca, had not returned. After wandering far and wide, he had landed on Ogygia, a remote and rugged island covered with forests. It was there that the nymph Calypso, daughter of Atlas, held him captive in her grotto, intending to make her husband. Odysseus, however, remained faithful to Penelope, the wife he had left behind in Ithaca. In the end, the gods on Mount Olympus came to sympathize with his fate, apart from Poseidon, god of the sea and time-honored enemy of the Greeks, who bore a grudge against Odysseus. Although he did not have the courage to completely destroy him, the sea god put every imaginable obstacle in the hero's way as he attempted to journey homewards, instead sending him drifting aimlessly over the ocean. Moreover, Poseidon was the one who had cast the hero ashore on Ogygia.

The immortals gathered in conference and decided that Calypso, ruler of the island, should set Odysseus free. Athena demanded that Hermes, messenger of the gods, be sent to Ogygia to inform the fair nymph of Zeus's irrevocable ruling that the long-suffering Odysseus should return home. Athena herself bound to her feet the golden sandals that carried her over land and sea. She then took up her trusty, sharp-pointed lance, with which she had defeated many a hero in battle, and descended from the rocky summit of Olympus. Soon she reached the island of Ithaca on the west coast of Greece, landing on the threshold of the absent Odysseus's palace. She then made her way inside, lance in hand, assuming the shape of Mentes, brave king of the Taphians.

Odysseus's house was a sad place. Beautiful Penelope, daughter of Icarius, and her young son Telemachus were no longer masters of the house Odysseus had left behind. When he failed to return, long after the news reached Ithaca that Troy had fallen and other heroes had arrived home, it became increasingly likely that rumors of his death were true. On Ithaca there lived no fewer than twelve other men as rich and powerful as Odysseus.

A further twenty from Zakynthos and fifty-two from Dulichium had arrived on the island, bringing with them a retinue including a herald, a singer, two expert cooks, and a large number of slaves. All these nobles were there in the hope of winning the hand of his young widow, whose suitors lingered in the palace, displaying their impudence and arrogance by devouring all the stores left by the missing hero. This mayhem had been tolerated for more than three years.

When Athena arrived in the guise of Mentes, she found the suitors playing checkers in front of the palace. They were seated on hides from Odysseus's cattle, which they had killed and skinned themselves. A maidservant brought a golden pitcher of water for the stranger to wash his hands and the same honest maid brought bread and meat, which was cut by a manservant, while a herald filled the cups until they were overflowing with wine. Soon afterwards, the suitors appeared, one after another, and took their places on elegant couches. The heralds sprinkled their hands, while the maidservants offered them baskets of bread. Then, as if they had never been fed, they set about the flavorsome feast. Then they demanded dancing and singing. The herald handed an elegant lyre to the bard Phemius, who plucked the strings and started to sing a heart-warming song.

While the suitors listened to the song, Telemachus leaned towards his guest and whispered to the goddess in disguise, "My friend, please do not reproach me for what I have to tell you. Do you see how these men fritter away another man's fortune with no intention of replacing anything? Everything you can see belongs to my father, whose bones may be rotting on some far-away shore or tossed about by the tide. He will not be coming home to punish them! But tell me, noble stranger, who are you, where is your home, and who are your parents? Were you perhaps a friend of my father's?" Athena replied, "I am Mentes, son of Anchialus and ruler of the island of Taphos. I came because I believed that your father had returned. Clearly this is not true, but I am convinced he is still alive. In fact, he is on some barren island where he is being held captive. Yes, I think I can predict that he will soon be released and will make his way home!

My dear Telemachus, you are truly your father's son. Your faces are the same, especially those sympathetic eyes! I can tell

ODYSSEUS: TELEMACHUS AND THE SUITORS

you I knew your father long before he left for Troy, but I have not seen him since. Tell me now, why is there such pandemonium in your house? Are you celebrating a wedding, or is this some other festive banquet?"

Telemachus answered with a sigh. "Oh, my friend, there was a time when our house was a respectable and prosperous place. But not anymore. All these men whom you see around us are courting my mother and wolfing down all our food. My mother refuses to marry again and will not even consider doing so. Meanwhile these gluttonous beasts are pillaging our house and before long, they will finish me off, too!" The goddess replied in sorrow and anger combined, "You poor young man! How much you need your father. I would strongly recommend that you think of ways to drive these infuriating vermin out of the palace. Let me give you a piece of advice. Tomorrow, simply stand up to them and tell them to get out of here and let each

*"And you, dear mother, go back to your
chamber and take care of business,
supervising the work of your women
with the spindle and the loom!"*

one make his own way home. Then you must tell your mother that if she wishes to marry again, she must return to her father. In his house, the marriage can be properly arranged, as can her dowry. Your task is to make ready your finest ship. Take twenty oarsmen and start your search for your long-absent father."

Meanwhile, in the grand hall, the sound of the lyre and a song could be heard. It was a ballad telling of the Greeks' terrifying homeward voyage from Troy. All the suitors listened attentively. The music drifted upwards to Penelope as she sat in solitude in her chamber. Wrapped in a heavy veil and accompanied by two lady's maids, she descended to the hall to join the suitors. One of her maids stood beside her and began to weep. Penelope also began to shed tears as she turned towards the singer Phemius. "You know many heartwarming songs, Phemius," she said. "Do warm my guests' hearts with them. But please, none of those lamentations that fill my own heart with sorrow. For even without them, all I can think of is the man, renowned throughout all Greece, who has not come home!" But Telemachus spoke lovingly to his mother. "Do not scold such a charming singer for delighting us with words that set his heart ablaze. We should not blame the bard but Zeus, who inspires him and his choice of songs! Let him sing of the Greeks! Odysseus is not the only one who has not lived to see the day of return; many other Greeks have perished. And you, dear mother, go back

"ALL THESE MEN YOU SEE AROUND US ARE COURTING MY MOTHER AND WOLFING DOWN ALL OUR FOOD."

to your chamber and take care of business, supervising the work of your women with the spindle and the loom! Words are the concern of men, of which I am one and hence the master of this house!"

Penelope was amazed and impressed by her son's intelligent and well-ordered words, spoken in a way she had not previously heard. Suddenly, the boy had grown into manhood. She returned to her room and wept in solitude for her husband. Telemachus joined the suitors, who by now had begun to stagger drunkenly about. He called out to them, his voice loud and clear, "Enjoy the feast, gentlemen, but there is no need for such an uproar. To enjoy music, it is better to stay silent! Tomorrow we shall call an assembly of the Greeks, at which I shall openly suggest that each of you returns to his own home. For the time has come for you to cease sitting around doing nothing. Go home and amuse yourselves among your own possessions before bleeding dry the entire estate of a stranger."

The suitors bit their lips on hearing such a speech. They could not have been more surprised at the young man's authoritative words. However, they refused to listen to his suggestion that they court Penelope at the home of her father, Icarius. After much wrangling, the meeting adjourned and the suitors slunk back to their couches, while Telemachus also returned to his chamber to rest.

ODYSSEUS
CALYPSO

Calypso bows to the will of Zeus:
Hermes, messenger to the gods, brings Calypso Zeus's command that Odysseus is
to be released so he can return home. When Poseidon discovers Odysseus drifting on a raft,
he plunges his trident into the sea to dispatch storms that shatter the makeshift vessel.
Naked and half-dead, Odysseus manages to reach the shores of an unfamiliar island.

Illustration by Newell Convers Wyeth

ODYSSEUS: CALYPSO

Hermes, Zeus's messenger, sped down from the ether to the sea. He glided across the waves like a seagull until he reached Ogygia, Calypso's island realm, to which he had been sent by the gods. He found the nymph with beautiful tresses at home. A fire blazed in her hearth and the fragrance of the smoke rising from the split cedar logs drifted across the island. Calypso sat in her chamber, singing in a melodious voice as she spun beautiful fabric with a golden shuttle. Her grotto stood in a grove of greenery, shaded by alders, poplars, and cypresses, in which many colorful birds, as well as hawks, owls and crows, built their nests. Clinging to the vaulted rocks were vines loaded with ripening grapes, their skins glistening from among the shadows. Four springs rose close together, winding their way hither and thither as they watered green meadows strewn with violets, parsley, and other herbs and flowers.

Before entering the grotto, the messenger stood admiring the beauty of the place surrounding the home of the nymph. Calypso immediately recognized the approaching figure, for despite living far apart, the immortals are not strangers to one another. Odysseus, however, was not at home. He was sitting in his usual spot on the shore and, with tears in his eyes, staring longingly out across the open sea.

When Calypso had listened courteously to the gods' message, she hesitated before finally speaking. "Oh, cruel and jealous gods! Do you not allow an immortal to love a mortal and then choose him as her husband? Does it offend you that I should enjoy the companionship of a man whom I saved from death when he, clinging to the broken keel of his ship, was flung ashore on my island? All his brave shipmates were sent to the bottom of the sea when their vessel was struck by lightning, but he alone swam ashore among the wreckage. I received the unfortunate castaway with kindness and fortified him with food. And yes, I did in the end offer him the gift of immortality and eternal youth. But since no one can flout Zeus's orders, let him return to the endless sea. But, please, do not expect me to be the one to send him away, for my ships have no oars and no one to man them! All I can do is to offer him my good advice on how to reach his native land unharmed."

Hermes was well satisfied with her answer and hastened back to Olympus. As for Calypso, she made her way to the shore where Odysseus sat in misery. She moved towards him and said, "My poor dear friend, you no longer need to sit here grief-stricken. For I shall let you go. Now stand up and build a raft! Hew some timbers, join them together with bronze, and construct a raised deck! I shall provide you with water, wine, and food. I shall give you clothing and raise a favorable wind off the land. And may the gods carry you safely home!"

Odysseus eyed the goddess with suspicion and said, "I am sure, lovely nymph, that you have quite different ideas! Never again shall I board a flimsy raft until you swear to me by the oath of the gods that you are not plotting to do me harm." But Calypso smiled and gently stroked his hand. "Do not torment yourself with such futile thoughts: the earth, the sky and the Styx shall be witness to my oath that I have no intention to cause you pain. I only advise you to do what I would do, were I in your situation." At that, she walked away, followed by Odysseus, and in the grotto she bade him a tender farewell.

The raft was soon built and, on the fifth day, Odysseus departed with the wind in his sails. He sat at the rudder which he handled with confidence and skill. He did not fall asleep but steadfastly kept his eyes on the constellations, chartering his course according to the signs that Calypso had explained to him before his departure. He journeyed onwards for seventeen days. On the eighteenth day, he at last sighted the dark mountains of Scheria. The land reached towards him, lying there like a shield in the equally dark sea. But now Poseidon caught sight of Odysseus from the hills of the Solymi. Having not been present at the most recent council of the gods, he now realized that they had taken advantage of his absence to free Odysseus from Calypso's clutches. "Well," he said to himself, "he has plenty more trouble ahead!" With that, he gathered the clouds together, churned up the sea with his trident, called upon tempests to wage war overhead, so that land and sea would be cloaked in darkness. Winds howled from every direction around the raft. Odysseus's heart and knees trembled, and he thought that it might have been better to have been slain by a Trojan spear. Amid his lamentations, a wave rushed

*"My poor dear friend, you no longer need to
sit here grief-stricken. For I shall let you go."*

down from above, sweeping the raft into a whirlpool. He struggled away as the rudder slipped from his grasp and the raft was smashed to pieces and the mast and the yards were driven back and forth by the raging sea. Odysseus was caught up in the breakers and his soaking wet tunic dragged him even further downwards. Finally, he rose back to the surface, spat out the brine he had swallowed, and swam towards the still floating timbers and found himself strong enough to climb onto them. As he floated on the remains of the raft, tossed hither and thither like a thistle in the wind, Leucothea, a sea goddess, took pity on the unfortunate seafarer. She rose up from the whirlpool like a seafowl, perched on the raft and said, "Let me advise you, Odysseus! Take off your tunic and let the plank take care of the storm. Wrap my veil about you, then swim and pour scorn on the terrors of the sea!" Odysseus took the veil, and the goddess disappeared. Although he doubted the truth of her words, he obeyed her instructions. While Poseidon sent him the most ferocious waves and fragments of the raft floated here and there, he sat like a horseman astride his plank, threw away the tunic Calypso had given him, wound the veil around his body, and a slipped into the water.

Poseidon gravely shook his head. When he saw the determined mortal bravely launch himself into the sea, he said, "Wander on through the sea surrounded by pain and sorrow. There is more than enough misery awaiting you!" With that, the god left the sea and retreated to his palace. For two days and nights Odysseus was at sea, until he finally reached a wooded shore where the high cliffs were battered by the waves. Before he had time to come to any decision, a massive wave swept him towards the coast. He gripped a protruding rock with both hands, only to be swept back into the sea by another wave. He sought his salvation again by swimming and finally found a comfortable, shallow cove where there was no river flowing into the sea. Here, he prayed to the river god, who heard him and calmed the current, thus enabling him to reach the land. Unable to speak or breathe, he sank to the ground. With seawater streaming from his mouth and nose and numbed by complete exhaustion, he lost consciousness.

When he recovered from his stupor and was able to breathe again, he unwound the goddess Leucothea's veil and gratefully cast it back into the waves so that it might return to its owner. Then he threw himself down among the reeds and kissed the earth. In his nakedness, he froze and shivered in the night air until dawn. He decided to climb a wooded hill and try to recover in the nearby woods. There he found a comfortable spot between two intertwined olive trees, one wild and one tame, whose foliage was so dense that no wind, rain, or rays of the sun could penetrate it. Odysseus gathered a pile of fallen leaves on which to lay down, and then covered himself with yet more leaves. His eyelids were soon weighed down by restful sleep, letting him forget the hardships he had suffered, but not yet think about the dangers still in store for him.

ODYSSEUS
POLYPHEMUS

Only a trick can save the travelers:
Polyphemus, the one-eyed Cyclops, has shut Odysseus and his companions
away in a cave. Some men do not survive but the rest succeed in getting the
giant drunk on wine and gouging out his eye with a stake. After an adventurous
flight from the cave, Odysseus and his men reach their ship safely.

Illustrations by John Flaxman, Zdeněk Burian, and Newell Convers Wyeth

ODYSSEUS: POLYPHEMUS

"Drink up, Cyclops!"

The next morning, I became curious about the land on the other side, whose inhabitants, the Cyclopes, I knew nothing about. I and a large number of my companions boarded the ship and made the crossing. When we landed at the farthest end of the shore, we saw a high cave, overgrown with laurel and surrounded by sheep and goats. Rammed into the earth were large rocks which, together with tall spruces and oaks, created an impenetrable fence. Behind it there lived a man of colossal physique, who kept to himself and tended his flocks well away from others of his kind, while he did nothing but plot heinous crimes. For he was a Cyclops. Of this we became aware as we surveyed the shore. I then chose twelve of my bravest comrades and told the others to stay on board guarding the ship. I took with me a skin of the finest wine, given to me by a priest of Apollo in Ismarus, a city of the Cicones, because I had spared him and his family.

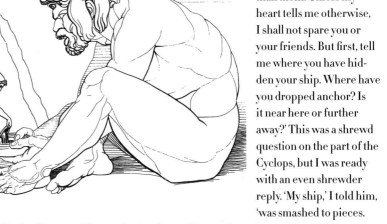

"At last the Cyclops came, carrying on his massive shoulders an enormous load of dried-out wood, which he had gathered to cook his supper. He threw it to the ground with a crash so loud that it startled us all and sent us scurrying to the farthest corner of the cave. Like all Cyclopes, he had only one eye brightly flashing away in the middle of his forehead, legs like the trunks of thousand-year-old oak trees, and arms and hands big and strong enough for him to play ball with blocks of granite.

"'Who are you, strangers?' he roared in a voice blasting out like thunder in the mountains. 'Where have you sailed from and what are you up to? Are you pirates by any chance?' His bellowing set our hearts trembling, but even so I pulled myself together and replied, 'Certainly not. We are Greeks sailing homewards after the fall of Troy and we have lost our bearings. So we come to you on bended knee, begging your protection and help. Yes, my friend, fear the gods and hear our plea. For Zeus is the protector of supplicants and takes revenge on those unwilling to help them!'

"But the Cyclops burst into hideous laughter. 'What a fool you are, stranger,' he said facetiously. 'You do not know who you are dealing with. Do you think we Cyclopes have the slightest interest in Zeus the Thunderer and all the rest of the gods? For we are mightier than them! Unless my heart tells me otherwise, I shall not spare you or your friends. But first, tell me where you have hidden your ship. Where have you dropped anchor? Is it near here or further away?' This was a shrewd question on the part of the Cyclops, but I was ready with an even shrewder reply. 'My ship,' I told him, 'was smashed to pieces. These other twelve and I were the only survivors.'

"After the monster had stuffed his fat belly full and quenched his thirst with milk, he threw himself flat on the cave floor to sleep. At this point I wondered whether I should set about him and thrust my sword into his side between the stomach and the liver. But I quickly thought of a better plan. How could killing him help us? At last, an idea came to me that I believed might actually work. In among the stalls lay the Cyclops's mighty cudgel made of green olive wood, which he had left there waiting for it to harden and be ready to carry with him. To us, it looked as long and as thick as the mast of a ship. From the cudgel I cut myself a staff of two arms' length, which I handed over to my comrades, who smoothed it down, sharpened it to a point and hardened it in the fire. Then I carefully hid the staff in a pile of

ODYSSEUS: POLYPHEMUS

The Cyclops took the jug without a word.

dung, of which there were large quantities scattered all over the cave. Then we cast lots as to who would be daring enough to help me pierce the monster's eye with the burning stake while he lay asleep. The lot fell to the four bravest, indeed the ones I, the fifth, would myself have chosen.

"At nightfall the repugnant shepherd returned with his flock. This time he did not leave any animals outside, instead driving them all into the cave. Maybe he was suspicious, maybe it was because, as it will soon be revealed, a god had decided to help us. Apart from that, everything stayed the same. He put the rock back in its place and then dined on two of our number. Meanwhile, I had filled a wooden jug with dark red wine from our wineskin. I then moved towards the beast and said, 'Drink up, Cyclops! Wine tastes wonderful after a tasty bit of human flesh. You will soon discover what fine wine we carried on board our ship. I brought it with me to enjoy with you in return for your kindness and for helping us to head homewards. But, no. You are a cruel, malicious tyrant. What mortal will even think of visiting you at any time in the future? You shall pay for your evil deeds!'

"The Cyclops took the jug without a word. He drank it straight down and it was easy to see how he savored the wine's strength and sweetness. When he finished, for the first time he spoke in a friendly manner. 'Stranger,' he said, 'give me another drink. And tell me your name so that I may offer you a gift. We Cyclopes also grow fine wine in our country. But now permit me to tell you who it is that stands before you. My name is Polyphemus.' So said the Cyclops and I was more than happy to give him more wine. Three times I filled the jug and three times he was dim-witted enough to drain each jug to the last drop. As the wine did its work and his mind began to cloud over, I sidled up to him and slyly asked, 'Do you want to know my name, Cyclops? I have a very strange name. My name is Nobody. Everyone calls me Nobody, my mother and father and all my friends know me by that name.' To which the Cyclops replied, 'Now I shall give you your gift. Nobody is the man I shall eat when I have gobbled up all his comrades. Do you approve of your gift, Nobody?'

"But these last words were incoherent, as he leaned backwards and, with his great ungainly neck bent, went crashing to the floor. Then amid his drunken snores, he puked up a mess of human flesh and wine. Then I quickly held my wooden staff in the smoldering ashes until it caught fire, spraying sparks as I drew it out. Then, with the help of my four friends, I plunged it into his eye, twisting it like a carpenter drilling timber for a ship. His eyelashes and eyebrows were caught in the blaze, while his eyeball sizzled like hot iron in water. The wounded monster's deafening howls sent us scurrying with fear to the farthest corner of the cave. Then he raised more tumult as he screamed and shouted to his fellow Cyclopes living up in the mountains. They came from all directions, surrounding the cave and asking what had happened to their kinsman. 'My friends, Nobody is murdering me! Nobody has cheated me!' When they heard these words, they shouted back, 'If Nobody is hurting you, if not a single soul has attacked you, what have you got to yell about? Your problem, friend, is that you are crazy, a disease for which we have no cure.' Having said that, they the hurried away. As for me, I laughed heartily.

"The blind Cyclops groped his way around his cave, every now and then whimpering with pain. In the meantime, having mulled over one plan after another, I at last found a way. All around us were fat, well-fed rams with thick, heavy fleece. Making hardly a sound, I rounded them up and bound them together in threes with willow stems taken from the mat on which the Cyclops slept. In each case, the ram in the middle carried under his belly one of our men, while the rams on either side hid the middle one's clandestine load. For myself, I chose the biggest ram of them all. I grabbed hold of his back and worked my way round to his belly where I firmly clung to his curly wool. And there we hung, suppressing our sighs as we waited for morning. At dawn, the rams were the first to go out to pasture, while the ewes remained bleating in the stalls, their udders about to burst as they waited to be milked. Their stricken master carefully ran his hands along each ram's back to make certain that no fugitive sat astride him. Stupid as he was, it never occurred to him to reach underneath, which if he had done, he would have discovered my ploy.

"The Cyclops let the rams out. And now all of us were outside. As soon as we were a short distance away from the cave, I first freed myself and then unfastened my friends. Sadly, only seven

Then Polyphemus grabbed a second, much larger rock and hurled it at us, again only just missing us.

of us were left to embrace one another joyfully, then mourn those we had lost. But I signaled to them not to weep aloud but to concentrate on driving the stolen rams back to our ship. Only when we were safely seated on our rowing benches and plowing through the waves, only a herald's cry from the shore, I shouted to the Cyclops who was climbing uphill with his flock, 'Let me tell you, Cyclops, that in your cave you have gobbled down the companions of a man of not inconsiderable importance! At last your insufferable deeds have been avenged and you have experienced the punishment of Zeus and the other gods!'

"On hearing these words the vicious beast raged even more savagely. He wrenched a huge rock from the mountains and hurled at our ship. So precise was his aim that he only just missed our stern. Even so, the splash created by the massive block of stone sent the waves rising so high that our ship was driven back towards the shore, and it took all our combined strength to row forward and away from the monster. Now I called to him for a second time, even though my friends, in fear of another rock, tried to stop me by force. 'Listen, Cyclops!' I shouted. 'If ever a human being should ask you who blinded you, you should give them a better answer than the one you fed to the Cyclopes. Simply say that you were blinded by Odysseus, conqueror of Troy, son of Laertes, who lives on the island of Ithaca!' The Cyclops wailed pitifully, 'Woe is me! The ancient prophesy has been fulfilled. Once there was a prophet, Telemus, son of Eurymus, who lived to old age in our homeland. It was he who told me that one day I would lose my sight to Odysseus. I always thought he would be a big strong fellow like me and that he would challenge me to a fight. And now this little runt, this weakling came along and befuddled me with wine and when I was dead drunk, he put my eye out!'

"Then Polyphemus grabbed a second, much larger rock and hurled it at us, again only just missing us. But we were able to resist the counterflow of the sea and confidently row forward. Soon we were back on the island where the rest of the ships lay safely at anchor in the bay. There, too, were our friends who had anxiously awaited us. As soon we landed, they greeted us with cries of joy. When we stepped ashore, our first task was to divide the sheep we had stolen from the Cyclops. However, in addition to my share of the loot, my companions presented me with the ram under whose belly I had escaped. I immediately offered him up to Zeus and burnt the sheep's legs in honor of the god. However, Zeus scorned the sacrifice and refused to be placated. It had been his will that I and all my friends should die.

"But at the time we had no idea. In fact we sat all day, happy to be together feasting and drinking until the sun sank into the sea, as if we had not a care in the world. Then we lay down to sleep to the soft sound of the waves."

ODYSSEUS

CIRCE

This enchantress's charms are irresistible:
On the island of Aeaea, many of Odysseus's companions fall victim to
Circe and are transformed into swine. To save Odysseus from a similar
fate, Hermes gives him a magic herb that protects him from Circe's spells.
He is able to transform his companions back into their original states,
and Circe allows them all to depart in peace.

Illustrations by Virginia Frances Sterrett and William Russell Flint

ODYSSEUS: CIRCE

This group soon came to the goddess Circe's splendid palace, constructed from carved stone.

hen we travelled onwards, all of us crammed together on a single ship, until we came to the island of Aeaea. Here lived a beautiful demigoddess. She was the sister of King Aeetes, daughter of the sun god and Perse, daughter of Oceanus. Her name was Circe and she lived on the island in a splendid palace. We, however, knew nothing about her. We dropped anchor in an inlet and then, exhausted by stress and strain, frustration and sorrow, we lay down on the grassy shore where we slept for two days and nights. On the morning of the third day, I took my sword and lance and set off to explore the island. After a while, I saw smoke rising from Circe's palace, but remembering the danger we had recently endured, I decided to return to my friends. For a long time we had survived on very little food, but all at once I saw a stag with tall antlers running out of the woods to quench his thirst at the nearby stream. I threw my lance at him, catching him in the back before the weapon came out at the belly. I rested my foot on the body and pulled the lance from the wound. Then I twisted a rope from willow stems and bound the feet together, ready to carry it back to the ship. It was so heavy that I had to lean on my lance as I walked.

"My companions cheered when I arrived with such a fine example of woodland game on my shoulders. The stag that had been so quickly slaughtered was roasted while we fetched the bread and wine that we had left on the ship to create a festive feast. It was then that I told them about the rising smoke I had seen, but my friends were dispirited by the news, for it reminded them of the cave of the Cyclops and the land of the Laestrygonians. I alone was not reduced to tears. Instead, I divided my surviving shipmates into two groups, one I myself would lead, while Eurylochus took charge of the other. Then we shook lots in a brazen helmet. The lot fell to Eurylochus, followed – somewhat reluctantly – by twenty-two men. Their task was to make their way towards the place where I had seen the smoke rising.

"This group soon came to the goddess Circe's splendid palace, which was constructed from carved stone and hidden away in an enchanting valley. But how shocked my comrades were on seeing wolves with long pointed teeth and lions with shaggy manes skulking around the walled court in front of the palace. They looked in terror at these evil-looking creatures, while trying to locate the quickest escape route from this strange place. But already they were surrounded by wild beasts which did them no harm, nor did they pounce as is the way of creatures of their kind. Instead, the wolves and lions moved slowly and softly, with tails wagging, just like dogs going to meet their master, knowing he has brought them a treat saved from the feast he has just attended. As we later discovered, these were in fact men whom the sorceress Circe had turned into animals.

"As the animals did nothing to prevent them, my friends again plucked up the courage to approach the palace gates. From there, they heard the sound of the beautiful voice of Circe, an accomplished singer. She sang as she worked, seated at her loom and weaving an exquisite mantle, which only a goddess could have designed. The first to catch sight of her in the palace and be thrilled by what he saw was the hero Polites,

a very good friend of mine. On his advice, our other friends called to the goddess to come out, which she did. She invited them in with a welcoming smile. All of them accepted her invitation, apart from their leader, Eurylochus. He was a shrewd, level-headed man who, based on past unpleasant experience, suspected some kind of trickery was afoot.

"Circe led the others into the palace and invited them to sit on luxurious chairs. Then she ordered servants to bring cheese, flour, honey, and Pramnian wine. She proceeded to mix these ingredients together to make delicious cakes, secretly adding noxious drugs to the batter. These would render her unfortunate guests unconscious and make them forget their homeland. After they had all partaken of the tempting delicacy, they were turned into bristly pigs. Then, as they started grunting, Circe herded them into sties and, instead of presenting them with tasty morsels, she threw them the acorns and Cornelian cherries that pigs enjoy.

"From afar, Eurylochus had watched some of what happened and guessed the rest. He hurried back to the ship as fast as he could to tell me and those left behind of our friends' the dreadful fate. When he reached us, fear had robbed him of speech and he could not utter a single word. His eyes were flooded with tears while grief still left him speechless. Astonished and concerned, we finally persuaded him to speak and he managed to find words to describe what had happened to our comrades. When he finished telling his terrible story, I immediately slung my sword and bow over my shoulder and asked him to lead me to the palace. He, however, replied by throwing his arms around my knees begging me not to go, nor to force him to go with me. 'Believe me,' he sobbed, 'you will not return, nor will you bring back our comrades. Oh, let us escape from this accursed place!' I permitted him to stay, but I did what I had to do and set off to the palace. On the way, I met a handsome young man blessed with the gentle charm of youth. He held a golden staff, by which I recognized him as Hermes, messenger of the immortals. He grasped me by the hand and said, 'My poor friend, why are you running through the woods when you do not know the way? Circe the sorceress has locked your friends in pigsties. It is more likely that she will lock you up alongside them. Do you want to set them free? Well, here is something that will help. Take this herb with you and she will be unable to harm you.' With these words he pulled from the soil a black root with milk-white blossoms, which he told me was known as moly. 'She will prepare for you a sweet delicacy flavored with wine, to which she will add her magic potion, but this herb will prevent her from turning you into an animal. When you see her dipping her magic wand into the mixture, draw your sword and rush towards her as if you intend to kill her. Then you can easily force her to swear a sacred oath not to harm you in any way. It will also mean that you can safely stay in her house and, once you have gained her confidence, she will not refuse to hand back your comrades.'

"So said Hermes before returning to Mount Olympus, while I hurried towards the palace, troubled and apprehensive. At my call, she opened the gates and politely invited me to enter which, enraged though I was, I duly did. Then she seated me in a splendid chair and placed a footstool beneath my feet. Immediately she filled a golden cup with her so-called 'sweet delicacy.' She could hardly wait for me to empty the cup and, as soon as I did, she touched me with her wand and said, 'Out you go to the pigsty and join your friends!'

"But I instantly drew my sword from its scabbard and rushed towards her as if about to kill her. Throwing herself to the floor, she screamed, 'Have pity on me! Who are you, colossal being? You, whom my potion leaves unchanged? No other mortal has the strength to withstand my magical powers. Are you perhaps the resourceful Odysseus whom Hermes predicted long ago I would meet? If you are, put your sword back in its sheath and let us be friends.' But I had not changed my threatening stance and replied, 'How can you, Circe, ask me to be friends with you when in this very house you have turned my companions into swine? Should I not suppose that your sympathetic behavior is nothing but a means of endangering me? I can only consider becoming your friend if you swear a sacred oath not to harm me in any way.' As I demanded, the goddess immediately

BUT ALREADY THEY WERE SURROUNDED BY WILD BEASTS.

swore an oath and I now felt at ease and spent a carefree evening there.

"In the early morning, her four handmaidens, all beautiful and of noble birth, set about tidying their mistress's chambers. One of them spread the chairs with fine purple fabrics, another placed beside them silver tables on which she set golden baskets. A third mixed wine and water in a silver jug and set golden cups on each table. The fourth finally brought in fresh spring water and set the cauldron on a tripod, which she then placed over a flame until the water boiled. This was to provide me with the refreshing bath, after which I rubbed my body with perfumed oil and then dressed.

"It was intended that I should enjoy the morning meal in Circe's company. Although there was good and abundant food spread before me, I did not extend my hand to serve myself, but sat silent and sadly opposite my beautiful hostess. When she finally asked me why I was so unhappy, I replied, 'How can a man, who still has feelings of what is just and what is fair, possibly relish such food and drink while knowing that his friends are living in squalor? If you wish me to delight in your company, then grant me the satisfaction of seeing them with my own eyes!'

"I did not have to plead for long, for Circe quickly left the room, wand in hand. Outside, she opened the doors of the pigsty and drove out my friends who crowded around us, still in the shape of swine. Then she walked to each one and anointed him with a salve. Immediately they shed their bristly hides and emerged again as men, this time even younger and more handsome than before. Eagerly, they rushed towards me holding out their hands, but started to weep bitterly as they remembered what they had been subjected to. The goddess then spoke reassuringly, 'Now, dear hero, I have done as you asked. So, in return, I beg you to bring your ship ashore and store your cargo in one of the caves along the shore, for you and your esteemed comrades are my honored guests!'

200

ODYSSEUS: CIRCE

Then she seated me in a splendid chair and placed a footstool beneath my feet.

"Touched by her welcoming words, I returned to the ship and the friends still on board. Having believed me dead, they now ran towards me. When I suggested we beach the ship and stay as guests of the goddess, they all agreed, apart from Eurylochus, who vigorously rejected the idea and exclaimed, 'Do you wish to associate with that witch of your own free will? Do you long to be turned into lions, wolves, and pigs and be expected to stand guard over her palace? Do you not remember what the Cyclops did to our friends when Odysseus was foolish enough to release us into his hands?' When I heard his unfair condemnation, I was sorely tempted to draw my sword and separate his head from his body, despite him being my kinsman. Fortunately, when my friends saw what I was about to do they grabbed me by the arm and brought me back to my senses.

"So we all set off. Even Eurylochus who, duly shocked by my threatening behavior, did not refuse to join us. Meanwhile, Circe had arranged baths for our friends, who were now anointed with perfumed oils and elegantly clad in fine garments. We arrived to find them merrily gathered together. It was such a happy reunion, marked by tears, embraces, and hearty greetings! The goddess sought to give us courage and treated us with such warmth that our spirits rose day by day and we spent the rest of the year at her palace. But as the end of the year approached, my companions reminded me that it was time to think about heading homewards. I took their words to heart and that same evening I spoke to Circe, my hands clasping her knees, pleading her to keep her word and send us home. The sorceress replied, 'You are right, Odysseus. It is not fitting that I should compel you to stay here with me. But before you return home, you must first travel to Hades, Persephone's realm of shades, and ask the soul of blind old Tiresias to predict the future. He was the prophet of Thebes, and Persephone has allowed him to retain his gift of prophesy even after death. The souls of the other departed are no more than hovering shadows.'

"On hearing Circe's decision, I broke down and wept. I dreaded having to visit the home of the dead. I asked her who would be my guide, for no man of flesh and blood had ever made a sea voyage to the underworld. 'Do not be troubled by the lack of a guide for your ship. Simply raise your mast and hoist the sails. The north wind will lead you there, then once you have crossed Oceanus, whose waters encircle the earth, you must land on a low-lying shore where you will see alders, poplars, and willows growing side by side. These stand in Persephone's grove and also mark the entrance to the underworld. Here is a valley near a rock where the currents of the Pyriphlegethon and Cocytus, the latter a branch of the Styx, join Acheron, which flows into the underworld. There you will find a cleft leading into the shadowland. There you must dig a pit and place in it honey, milk, wine, water, and flour as offerings to the souls of the dead. When you return home to Ithaca, you must also vow to make another offering to the departed, as well as sacrificing a black ram to Tiresias. After that, slaughter two black sheep, a ram, and a ewe. Then let your eyes follow the rivers as they become one, while your comrades burn the animals in honor of the gods, to whom you must also pray. Then the souls of the dead will appear to you and these phantoms will try to approach the light and taste the

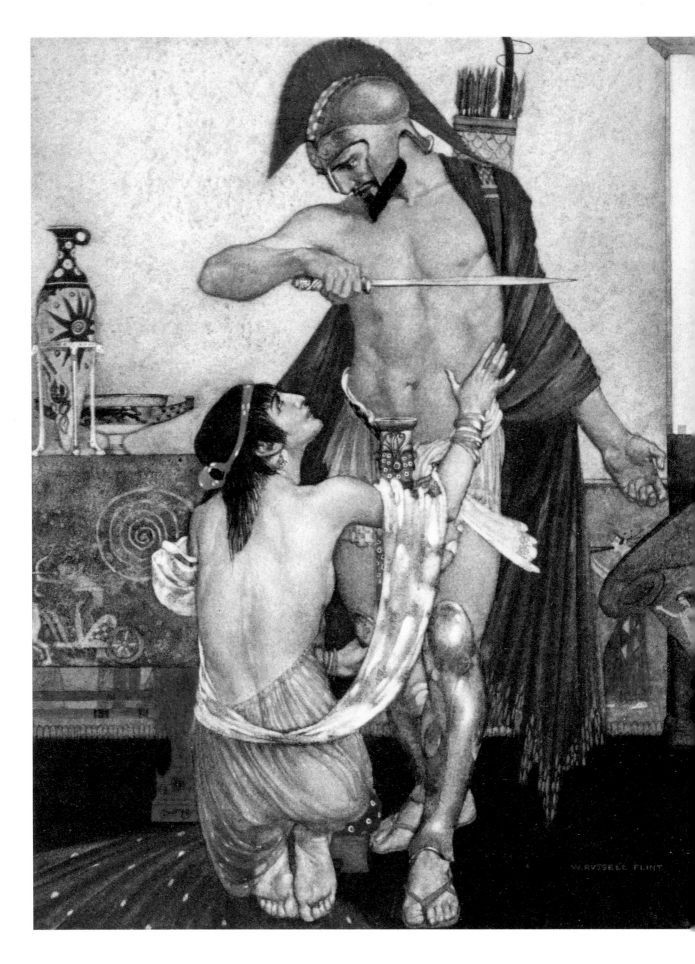

W. RVSSELL FLINT

ODYSSEUS: CIRCE

But I had not changed my threatening stance.

blood of the sacrificial beasts. You, however, must raise your sword to urge them back, and not let them any closer until you have consulted Tiresias, for he will soon appear, prepared to discuss your journey home.'

"These words gave me some reassurance. The next morning I called my friends together, ordering them to prepare to set sail. Now, the youngest on board, Elpenor by name, who was neither very brave nor very bright, had imbibed rather too much of Circe's sweet wine last evening. He slunk away from the others to cool his overheated face and then stretched out on the flat roof of the palace, where he fell asleep and spent the whole night undisturbed. When he was woken by the commotion caused by his friends as they rushed about preparing to set sail, he was still in a daze and he forgot where he was. Instead of making for the stairs, he walked to the edge of the high roof and crashed to the ground, breaking his neck as his soul descended into the underworld.

"I gathered my companions around me and said, 'I know, my dear friends, that you think we are about to leave for our beloved homeland. Alas, this is not the case, for the goddess Circe requires us first to travel in quite another direction. We must visit the terrible realm that is Hades and ask Tiresias, the Theban prophet, for advice about our journey.' When my comrades heard this, their hearts nearly broke with sorrow, as they wept and wailed and tore their hair from their heads. But there was nothing we could do, so I immediately ordered them to follow me to the ship. Before our arrival, Circe had placed on board the two sheep we were to sacrifice, together with honey, wine, and flour. As we arrived, she slipped past us, bidding us a silent farewell. But we pushed the ship into the sea, raised the mast and sails and sat down despondently on the rowing benches. The fair wind that Circe had sent us swelled our sails and soon we were back on the high seas."

ODYSSEUS

THE REALM OF SHADES

The voyage continues:
Odysseus meets the soul of Tiresias, the blind soothsayer, who prophesies his return
home and the rest of his life. Odysseus also meets the shades of others, including his mother,
Agamemnon, Achilles, and Patroclus. Achilles laments to him that he would rather
be a beggar on earth than king of the underworld.

Illustrations by Newell Convers Wyeth and John Flaxman

After a moment's pause, Odysseus continued telling his story to the eagerly listening Phaeacians: "The sun dipped down into the sea as a favorable wind drove us to the end of the world, to the land of the Cimmerians, a place cloaked in constant mist and never lit by the rays of the sun. Then we came to Oceanus, the river that encircles the earth. We soon arrived at the rock where the rivers of the dead come together. There we made our offerings, exactly as Circe instructed us to do. As soon as the blood began to flow from the throats of the sheep, the souls of the departed rose up from a crevice in the rocks and came towards us. Among them came young men and old, young women and children, and many heroes with gaping wounds and bloodstained armor. They approached us in droves and flapped around us with their eerie sobs and sighs, as shades are wont to do. They hovered above the sacrifice pit. I confess I was horror-stricken. I told my companions to do as Circe advised and quickly burn the sheep and pray to the gods. I drew my sword from its scabbard to scare the shades away from the blood before I was able to speak to Tiresias.

"But before he arrived, I was approached by the soul of our friend Elpenor, whose body lay unburied in Circe's residence. Tearfully, he bemoaned his plight, begging me to sail back to the island of Aeaea so that he might have a civilized burial. I promised him I would do so, and his shade sat down facing me. There we were, the young man's shadow on one side, me with my sword held across the sacrificial blood on the other. Soon, we were joined by the soul of my mother, the beautiful Anticlea, who was still alive when I set off for Ilium. Silently, she sat down and stared at the blood, never once recognizing or acknowledging me as her son.

"Then there appeared the shade of Tiresias of Thebes, a golden staff in his right hand. He immediately recognized me and said, 'Noble son of Laertes, what has persuaded you to leave the sunlight and visit a place as distressing as this? Please withdraw your sword from the pit so that I may drink of the sacrificial blood and thus be able to predict your fate.' Obeying his wish, I replaced my sword in its sheath. The shade of Tiresias drank the dark blood and immediately began his predictions. 'What you are trying to discover, Odysseus, is whether I shall foretell a happy homecoming for you. But there is a god determined to make it as difficult as he can for you, and you have no escape from the hand of the immortal they call the Earth Shaker. For you became his sworn enemy when you blinded his son Polyphemus. Even so, your return journey will not be cut short. You and your comrades must not succumb to despair. First, you will land on the island of Thrinacia. Provided that you do not disturb the sun god's sacred herds of sheep and cattle, you will reach home safely. But should you harm those animals I predict that you, your friends, and your ship will be destroyed. And even though you may escape, you will arrive home alone and on a foreign ship. And on your return, you will find nothing but trouble: swaggering wastrels, frittering away your riches and courting your wife Penelope. You will kill all of them, whether in secret or for all to see. Then, in the evening of your life, you will pick up your oar and wander ever onwards until you come upon people who know nothing of the sea, have no ships, and do not season their food with salt. And when you are in some foreign land and you meet another wanderer who tells you that you are carrying a winnowing fan on your back, throw your oar to the ground, make an offering to Poseidon, and then make your way back home. Then,

> ## "WHAT POSSESSED YOU, DEAR SON, YOU WHO ARE STILL ALIVE, TO COME HERE TO THIS NIGHT OF DEATH?"

All the other souls, who meanwhile had partaken of the blood, were prepared to talk to me.

while your kingdom prospers, you will die peacefully of old age, far from the sea.'

"That is what the prophet told me. I thanked him and asked him another question. 'Tell me,' I said. 'Sitting there is my mother's shade. What can I do to make her recognize me?' The seer replied. 'Simply seize the moment. Let her drink some sacrificial blood and she will soon break her silence.' I drew back from the pit, bearing my sword. Suddenly she recognized me. 'What possessed you, dear son, you who are still alive, to come here to this night of death? Were you not held back by the ocean and the other terrifying rivers? When Troy fell, did you merely wander about rather than return to your home on Ithaca?' After having answered her questions, I asked my mother how she had died, for she was still alive when I had left for Troy. Then with my heart beating with fear, I asked about the others I had left behind. My mother's shade responded. 'Your wife is steadfastly faithful and weeps for you night and day. Carrying your scepter is none other than your son Telemachus, who also attends to your property. Your father Laertes has gone to live in the country and no longer returns to the city. At home he does not sleep in a princely chamber or a soft couch. Like any other farmhand, he slumbers beside the hearth fire on a bed of straw for the whole winter, wearing the most dreadful clothes. In summer he sleeps under the open sky on a pile of brushwood. He does all of this out of grief for your fate. As for me, my beloved son, I died of sorrow for you. It was no illness that carried me away.'

"As she spoke, I trembled with longing. But when I tried to embrace her, she melted away, like a figure in a dream. Then there appeared other shades, many of them wives of famous heroes. All of them drank from the sheep's blood, then proceeded to tell me their stories. As the women vanished one by one, I

"I SAW A SHADE THAT MADE MY HEART MISS A BEAT. MOVING TOWARDS ME WAS THE SOUL OF AGAMEMNON."

saw a shade that made my heart miss a beat. Moving towards me was the soul of Agamemnon, the great prince of nations. He ambled dejectedly towards the pit and drank from the blood. Then he looked up, recognized me, and began to weep. In vain he stretched out his hand to me, but his arm was too weak to reach that far. Sinking back into the distance, he answered my eager questions. 'Noble Odysseus,' he said, 'you may believe that I was destroyed in anger by the god of the sea, or that enemies overpowered me at a feast. But my wife and her lover Aegisthus killed me in the bath, as if slaughtering an ox in a stall. Me, the husband who had come home yearning to see his wife and children. Therefore I would advise you, Odysseus, do not place too much trust in your wife, and do not let affection entice you to tell her your every secret. But you are a fortunate man who has an understanding and virtuous wife. And Telemachus, the little child she was still nursing when you and I left Greece is now a fine young man who will welcome his father home with wholehearted familial love. My despicable wife did not even allow me the pleasure of seeing my son before she murdered me! So take my advice. Land quietly and unannounced on the coast of Ithaca, for no woman can be trusted!'

"With these discouraging words, the shade of Agamemnon turned and disappeared. Then came the souls of Achilles and his friends Patroclus, Antilochus, and the great Ajax. Achilles, who was the first to drink, recognized me in amazement. I told him why I had come, but when I suggested that he, the most famous of all Greeks and the greatest among the dead in Hades, must be happy there, he replied peevishly, 'Odysseus, it is futile to try to find reassuring words about death. I would prefer to work in the fields as a common laborer with neither property nor heritage than to rule over flocks of the dead.' Then he eagerly asked

for news of his son Neoptolemus, who was living the life of a hero. His father was highly gratified to hear of his many good deeds and acts of bravery. Now he walked away with a spring in his step until he was lost from sight.

"All the other souls, who meanwhile had partaken of the blood, were prepared to talk to me. Only the shade of Ajax, who took his own life after I had defeated him in the fight over the weapons of Achilles, angrily turned away. But I spoke to him kindly, 'Oh, son of Telamon, can you not forget your anger even in death? I am speaking of your anger about the weapons of Achilles, which the gods had handed over to the Greeks, only to put a curse on them. Because of this we lost you, a tower of strength on the battlefield, and mourned for you as we did for Achilles. We were not to blame for your death. You were killed

by a stroke of fate, dealt to us all by Zeus. Therefore, noble prince, restrain your wrath. Come nearer and speak to me!' The shade did not reply but turned back into the darkness to join the other departed souls.

"Then I saw the shades of heroes long since dead: Minos, judge of the dead; Orion, the mighty hunter who held back the phantoms of lynxes and lion with his club in his hand; Tityus, on whose liver two vultures pecked away, one on either side, as punishment for his crime; Tantalus, who stood in water reaching up to his chin but was never able to quench his thirst. Before he could reach for a drink, the waves shifted and dried up, revealing the black riverbed under his feet. Above his head he could see thriving fruit trees that bore pears, figs, pomegranates, olives, and apples. But before he could touch them, the wind swept

Then I saw the shades of heroes long since dead.

through the branches, lifting them heavenwards and leaving him to clutch into thin air. I also saw Sisyphus, struggling in vain to push a massive rock up a mountain. He rolled the great boulder up the mountainside, leaning his entire weight against the rock and working with his arms and legs. But whenever he thought he had reached to top, it slipped out of his hands and rolled back downwards, filling him with humiliation. So he began again, his limbs drenched with sweat, a cloud of dust rising around his head. Next to him stood Heracles, but only his shadow, for he himself resides on Olympus, home to his wife, the goddess of eternal youth. His shadow, however, stood there looking as dark as night while fitting an arrow to the bowstring and looking around in fear, as if he was about to fire it at an approaching enemy. Around his shoulders hung a splendid sword belt, adorned with the shapes of various animals. Then he, too, disappeared and along came a whole pack of other heroic shades. I would have been happy to spot Theseus and his friend Pirithous among them, but suddenly the terrible clamor caused by these countless souls filled me with terror. It was as if the Medusa had suddenly turned her hideous head towards me. My comrades and I hurried towards our ship moored on the shore of Oceanus. Then, as I had promised Elpenor's shade, we sailed back to Circe's island."

"BUT WHEN I TRIED TO EMBRACE HER, SHE MELTED AWAY, LIKE A FIGURE IN A DREAM."

ODYSSEUS
THE SIRENS

Fatally beguiling melodies:
On their voyage, Odysseus and his companions reach the island
of the sea demons known as Sirens. To avoid being seduced by their
sweet but perilous singing, Odysseus's companions plug their ears with wax.
Bound to the mast, Odysseus listens entranced to the music, and only
survives because his companions refuse to free him from his bonds.

Illustration by Newell Convers Wyeth

ODYSSEUS: THE SIRENS

"Bring your ship ashore and hearken to our song."

Odysseus continued: "After we had burnt the body of our unfortunate comrade and buried his remains in the soil of the island of Aeaea, we built a burial mound for him and erected a pillar on it in his memory. Circe warmly welcomed us and gave us abundant stores for our continuing journey. She also alerted us to the kind of dangers we would be obliged to face.

"Our first adventure – one which Circe had foretold – awaited us on the island of the Sirens. These are nymphs who sing so sweetly that their songs bewitch everyone who hears them. They sit on the green shore singing their magical melodies to any passing ship. Anyone enticed by them is marked for death, which explains why moldering bones can be seen strewn along the shore. As we neared the island of the alluring nymphs, our ship stood still, for the following wind, which thus far had driven us gently onwards, suddenly ceased to blow and the sea lay smooth as a mirror. My comrades lowered the sails, folded them, laid them down on the ship, and then took up the oars

to row the ship forward. I, for my part, remembered Circe's words when she advised me, 'When you are close to the island of the Sirens, stop up your friends' ears with wax so that they can hear nothing. If you yourself are captivated by a longing to hear the Sirens' song, order your men to shackle your hands and feet and tie you to the mast. Then, the more passionately you command them not to loosen them, the more they will tighten the ropes even further!'

"Now I remembered her advice. I cut a slab of wax and then kneaded it with my fingertips to soften it, before using it to plug my travelling companions' ears. At my command they tied me to the mast, then returned to their oars and confidently rowed ahead.

"When the Sirens saw the ship, they stood like charming young maidens along the shore, their sweet voices harmonizing as they sang these words:

Come, great Odysseus, exalted across all Greece,
Bring your ship ashore and hearken to our song.
For no darkened ship has ever rowed past,
Without our honey-sweet voices enchanting the crew,
Who would gladly return and discover more.
For we know all that happens on the Trojan plains
Where, by gods' will, sons of Greece and Troy have prevailed,
We know all that comes to pass on this fertile earth.

"So they sang and, as I listened, my heart swelled within me as I longed to draw near to them. I made a gesture with my head, telling my friends to unleash me.

"With their deaf ears, they rowed even harder and two of them, Eurylochus and Perimedes, came and bound me even tighter, as I had ordered them. Not until we were safely out of reach of the Sirens' songs did my colleagues free their ears of wax and free me from by bonds. I thanked them with all my heart for their kindhearted stubbornness."

ODYSSEUS
SCYLLA AND CHARYBDIS

A deadly whirlpool and a murderous rock:
To avoid Charybdis, a maelstrom that devours everything caught up
in it, Odysseus steers his ship to the opposite shore where Scylla, no less
ominous, lurks. When the ship comes too close, the monster grabs six
of his companions from the deck and crushes them.

Illustrations by John Flaxman and Henry Justice Ford

ODYSSEUS: SCYLLA AND CHARYBDIS

"She can seize one man between each set of jaws and drag them from the ship before anyone has realized she was so close."

We had only rowed a short way forward when I sighted distant sea spray and heard the rumble of the surf. It was Charybdis, a whirlpool which, three times daily, burst out from beneath a cliff and then rushed back, taking with it any passing ship. My terrified comrades dropped their oars and let the tide carry us along. Then the ship stood still. I leapt from my seat and stepped swiftly from man to man, seeking to encourage them. 'Dear comrades,' I said. 'We are not novices when faced with danger. No peril could be worse than that which we endured in the Cyclops's cave. There, my own wits helped us all to escape. So all of you listen to me. Stay sitting on your bench and row straight towards the surf as fast as you can.' Then, since they had already seized their oars from the sea, I issued the traditional command, 'Strike

oars!' Then I continued. 'I firmly believe that Zeus will help us. You, our helmsman, gather all your senses and steer the ship through spray and surf as best you can! Stay near the rocks so that we are not caught up by the whirlpool!' Thus I warned my friends of the whirlpool Charybdis, following what Circe had told me. But I thought it wisest not to repeat her words of warning against the even greater threat posed by the monster Scylla. For I feared they might again drop their oars and then huddle together inside the ship.

"However, I had forgotten another piece of advice that Circe had given me. On no account, she told me, should I don armor to fight against the monster. I did, in fact, put on full armor, take two spears, and stand on deck ready to confront the approaching beast. But although my eyes were sore from looking intently around, I could not find her and waited full of fear as the ship

Never has a ship passed by without losing some of the crew.

sailed ever closer to the whirlpool. Circe had described Scylla thus: 'She is not a mortal foe but rather an immortal catastrophe. She cannot be defeated by acts of bravery. The only means of escaping her is to fly away. Her home is opposite Charybdis. It stands high on a steep, smooth rock with a jagged point always hidden in dark clouds where no ray of sun can reach it. In the middle of the rock is a cave as black as night. Here Scylla lives, only announcing her presence by ferocious barking which echoes across the water like the squealing of a newborn dog. The monster has twelve misshapen feet and six necks resembling snakes, on each one a hideously smirking head with three rows of gnashing teeth to tear their prey to shreds. Half her body is hidden inside the cliff, while she stretches her heads outside the cave and fishes for seals, dolphins, and other large creatures of the sea. Never has a ship passed by without losing some of the crew. She can seize one man between each set of jaws and drag them from the ship before anyone has realized she was so close.'

> # "SHE IS NOT A MORTAL FOE BUT RATHER AN IMMORTAL CATASTROPHE. SHE CANNOT BE OVERCOME BY ACTS OF BRAVERY."

"This was the image I could see in my mind's eye, but my search for it was in vain. And now the ship was drawing closer to Charybdis, which was greedily sucking up the sea and spewing it straight out again. The water boiled like a cauldron over the fire, and white spray flew into the air. But when the tide turned towards the sea, swallowing up the waves, the water turned muddy. Then a crash like thunder shook the rocks and deep below there appeared a chasm of black slime. Then, as we fixed our eyes in horror and dismay at this sickening spectacle, our helmsman inadvertently steered left, bringing us too close to Scylla and she snatched six of my bravest comrades from the deck in one fell swoop. I saw them struggling between the monster's teeth, hands and feet flailing. They called me by name, begging me to help as she dragged them into the air. The next moment they were crushed to pulp. On my travels I have endured many things, but never have I witnessed a more a heartbreaking sight!"

ODYSSEUS
SHIPWRECK

Crime does not go unpunished:
The cattle sacred to the Sun god, Helios, on the island of Thrinacia must not be touched.
When faced with a shortage of provisions, Odysseus's companions ignore their
leader's warning and slaughter the fattest cattle. The gods on high retaliate at once.
Zeus sinks the ship with a thunderbolt – only Odysseus survives.

Illustration by Newell Convers Wyeth

Now we had safely left Charybdis's whirlpool and Scylla's rock behind us, the sunlit island of Thrinacia lay before us. While still at sea, we heard the lowing of the sun god's cattle and the bleating of his sheep. Having lived through so great a misfortune, I immediately thought of the warning Tiresias had given to me in the underworld. I told my comrades that both Circe and the blind prophet had advised me to flee the island of Helios, where an even worse fate threatened us. This saddened my companions beyond measure and Eurylochus responded angrily, 'Odysseus, you are a cruel and obstinate man, as hard as nails! Weak and weary as we are after our ordeal, do you seriously intend to deny us the chance to set foot on land or refresh ourselves with food and drink? Or must we sail blindly through the darkness of night across the sea's black waters? What if we are struck by a southerly gale or a howling wind from the west? At least let us anchor near this friendly shore that beckons us so hospitably!'

"While I was obliged to listen to his protests, I did, in fact, know that a hostile god was determined to do us harm. So I replied, 'Eurylochus, it is not difficult for you to convince me, for I am one man among many. So I shall defer to you. But first, each one of you must swear a sacred oath not to slaughter a single one of the sun god's sheep or cattle, however many you see. It is far better to be satisfied with the victuals which Circe has kindly given us!' All the men were willing to take the oath. So we sailed into the bay, from which fresh water poured into that of the sea, and set foot on the shore. It was not long before our meal was ready. When we had eaten, we mourned our shipmates devoured by Scylla, but in the midst of our tears, we weary seafarers were overtaken by sleep.

"It was when two thirds of the night had passed that Zeus sent a violent storm. At daybreak we brought our vessel to safety in a grotto. Once again, I warned my companions not to lay a hand on the sun god's livestock, for I knew the stormy weather would force us to stay on the island somewhat longer than planned. In fact, the unremitting southerly wind, alternating with easterly squalls, meant we were trapped there for a whole month. As long as Circe's supply of food and wine

lasted, we were safe enough. But when our supplies ran out and we began to feel hungry, my comrades started to catch fish and birds while I set off along the shore in the hope of meeting any god or any mortal who could help us in our plight. Once I was some distance away from my friends and completely alone, I washed my hands so that I could pray with clean palms outstretched, then fell to my knees to beg all the gods to come to our rescue. But the only favor they granted was to send me to sleep.

"In my absence, Eurylochus stood up and gave our comrades some disturbing advice. 'Listen to me, my poor afflicted friends!' he said. 'Any kind of death is terrifying, but death by starvation is the worst fate. Well then, what if we were to take Helios's finest cattle to sacrifice to the gods and use the remaining meat to satisfy our hunger? Then as soon as we reach Ithaca we can pacify the god by building him a fine temple and filling it with beautiful votive offerings. But should he be so angry that he sends a tempest and sinks our ship to the seabed, I for one would prefer to die quickly by drowning than slowly starve to death on this desolate island!'

"His words impressed my hungry comrades. They immediately set about choosing the finest specimens from the sun god's herds which grazed nearby. Then, after slaughtering the beasts with their own hands, they wrapped the entrails and the long bones in fat and offered them up to the immortals. As they had no wine left, they sprinkled them with spring water. The meat that remained in abundance was put on spits to roast. They had just sat down to eat when the god of sleep awakened me and I could smell roasting from afar. Then I shouted up to heaven, 'Oh father Zeus and all you other immortals! You have cursed me by sending me to sleep. What crime did my friends commit while I was sleeping?'

"Meanwhile, one of the sun god's servants told him of the violence that had occurred in his sanctuary. So angry was he that he gathered the immortals together on Mount Olympus and accused them of being behind these wrongdoings. Helios threatened to drive his chariot down to Hades and never again shine for the gods and mortals on earth if the culprits were not harshly punished. On hearing this, Zeus rose from his throne

My companions toppled from the ship and thrashed around like drowning crows as they all sank, one by one.

and said angrily, 'Do not cease shining for gods and man, Helios. When those unpardonable robbers are on board, I myself shall strike the ship with a thunderbolt and sink it to the bottom of the sea!' I heard Zeus's words from the noble goddess Calypso, who in turn had heard them from Hermes, the messenger of the gods.

"When I rejoined the ship, I reprimanded my companions severely. But it was too late. The slaughtered cattle lay before me and certain terrible signs made it clear that a crime had been committed. Their hides crept about as if they were alive and meat on the spits bellowed, as live cattle do. But my famished comrades paid no attention. For six days they feasted. Not until the seventh, when the storm seemed to have passed, did we climb aboard and steer out to the open sea. When we had long since sighted land, Zeus spread blue-black clouds directly over our heads and turned the sea beneath us to an even darker hue. Suddenly, a furious gale swept in from the west, breaking both the ropes securing the mast, which then crashed downwards onto the deck, taking the sails with it. The whole weight struck the helmsman on the head, cracking his skull. He plunged like a diver into the sea and his body was swallowed by the waves. Then amid a crack of thunder the ship was struck by lightning that filled the air with sulfurous fumes. My companions toppled from the ship and thrashed around like drowning crows as they all sank, one by one. Soon I was all alone on the ship, pacing back

and forth until the sides broke away from the keel. The fallen mast had crashed straight down onto the bare keel. I still had my wits about me, so I grabbed a piece of the rigging made of ox hide and bound the mast and keel together to make a raft, on which I sat, calling on the gods as the stormy sea tossed me hither and thither.

"At last the storm abated and the west wind died down. But then the south wind began to howl, filling me with yet more terror, for now I was in danger of being swept back to Scylla and Charybdis. And that is what happened! Dawn had barely broken when I caught sight of Scylla's pointed rock and Charybdis's whirlpool, which swept my mast away into the abyss. I grabbed hold of the bough of a fig tree hanging over the cliff, where I hung like a bat until my mast and keel reappeared. The moment I saw them, I slipped down onto my raft and perched on the narrow keel. I used my hands to row as fast as I could to escape from the churning water. But I would have been lost if Zeus in his mercy had not steered me away from Scylla and her rock and guided me to safer waters.

"For nine days I drifted about on the sea and on the tenth night the benevolent gods finally brought me to the island of Ogygia where Calypso resided. There, the noble goddess took care of me and restored me to health. But why do I need to tell you all this? It was only yesterday that I described my last adventure to you, oh king, and your good lady!"

ODYSSEUS
SHELTERED
BY THE SWINEHERD

Back in Ithaca:
Disguised as an old beggar, Odysseus is hospitably taken in by his faithful
swineherd, Eumaeus, who deplores the scandalous behavior of the suitors
for Penelope's hand at Odysseus's palace but does not recognize Odysseus.
The returned king does his best to console his faithful servant, and swears
to him that Odysseus will return and avenge the wrongdoings.

Illustration by Newell Convers Wyeth

ODYSSEUS: SHELTERED BY THE SWINEHERD

Thus disguised, Odysseus wandered unrecognized over the hills and through the forest to the place his patron goddess had described. More importantly, it was there he would find the most loyal of his servants, Eumaeus the swineherd. He found him in a field on a high plateau, tending his pigs. There, the old man had built an enclosure for them with his own hands. It was walled in by heavy stones that he himself had dragged up the steep slopes. Inside, twelve pens were lined up, each one housing fifty sows kept for breeding. The boars, much fewer in number, were kept outside the pens. The reason there were so few male animals was that, day after day, the suitors of Odysseus's wife Penelope demanded a fatted boar for their feasts. Now only three hundred and sixty remained. The herd was guarded by four dogs, all looking as fierce as hungry wolves.

The swineherd was busily cutting out fine ox hide to make sandals, while his helpers were scattered about, three of them looking after the swine out at pasture while the fourth had been sent to the city to deliver Penelope's ill-bred suitors' daily order.

The dogs were the first to notice Odysseus as he approached. Barking ferociously, they bolted towards him, who in turn merely laid down his staff and sat down. He would certainly have had to suffer the humiliation of being attacked by his own dogs on his own property, but the swineherd sped out of his hut, dropped the ox hide he was working on, and threw stones to scare them away. Then he turned to his master, who he thought was a beggar, and said, "Honestly, old man, a second or two more and they would have torn you to pieces, and I would have had yet another sorrow to bear. Is it not enough that I must helplessly grieve for my poor master who is somewhere far away? Here I sit, fattening pigs for other people to feast on, while he may well be living in poverty, without even a little piece of dry bread, as he wanders through foreign lands – that is, if he can still see the light of day. Come into my hut, my poor friend, and let me offer you food and wine. Then, when you have satisfied your hunger, you can tell me where you are from and what it is you have suffered that makes you look so forlorn!"

Together they entered the swineherd's hut, where he scattered leaves and brushwood on the floor. He spread his own bed cover, a large, shaggy sheepskin, over them and invited the visitor to rest. When Odysseus thanked his friend for his warm welcome, Eumaeus replied, "Well, old man, you should never turn a guest away, however little you can offer him. I confess that I can offer very little. If my good master had stayed at home, I would have done much better. He would have made sure that I had a house, land, and a wife, which would have meant I could receive strangers more graciously. But now he is gone. He may even be dead. Would that Helen and her kin came to harm, since she is responsible for the death of so many brave men!"

As he said this, the swineherd wrapped a girdle around his tunic and went out to the pens where large numbers of piglets were kept. He picked up two and slaughtered them to cook in honor of his guest. He cut up the meat, sprinkled it with white flour, then threaded it on the spit to roast until it could be presented, freshly cooked, to his visitor. From a large jug he poured honey-sweet, mature wine into a wooden tankard, then sat down opposite his guest and said, "Eat and enjoy, stranger! It is the best I can offer! It is only the meat of young pigs because the suitors grab all the fatted boars. Such brutes they are! They fear the gods even less than pirates do. They have most likely heard that my master is dead, for the way in which they go about courting his wife is not that of civilized people. They never go back to their own homes, but stay here, frittering away the wealth of a stranger. They slaughter his cattle not once or twice a day, but every hour, while they empty one wine barrel after another. Oh, but my master was as rich as twenty others put together, with twelve herds of cattle and just as many herds of sheep, pigs, and goats on his farms, some tended for him by shepherds, some by hirelings. In this region alone, there are eleven flocks of goats, watched over by trustworthy men, but each of them is forced to deliver a choice billy goat to the suitors every day. I am the chief swineherd and even I am obliged daily to choose the finest boar and send it to those gluttonous brutes!"

As the herdsman talked, Odysseus quickly ate the meat and drank the wine like a man who did not know what he was doing. Nor did he speak a word. His mind was otherwise occupied as he considered how best to take his revenge on the suitors. When he had eaten and drunk his fill, and the herdsman had filled his cup

ODYSSEUS: SHELTERED BY THE SWINEHERD

*"Come into my hut, my poor friend,
and let me offer you food and wine."*

again, he drank to his host's health and then said in a kindly voice, "Do tell me more about your master, dear friend. It is quite possible that I know him and that I have met him somewhere, for I have travelled many miles around the world."

But the swineherd found this hard to believe and asked, "Do you think some wandering stranger could really make us believe what he told us about our master? It has often happened that vagabonds who came here looking for food and shelter have reduced my mistress and her son to tears with tales of my master, when all they really wanted was for someone to feed them well and give them a cloak or a tunic. I am certain that dogs and birds have already torn his flesh from his limbs, or fish have eaten it and his bare bones are lying on some pebble beach. Alas, I shall never again have so fine a master. He was almost too kind, almost too thoughtful. When I think of him, I do not think of him as my master but as an elder brother."

"Well then, my friend," Odysseus replied. "Because your heart refuses to believe your master will return, I swear to you that he will! I am an honest man who loathes and detests liars. I am not one to tell tales simply to be given a cloak or a tunic. So listen when I swear by Zeus, by your hospitable table, and by the herds of Odysseus, that within a month he will enter his house and punish the shameless intruders who have dared to blight the lives of his wife and son."

"Old man," said Eumaeus, "I shall only be obliged to reward you when Odysseus comes home. Settle down and drink your wine and let us speak of something else. I shall not make you stick to your oath. I no longer have any hope for Odysseus, but I am deeply troubled by his son Telemachus. I had always hoped to see him grow into his father, in both body and spirit. But a god or mortal has filled his head with very strange ideas. He is on his way to Pylos to inquire after his father. Meanwhile, the suitors are lying in ambush, waiting to kill the last descendent of the ancient line of Arcisius. Now tell me all your troubles. Who are you, and what has brought you to Ithaca?"

To amuse himself, Odysseus told the swineherd a long story in which he portrayed himself as the poverty-stricken son of a wealthy man on the isle of Crete and dreamt up some entertaining adventures. He also claimed to have fought in the Trojan War, which was where he met Odysseus. On the homeward voyage, a violent storm had cast him ashore on the coast of the Thesprotian kingdom, whose king passed on news of Odysseus who, he said, had recently been his guest but had already left to travel to the oracle of Dodona and receive Zeus's commands before the beggar arrived.

After he had spun this web of lies, the swineherd appeared to be deeply moved. "Unfortunate stranger, the way you have described your beleaguered travels has truly touched me! But somehow I do not believe what you have told me about Odysseus. Why do you have to lie? I refuse to believe anything since I was lied to years ago by a man from Aetolia, a murderer on the run who wanted my help. He swore to me that he had seen my master with Idomeneus on the island of Crete where he had come to repair his ship, which was severely damaged in a storm. The man assured me that Odysseus and his shipmates would be back by summer, or at the latest by autumn. Which means, my ill-fated friend,

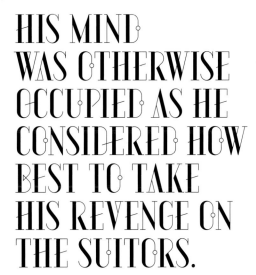

HIS MIND WAS OTHERWISE OCCUPIED AS HE CONSIDERED HOW BEST TO TAKE HIS REVENGE ON THE SUITORS.

please do not try to convince me by lying. You can still enjoy my hospitality."

Odysseus replied, "Good swineherd! You are an honest man, so let us strike a bargain. If your master does return, you shall give me a cloak and a tunic for me to wear when I go to Dulichium, somewhere I wish to go. If he does not, you can tell your helpers to toss me over a cliff and into the sea, as an example to other beggars who think they can lie." The swineherd retorted, "That would hardly make me look good, if I were to kill a guest I had invited to eat and rest in my own hut. Never again could I pray to Zeus! But it will soon be time for supper. The other men will arrive soon and we can enjoy our meal together." And indeed, before long they heard the grunting of the pigs as the herdsmen drove them into the pens. Then the swineherd ordered a five-year-old fatted boar to be slaughtered in honor of their guest. Some of it was offered up to the nymphs and the god Hermes, and some was brought into the hut. The best part of the beast, cut from the back, was served to the guest, even though his host thought he was no more than a beggar.

ODYSSEUS

THE BEGGAR IN THE HALL

Fate takes its course:
Odysseus enters his own palace as a beggar to find the suitors feasting and living
at his expense. Only a few offer him something to eat. Another beggar tries to drive him
away with threats. It results in a fight between the two beggars, with the suitors bellowing
insults from the sidelines. Odysseus fells his opponent, but does not kill him.

Illustrations by Newell Convers Wyeth

ODYSSEUS: THE BEGGAR IN THE HALL

Page 225
At this moment, the goddess Athena, invisible to all, approached Odysseus.

Telemachus was the first to see the swineherd as he came into the great hall and beckoned him to approach. Eumaeus looked around cautiously and picked up the empty stool on which the carver would sit as he prepared meat for the suitors' feasts. At a sign from Telemachus, he carried it to the young master's table and sat down opposite him while a herald immediately served him with meat and bread. Soon after, Odysseus hobbled in, clutching his staff, and sat down on the ash wood threshold inside the door, leaning against one of the beautifully carved doorposts. As soon as Telemachus saw him, he reached for a whole loaf from the basket in front of him and picked up a large piece of meat which he handed to the swineherd, saying, "Here, my friend. Take these gifts to the stranger and tell him not to be ashamed to go and beg among the suitors." Odysseus received the gifts, raising both of his hands as a gesture of thanks, then laid the food on the sack at his feet and began to eat. Throughout the feast, the singer Phemius had delighted the guests with his songs. Now he was silent, for nothing could be heard amidst the racket in a room full of inebriated revelers. At this moment, the goddess Athena, invisible to all, approached Odysseus and urged him to beg for a crust from each suitor, thus learning to distinguish between the fair-minded and the louts. Even so, the goddess planned to do away with them all. The only difference would be that some would suffer less than others. Odysseus followed the immortal's instructions, moving from man to man, pleading with an outstretched hand, as if he had been a beggar all his life. Some were compassionate and gave him food, while other suitors merely asked each other where the man might have come from. Then Melanthius the goatherd said, "I have seen the old fellow before. The swineherd brought him here." The suitor Antinous turned angrily towards Eumaeus and addressed him in an uncouth manner. "You revolting swineherd. Tell us why you have brought this person into the city! Do we not have enough good-for-nothings without you dragging another glutton into the hall?" "You, sir, are a callous brute," said Eumaeus calmly. "All the city's great and good compete with each other to invite interesting people to their palaces such as seers, doctors, master builders, and singers like the one who has charmed us with his music tonight. But no one invites a beggar. He comes uninvited but that is no reason to throw him out! And that will not happen here as long as Penelope and Telemachus reside in this house." But Telemachus told him to stay silent, saying, "Do not trouble to answer him, Eumaeus. You know how offensive this man can be when he wants to insult others. As for you, Antinous, you are not my guardian! You, therefore, have absolutely no right to tell me to throw a stranger out of my house. I believe it better to give him everything he needs and not be stingy with anything that is mine to give. But of course, you prefer to stuff yourself with food rather than share it with others!"

"Do you hear how this impertinent brat pokes fun at me?" Antinous shouted. "But if all the suitors would give the beggar as much as I have, he would not have come back to this house to beg for another three months!" With that, he grabbed his footstool, and when Odysseus passed on his way back to the threshold, he asked for alms yet again and began to bemoan his lengthy wanderings through Egypt and Cyprus. Antinous exclaimed malevolently, "What demon has sent us this barefaced scrounger? What do I care about Egypt or Cyprus? Get away from this table!" Then, as Odysseus stepped back muttering to himself, Antinous flung the footstool at him, striking him on the shoulder close to the neck. But Odysseus stood there, steady as a rock, silently shaking his head as he decided how best to react. First, he went back to the threshold where he placed his bag full of gifts on the floor, and then sat down, loudly complaining about Antinous's insulting behavior to all those present. The latter shouted back, "Shut your mouth and stuff your gut, you loathsome foreigner! Get out of here before I drag you hand and foot over the threshold so hard that your limbs bleed!"

Such a boorish confrontation even offended the suitors, one of whom rose to his feet and responded, "Antinous, you are wrong to throw things at this unfortunate stranger. It does no good at all. What if he were a messenger from the gods in the shape of a mortal? Such things do happen!" But Antinous did not heed the warning. Telemachus suffered in angry silence as he saw his father thus abused.

ODYSSEUS: THE BEGGAR IN THE HALL

Through the open window of her chamber, Penelope could hear everything happening in the great hall and, on hearing how the beggar was being treated, she felt sorry for him. In secret, she summoned the swineherd to her quarters and bade him to bring the stranger to her. "Perhaps," she added, "he may have news of my husband or he may even have seen him, for he appears to be wandering all over the world." "Yes," Eumaeus replied, "if the suitors had stopped shouting and listened, there is much he could have told them. He has stayed with me for three days and has enchanted me with his stories, which he tells like a singer performing his songs. He comes from Crete and claims that his father and the father of Odysseus would each occasionally offer hospitality to the other. He also believes that Odysseus is in the land of the Thesprotians and will soon be home, laden with treasure." At this, Penelope was deeply moved. "Go and bring the stranger so that he can tell me his stories," she said. "Those suitors and their appalling manners! What we need is a man like Odysseus used to be. If only he were here, he and Telemachus would soon punish them for what they have done!" Just as she finished speaking, Telemachus sneezed so loudly that it echoed all around the great hall. Penelope could not help smiling as she said to the swineherd, "Did you hear my son sneeze? That must be a good omen, so please send the stranger here immediately!"

Eumaeus passed Penelope's instructions on to the beggar, who replied, "I would gladly tell the queen as much as I know of Odysseus, and I do know a great deal about him. But the suitors' behavior terrifies me. When that evil man over there flung a footstool at me and hit me on the shoulder, neither Telemachus nor anyone else came to my aid. Therefore, please ask Penelope to wait until sunset, when I shall ask her to permit me to sit beside her warm hearth, for these rags of mine do let in the cold. Then I will tell her all I possibly can." Penelope was very eager to meet the stranger, but even so she realized he was right and decided to be patient.

Eumaeus returned to the great hall, where he was surrounded by suitors but was able to approach Telemachus and whisper in his ear. "Master, I am going back to my hut now. Do whatever is necessary here but, for your own protection, you must be con-

stantly on your guard against these malicious individuals. They may harm you at any moment." But Telemachus begged him to stay until nightfall and he agreed. Then he left, promising to return on the following day with some of his best fatted boars.

The suitors were still at the table when an infamous beggar from the city wandered into the great hall. He was famous as a huge eater and although tall and broad-shouldered, he was physically a weakling. His real name was Arnaeus, but the city's youngsters called him Irus, playing on the name of Iris, messenger to the gods, since, for a modest sum, he would carry messages. It was suspicion that led him to the house, for he had heard that a rival beggar had appeared there. Now, he set out to do what he intended, namely to drive Odysseus out of his own house. "Get away from the door, old man," he shouted on entering. "Can you not see how they are waving their arms about telling me to haul you out by your feet? Go on then, get yourself out of here before I pick you up and throw you out!" Scowling at him, Odysseus said, "There is room for both of us on this threshold. You look as poor as I do. There is no need to envy me, for I will not begrudge you your fair share. Do not make me angry and do not challenge me to a fist fight. Old I may be, but I can soon make the blood flow from your chest and your lips, and you will be in no state to disturb people in this house tomorrow." This made Irus even crazier. "You greedy pig! What is all this about? You sound like some old fishwife. A few clouts left and right will smash your face in and all your teeth will fall out, like a pig spilling corn. Do you still fancy fighting me, even though I am much younger than you?"

The suitors burst out laughing as they heard the two of them quarreling and turned to watch the wrangling beggars. Antinous spoke. "How is this for an idea, friends? Look over there. Do you see those goat bellies stuffed with blood and fat roasting over the fire? Let us offer them as a prize for these noble heroes. The victor shall eat as much as he can, and in the future he will be the only beggar allowed into this hall!"

All the suitors approved the plan. Meanwhile, Odysseus, still portraying himself as a timid old man enfeebled by constant hardship, entreated the suitors not to use their younger hands to intervene in Irus's favor. To this, they readily agreed.

ODYSSEUS: THE BEGGAR IN THE HALL

Both men raised their fists and began to fight.

Then Telemachus rose and said, "Stranger, if you succeed in defeating this man, then you need not fear anyone. For I am the host and anyone who injures you will have me to deal with." All the suitors applauded to this. Odysseus girded up his ragged garments and rolled up the sleeves, revealing muscular arms and thighs, broad shoulders and chest, for Athena had secretly made him even more powerful, so much so that the spectators gaped at him and whispered among themselves. "What sturdy haunches the old man has hidden under his rags. Poor Irus is going to have a rough ride!" At this point, Irus was losing his nerve. The servants had to force him to prepare for the fight and his limbs were shaking. Antinous, who had expected a rather different contest, angrily shouted at him. "Why did you not keep your big mouth shut? Better to have never been born than to tremble before a poor feeble old man! I will tell you now. If he wins, you will be put on board a ship and sent to Epirus to King Echetus, whom all men fear. He will cut off your ears and nose and throw them to the dogs!" The more Antinous yelled at him, the more Irus trembled. But they pushed him forward, and both contestants raised their fists and began to fight. For a moment, Odysseus pondered whether he should kill his pitiful opponent outright with a single blow or strike him only gently so as not arouse the suitors' suspicions. This seemed to make more sense, so when Irus struck him on the shoulder, Odysseus responded with a light tap behind the ear. Even so, it crushed the bone, sending blood spraying from his mouth and Irus fell to the floor, writhing in pain with his teeth chattering. Amid the suitors' raucous laughter and handclapping, Odysseus dragged him away from the threshold, through the courtyard and out through the gate. There he propped him up against the wall, put a staff in his hands and said disdainfully, "Stay there and keep an eye on the dogs and pigs!" Then he returned to the great hall and sat back down with his sack on the threshold.

His victory had earned the suitors' respect. They came to up to him, laughing, smiling, and holding out their hands to him, and they said, "May Zeus and the immortals give you what you desire, stranger, for you have rid us of a troublesome pest, whom we shall ship to the land of King Echetus, where he may well find peace!" Antinous himself laid before him a large goat belly stuffed with fat and blood, while Amphinomus brought two loaves from the basket and filled a cup with wine to drink a toast to the victor with these words: "To your good health, old man. May your future be free of worries!" Odysseus looked him in the eye and replied in a solemn voice, "Amphinomus, you strike me as a young man of considerable intelligence and I know you to be the son of a distinguished father. Take to heart what I am about to say to you! There is nothing more futile and uncertain on earth than man himself. While he is favored by the gods, he does not believe that the future holds any danger. But when struck by sorrow he finds he is not brave enough to bear it. I speak from experience. In those happy days when I could trust in my youthful strength, I did many things I should not have done. Therefore I warn each and every one of you: your youthful exuberance must not lead you behave lawlessly. I also advise you to accept the gifts of the gods with humility and serene gratitude. For this reason, it is not wise for suitors to behave in such a malevolent and unruly manner and offend the wife of a man who has long been away from home. A man who, I have reason to believe, will soon return. Indeed, he may not be far away! Amphinomus, may some god take you away from this house before he arrives and finds you here!" Odysseus poured a libation as he spoke, which he drank and handed the cup back to the young man. The suitor grew thoughtful and bowed his head as he walked with a heavy heart through the hall as if he guessed that some terrible fate awaited him. But he was not to escape the punishment that Athena had decreed.

ODYSSEUS
ALONE WITH PENELOPE

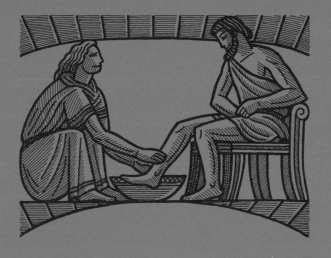

The first encounter after twenty years:
Penelope summons the stranger to her presence. He tells her a fabulous story,
and foretells the return of Odysseus, but does not reveal his identity to Penelope.
While washing his feet, his old nurse, Eurycleia, recognizes the boy
she once took care of from a scar. She keeps quiet on Odysseus's orders.

Illustrations by William Russell Flint and Walter Crane

Telemachus left and Penelope came out of her chamber, as beautiful as Artemis and Aphrodite. On reaching the great hall she saw that her favorite chair, a fine piece of furniture exquisitely inlaid with silver and ivory and covered with sheepskin, had been placed for her by the hearth, where she preferred. A group of maidservants arrived to clear food and cups from the tables, which they set to one side while they attended to the fire and the lights. Now, Melantho the maidservant mocked Odysseus for the second time. "Stranger," she said. "Do you intend to stay here all night and prowl around the palace? Be satisfied with what you have been given and go straight through the door this minute, if you do not want a fire stick thrown at you." Odysseus glared angrily at her and replied, "I cannot understand why you treat me in such a hostile manner simply because I am dressed in rags and obliged to beg for my food. Is that not the fate shared by all those who wander homeless through the world? There was a time when I lived happily in a fine house and I always gave wandering strangers whatever they needed, no matter how they looked. I also had plenty of servants. But Zeus took all that away from me. So think, young woman, this could happen to you. What if the queen became seriously displeased with you? What if Odysseus returned? There is still some hope that he will! And what if Telemachus, who is no longer a child, punished you in his father's stead?"

Penelope heard what the beggar said and scolded the arrogant maidservant. "You shameless young woman. I am well aware of your ignorant cast of mind. I also I know what you are up to and I shall make you pay for it! Did you not hear me say I would honor this stranger and receive him in my own chambers, where I would ask him about my husband? Are you not ashamed that all you have done is mock him?" Melantho crept away, humiliated, as the housekeeper entered with a stool for the beggar, whom Penelope began to question. "First of all, stranger, please tell me your name and who your parents are," she asked. He replied, "Your Majesty, you are a woman beyond reproach and your husband is a man greatly honored; your people and your country are widely praised. As for me, ask me whatever pleases you, but not about my lineage or my native land, for I have suffered so much pain that I do not wish to be reminded of home. If I were to tell you everything, I would be bound to weep and wail and your maidservants would – quite justifiably – rebuke me." At this Penelope continued. "Stranger, I too have had much to endure since my beloved husband left me. You saw for yourself how many men are trying to win my affection when in fact all they do is drive me mad. For three years, I have avoided them by means of a ruse, which I have had to abandon." She then told him about her web and how her own handmaidens had betrayed her. "Now I can no longer shun a second marriage; my parents are coercing me, and my son is infuriated because his inheritance is being squandered. You can understand my situation. So you see, there is no need to keep your identity secret. After all, you were not born of a famous oak or rock!"

"If you insist, I shall tell you," Odysseus replied, and so he playfully revived his tall tale about Crete. This seemed so close to the truth that it had Penelope in floods of tears, while Odysseus was full of pity for her. Nevertheless, his eyes remained fixed behind his lids, as if made from horn or iron, and he was calm enough hold back his tears. When the queen had wept long enough, she spoke again. "Now you must give me some proof that my husband truly was a guest at your house. Tell me what he was wearing, how he looked, and who was with him." "It is difficult to say, since it was nearly twenty years ago that the hero landed on Crete," Odysseus replied. "But I do seem to remember what he was wearing. A mantle of purple wool fastened by a golden buckle skillfully embossed with the image of a dog

ODYSSEUS PULLED HIS LEGS BACK INTO THE SHADOWS. BUT ALL IN VAIN.

with a fawn struggling between its front paws. Under the purple mantle he wore a tunic of the finest snow-white linen. He was attended by a hunchbacked herald with curly hair and dark skin, whose name was Eurybates." Again, the queen could not help but weep, for in her mind's eye she recognized every detail. Odysseus consoled her with a new tale, in which the beggar mingled fact with fiction. It was true that her husband landed on Thrinacia and stayed in the land of the Phaeacians. The beggar claimed to know about the king of the Thesprotians, with whom Odysseus had stayed when on his way to consult the oracle at Dodona, and he saw for himself how Odysseus left great treasure with the king for safekeeping. Overall, he felt sure that her husband's return was as good as certain.

But Penelope could not be persuaded. Sadly bowing her head, she said, "I do not believe this will ever happen." She was about to instruct her maidservants to wash the stranger's feet and to prepare a comfortable couch for him. However, Odysseus was unwilling to accept the services of these untrustworthy creatures and simply asked for some straw to sleep on. "Unless you have a kind, faithful old grandmother who has been through as much as I have, and who is willing to wash my feet!" "Come, my good Eurycleia!" Penelope called. "You were the one who brought up little Odysseus. Now please wash the feet of this man who must be of a similar age as your master." Eurycleia looked at the beggar. "Ah," she said. "Perhaps Odysseus has hands and feet like these. For those who know suffering age before their time." As she spoke, the old woman's eyes filled with tears and, as she approached to wash the stranger's feet she said, "Many strangers have visited us, but I have never seen one more like Odysseus than you! You not only have the same feet, but also the same voice and the same build."

"Yes, everyone who has seen both of us says the same," Odysseus replied without thinking, as he sat by the hearth while she mixed hot and cold water in a basin. As she worked, Odysseus moved carefully away from the light, to prevent her seeing a deep scar above his right knee. This dated back to his youth when, while out hunting, a boar had thrust its tusk sideways into the flesh. He feared that the old woman would recognize him if she saw it, so he pulled his legs back into the

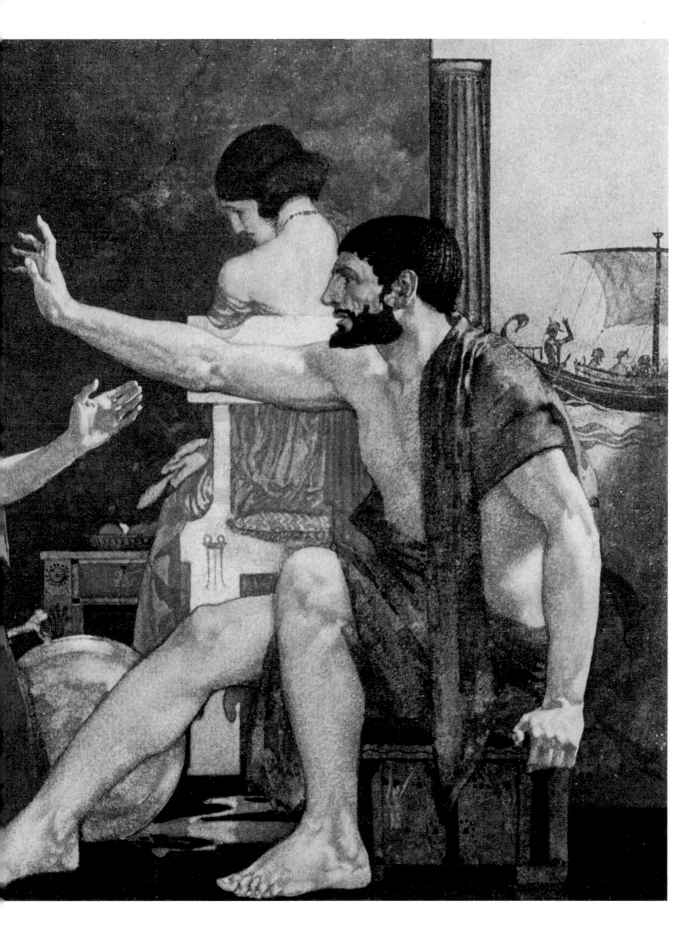

ODYSSEUS: ALONE WITH PENELOPE

Eurycleia looked at the beggar.
"Ah," she said. "Perhaps Odysseus
has hands and feet like these."

shadows. But all in vain. When she ran the palm of her hand over the leg, she immediately felt the scar and with that first shock of joy, she let the foot slip through her hand and into the basin so that the metal clanged and the water spilled. Her breath faltered and for a moment she lost her voice, while her eyes filled with tears. Then, grasping the hero's knee she cried, "Odysseus, my son, it is really you! I felt the scar with my hand!" But with his right hand, he caught her by the throat and with his left he dragged her towards him and whispered, "Old woman, do you want to destroy me? What you say is true, but no one in the palace must know. If you do not keep your mouth shut and I succeed in getting the suitors under control, you will share the same fate as those uncivilized young females!"

"What kind of nonsense is that?" asked Eurycleia calmly as he let go of her neck. "I would have you know that my heart is as firm as rock and iron. But beware the rest of the maidservants in the palace. I shall tell you the names of all those who have no respect for you." Odysseus replied, "That will not be necessary. I know who they are, so it need not concern you." Meanwhile Eurycleia went to fetch a second footbath, for the first one had spilled until almost empty. After she had washed and anointed his feet, Penelope came to talk to him for a while. "My heart swings back and forth, kind stranger," she said. "Shall I simply stay here to be with my son and manage the estate, all for the sake of my husband, who may still be alive? Or should I marry the most noble of the suitors, the one who will provide the richest dowry? While Telemachus was still a child, I refused to marry; but now he is a young man. He himself wants me to leave because otherwise his inheritance will become completely worthless. But I have had a dream, which you, who seem to be such a wise man, can explain to me.

"Here, I have twenty geese and I always enjoy watching as they eat their grain mixed with water. In the dream, an eagle came down from the mountains and broke all their necks. There they lay dead on the ground, while the bird of prey soared back into the air. I began to sob aloud but the dream continued. Then it appeared that women from the neighborhood had come to console me in my grief. Suddenly the eagle came back, then perched himself on a ledge and began to speak in a human voice, 'Be of good comfort, daughter of Icarius. This is not a dream but a vision,' he explained. 'The geese are the suitors and the eagle is me, Odysseus, who has returned to do away with them all.' I heard what he said and then I awoke and immediately went to ensure that my geese were safe, and there they were, feeding quietly at the trough." "Your Majesty," the beggar replied. "What Odysseus told you in your dream is what is sure to happen. The vision cannot be interpreted in any other way. He will return and no suitor will survive."

But Penelope sighed and said, "Dreams are like bubbles floating through the air and tomorrow will be the day I dread, when I am to leave my husband's house. I shall arrange a competition like one my husband used to organize. He would set twelve axes in a row, one behind the other. Then he would step back with his bow and arrow and shoot an arrow through the hole in each one. If any of the suitors can achieve that feat using Odysseus's bow, I shall marry him."

"An excellent idea, honorable queen," said Odysseus decisively. "The contest must take place bright and early tomorrow, for Odysseus will arrive ahead of the suitors, ready to bend the bow and shoot the arrow through the holes in the twelve axes."

ODYSSEUS

THE CONTEST WITH THE BOW, AND THE HERO'S REVENGE

Exacting terrible revenge:
The suitor who can bend Odysseus's bow and shoot an arrow through the holes
formed by twelve axes set up in a row is to marry Penelope — these are the conditions
that she sets. None of the suitors can handle the bow; only Odysseus can bend it.
After successfully fulfilling the conditions of the competition, he reveals himself
to the suitors. For them, the game is up; all are massacred.

Illustrations by Newell Convers Wyeth and Henry Justice Ford

Penelope knew that the moment had come. Holding a skillfully fashioned bronze key with an ivory handle in her hand, she led her maidservants to a distant storeroom where all King Odysseus's precious possessions in bronze, gold, and iron were kept. These included his bow and a quiver full of arrows, both gifts from a good friend in Lacedaemon. Penelope unlocked the door and slid back the bolts. Doing so made a racket as loud as a bellowing bull in the middle of a field. Penelope stepped into the storeroom and examined the cases containing clothing and various devices. She found the bow and quiver hanging on a nail and stood on tiptoe to take them down. Grief overwhelmed her and she threw herself into a chair where she sat weeping, bow and quiver on her lap. At last she stood and left the room, followed by maidservants carrying the weapons in a chest. She continued to the great hall, where she was quickly surrounded by suitors. Calling for silence, she began. "Well, gentlemen, for some time you have competed for my hand. Now steel yourselves for a real contest. Here is the great bow of my noble husband. Whoever among you can most easily bend it and shoot an arrow through the holes in twelve axes set up one behind the other can claim me for his wife. With that man I shall leave this palace, which was home to my first husband."

She then bade the swineherd to arrange the bow and arrows so that the suitors might see. As he lifted them from the chest, his eyes filled with tears and the cowherd also wept. At this, Antinous angrily protested. "You dim-witted peasants! Why must you break our queen's heart with your tears? By all means stuff your faces with our food, but save the sniveling for outside! We suitors are faced with a difficult contest, for

> "WELL, GENTLEMEN, FOR SOME TIME YOU HAVE COMPETED FOR MY HAND. NOW STEEL YOURSELVES FOR A REAL CONTEST."

to me it looks far from easy to bend. Not one of us here is as strong as Odysseus. I remember him well, but when he left I was only a little boy who could barely speak." Antinous said this, but in his heart he could see himself already stretching the bowstring and shooting the arrow through the holes in the axes. But Fate had decreed that Odysseus would be the one to launch the first arrow.

Then Telemachus rose and said, "It seems Zeus has been meddling with my brain! My mother has announced that that she will leave this house to follow some suitor or another and I just sit here grinning. Well then, suitors, you are about to compete for a woman unequalled in the whole of Greece. But of course you are aware of that and you have no need of my recommendations. So just get on with drawing the bow! I wish I could take part in the competition, for if I were to defeat all of you, my mother would not leave this house!" Having spoken, he cast off his purple mantle and took out his sword to draw a straight furrow along the floor of the hall. Into it, he bored a dozen holes in which he planted each axe, then stamped down hard on the surrounding earth. All the onlookers admired his strength and precision. Then he reached for the bow and positioned himself on the threshold. Three times he tried hard to bend it, three times he failed. As he drew the bowstring for the fourth time, a gesture from his father made him pause. "For pity's sake!" he cried. "Either I am a weakling or too young and unable to defend myself from an attacker. Go on, you try it. You who are stronger than me!" At which he propped the bow and quiver against the doorpost and went back to the chair on which he had been seated.

With a look of triumph on his face, Antinous stood up and said, "Come, friends, let us proceed, moving from left to right

The shaft did not miss a single axe as it passed through each hole, from the first to the last.

as the cupbearer does when he serves us." The first to stand was Leiodes, the man who poured sacrificial libations and always sat in a corner of the hall beside the big mixing vessel. He was also the only one among the suitors to hate all the rest of them and be disgusted by their hooligan antics. He made his way to the threshold and tried in vain to bend the bow. "Let another man try," he said, his hands dropping limply to his sides. "I am not the right man for this task. Perhaps none of us are." At that, he rested the bow and quiver against the doorpost. But Antinous berated him, "What an infuriating pessimist you are, Leiodes. Just because you failed to bend the bow, are you suggesting no other will succeed?" He called to the goatherd. "On your feet, Melanthius! Light a fire, put a chair in front of it, and bring us a big lump of fat from the kitchen. The bow is too cold and too dry, so we shall warm it and grease it to make things easier for us." The goatherd did as instructed, but to no avail. One after another, the suitors tried, but failed, to bend the bow. Finally, there remained only the two most vociferous, namely Antinous and Eurymachus.

Then it so happened that, on leaving the palace, the cowherd and the swineherd found themselves followed close behind by the hero Odysseus. As they shut the courtyard gate behind them, he caught up with them and, speaking with kindness and understanding, he said, "My friends, I should like to have a word with you, but only if I can trust you both. Otherwise I must remain silent. How would it be if a god suddenly brought Odysseus home from foreign shores? Would you side with the suitors, or with him? Tell me frankly. How do you truly feel?" The first to respond was the cowherd. "Oh Zeus on Olympus," he exclaimed. "If my dearest wish were granted and the hero returned, then you would see me raise my

THE GOATHERD DID AS INSTRUCTED, BUT TO NO AVAIL. ONE AFTER ANOTHER, THE SUITORS TRIED, BUT FAILED, TO BEND THE BOW.

fists in his defense." Likewise, Eumaeus called upon all the gods to send Odysseus home.

When he was convinced of their loyalty, he said, "Well then, listen when I tell you: I am Odysseus! After twenty years of unspeakable hardship, I have returned to my native land only to see that out of all my servants, you two alone are ready to welcome me. Nor have I heard any of them praying to the gods to bring me home. Therefore, when I have dealt with the suitors, I shall duly reward you. I shall give each of you a wife and plenty of land and build you a house close to my own, and Telemachus will treat you like brothers. And to prove to you I am telling the truth, I shall show you the scar left by a boar who wounded me while I was out hunting as a boy." He then moved his ragged clothes to one side to reveal the long scar. At this, the two herdsmen began to weep, throwing their arms around their master and kissing his face and shoulders. Odysseus kissed his faithful servants, and then said, "Take care, dear friends, not to show any sign of your emotions, for no one at the palace must suspect my presence. So let us enter one at a time. The suitors will not be willing to hand the bow and quivers to me, but you, Eumaeus, can stroll calmly across the room, take up the bow and hand it to me. At the same time, order the handmaids to lock themselves safely in the women's quarters and, if they hear the sounds of men shouting and groaning from the great hall, on no account should they come rushing out, but quietly continue with their work. Meanwhile, you, my loyal Philoetius, will be responsible for the courtyard gate. Bolt it shut and secure the lock with a rope." After giving his instructions, Odysseus returned to the hall, followed by the two herdsmen, one behind the other. Eurymachus was attempting to warm the bow. He turned it indefatigably over the fire but still failed to bend it. He sighed cantankerously and said, "This is so frustrating! Not so much because of Penelope. There are plenty of Greek women in Ithaca and other places. What is truly annoying is that we look so feeble compared with Odysseus. Our grandsons will never let us hear the last of it!" Antinous, however, chided his friend and said, "Do not talk like that, Eurymachus. Today the people are celebrating the feast of Apollo. In fact, this is not the time to be stretching bowstrings. Let us forget the contest for now, leave the axes where they are and drink a cup or two instead. Tomorrow we can make an offering to Apollo and try again!"

Now Odysseus turned and spoke to the suitors. "You are quite right to rest today. Let us hope that tomorrow Apollo, the long-range archer, will grant you victory. Meanwhile, allow me to try the bow and see whether any of the strength of my younger days still remains in my poor old limbs." To which Antinous replied, "Stranger, have you lost your mind? Or did you drink too much wine? Do you want to start a fight, as the centaur Eurytion did at the wedding of Pirithous? Remember he was the first to fall, so you may well be cut down as soon as you bend the bow, and no one among us will intercede for you." Now Penelope intervened in the dispute. "Antinous," she said softly, "would it not be unseemly to exclude the stranger from the contest? Are you afraid that if the beggar succeeded in bending the bow, he would carry me away as his wife? I doubt whether he holds out any such hope. Nor should any of you worry. Such a situation is quite impossible!" Eurymachus answered her, "We have no such fear, oh queen. What concerns us is the gossip among the Greeks who will think that those who courted the wife of the immortal hero were weak men, unable to bend the bow. Worse still, that a beggar appeared out of nowhere,

promptly bent the bow and then, with consummate ease, shot the arrow through the twelve axes."

"The stranger is not as lowly as you imagine," said Penelope. "Look at him more closely and you will see how tall and powerfully built he is. Moreover, he claims to be of noble stock. So give him the bow! Should he successfully bend it, his only rewards will be a mantle, a tunic, a spear, a sword, and sandals for his feet. Then he can go wherever his heart desires."

Then Telemachus butted in. "Mother, I alone have the right to decide whether to hand over the bow or refuse to do so. And if I chose to give it to the stranger, no one could prevent me. As for you, mother, go to your chamber and work your spindle and your loom. Shooting arrows is men's business." Penelope was astounded by her son's attitude, but nonetheless did as he said.

And now the swineherd took up the bow in his hands, despite the suitors' angry cries. "Where are you going with that, you raving madman? Do you honestly want to be torn to shreds by your own dogs out there by the pigsties?" Shocked by these words, Eumaeus laid the bow down for a moment, but Telemachus called out threateningly, "Bring it here, old man! I am the only one giving orders here and if you fail to obey me, I shall drive you away amid a shower of stones, even though I am much younger than you. Would that I could do the same to the suitors!" The suitors forgot their anger in a moment of laughter. The swineherd handed the bow to the beggar, then quietly bade Eurycleia to lock the handmaids in the women's quarters and bolt the doors, while Philoetius hurried out of the palace and carefully locked the courtyard gates.

Odysseus, meanwhile, examined the bow from every angle. He wanted to see whether worms had eaten away the wood or if

> "ARE YOU AFRAID THAT IF THE BEGGAR SUCCEEDED IN BENDING THE BOW, HE WOULD CARRY ME AWAY AS HIS WIFE?"

ODYSSEUS: THE CONTEST WITH THE BOW, AND THE HERO'S REVENGE

anything else had affected it over the years. The suitors whispered to one another, "This vagrant seems to know something about bows. Maybe he has a similar one at home, or maybe he wants to copy one for himself. Look at the way his fingers move as he examines it."

After Odysseus had closely examined the mighty bow, he strung it very lightly, as a singer strings his lyre. He plucked the string with his right hand to test its tautness, producing a high, clear sound, like the chirping of a swallow. When they heard it, the suitors all winced as if in pain and turned pale. But Zeus sent a clap of thunder down from heaven – always a happy omen. Then Odysseus stood at the table working on an arrow which had slipped from the quiver. He gripped the bow, drew the string, checked the notch, then fitted the arrow and loosed it, aiming with an expert eye. The shaft did not miss a single axe as it passed through each hole, from the first to the last. Then the hero spoke. "Now, Telemachus. The stranger you admitted to your palace has not shamed you. My strength has not weakened, despite the suitors and their insults. But now it is time to serve these gentlemen their evening meal. Let us take care of it before dark so that later we can have the music of the lyre, singing and whatever befits a celebratory feast."

With these words, Odysseus gave his son their agreed-upon sign. Quickly, Telemachus slung his sword over his shoulder, took hold of his spear and, fully armed, hurried to stand beside his father's chair.

Then Odysseus tore the rags from his arms and sprang onto the raised threshold, firmly holding the bow and the quiver full of arrows in his hand. There he poured them out close to his feet and called to the suitors gathered below. "Listen, you suitors! The first contest is now over. Now for the second! This time it is I who will choose a target which no archer has ever hit. I cannot imagine I shall miss." As he spoke he aimed at Antinous, who was just lifting his two-handled golden cup to his lips. Odysseus's arrow hit him in the throat, its point going straight through the back of his neck. The cup dropped from his hand as a thick spurt of blood flooded from his nostrils, and as he fell, his foot caught the table, dragging it and sending everything on it rolling to the floor. When the suitors saw him fall, they leapt from their chairs with ear-splitting screams and ran towards the walls in an attempt to seize weapons, but there was neither spear nor shield to be seen. Now they started to hurl abuse at Odysseus. "Why do you shoot men, you infernal stranger? You have killed our most noble companion. But that was your last shot. Soon the vultures will

ODYSSEUS: THE CONTEST WITH THE BOW, AND THE HERO'S REVENGE

While his arrows lasted, Odysseus shot one suitor after another, with each one falling on top of the rest.

eat your flesh!" They said this in the belief that he had shot Antinous accidentally. They had no idea that they also faced the same threat. But, in a voice like thunder, Odysseus called down to them. "You dogs! You thought I would never return from Troy, so you squandered all that was mine, seduced my servants, and courted my wife with no certainty that I was dead and with no fear of men or gods! But now the day of your destruction has come!"

On hearing those words, the suitors turned pale with fear. Each one looked about, silently searching for a means of escape. Only Eurymachus remained composed and said, "If you truly are Odysseus of Ithaca, your anger is justified, for many wrongs have been done inside the palace and on your land. But the man most blameworthy is already dead, shot by your arrow. For it was Antinous who instigated all these misdemeanors, and he was not even courting Penelope in earnest. His only interests were firstly, to become king of Ithaca and secondly, to murder your son in secret. Now that he has got what he deserved, spare us your anger, for we are of equally good breeding. Each one of us will bring you twenty bullocks to compensate for those we have eaten, and as much bronze and gold it will take to regain your esteem!" "No, Eurymachus," replied Odysseus "even if each of you were to offer me all your inheritance, I shall not rest until you all have died to atone for your depravities. The choice is yours, fight or flee, but none of you shall escape me!"

The suitors were paralyzed with fear. Their hearts beat wildly and their bodies quaked. Eurymachus spoke again, this time to his comrades. "No one can stop this man. Draw your swords, use the tables to shield yourselves, then let us try to throw ourselves at him and send him crashing from the threshold. Let us then spread ourselves around the city and raise help from our friends there." As he spoke, he unsheathed his sword and leapt forward with a wrathful shout. At that moment, the hero's arrow pierced his liver. His sword slipped from his hand and he fell over a table, taking with him food and cups, which rolled to the ground as his face hit the floor. In a final convulsion, he kicked away a chair and then lay dead on the floor. Now Amphinomus rushed at Odysseus using his sword to clear a path for himself, but Telemachus's spear struck him between the shoulder blades,

throwing him face-down onto the ground. Telemachus then jumped to separate himself from a multitude of suitors and took his place on the threshold beside his father, for whom he had brought a shield, two lances and a bronze helmet. He then hurried through the door into the armory from where he picked additional weaponry for himself and his friends. He chose four shields, eight lances and four helmets with horsehair crests. Now he and the two loyal herdsmen were suitably armed. The fourth set of weapons he took to his father and now all four allies stood shoulder to shoulder.

While his arrows lasted, Odysseus shot one suitor after another, with each one falling on top of the rest. Then he leaned the bow against the doorpost, threw his shield around his shoulder, set the helmet with its horsehair crest waving to and fro, and grabbed two hefty lances. In the great hall there was a side door opening to a passage leading to the rear of the palace. However, the door was so narrow that only one man at a time could pass through. Odysseus had appointed Eumaeus to keep watch on the door, but when the swineherd went to arm himself, it was briefly unguarded. One of the suitors, Agelaus, noticed this and said to those near him, "Why do we not escape through the side door and get to the city, where we can find help and soon rid ourselves of this man?" "That will not work!" said Melanthius, the goatherd who had sided with the suitors. "The door and the passage are so narrow that there is only room for one man at a time. Instead, let me slip out quietly on my own and fetch enough weapons from the upstairs room." The goatherd went back and forth time after time, bringing with him twelve shields, with just as many helmets and lances. Suddenly, Odysseus saw his enemies clad in armor and brandishing long spears. Startled, he turned to his son Telemachus and said, "This is the work of one of the false handmaids or that evil goatherd!" Telemachus confessed to his father, "I am the one to blame, Father. When I brought us more weapons, I was in such a hurry that I left the storeroom door ajar." The swineherd hurried up to the room to close it firmly, but through the open door he saw the goatherd helping himself to more weapons, so he ran straight back to tell Odysseus. "Shall I take him alive or finish him off?" he asked his master. "Take the cowherd with you," he replied. "Both of you,

seize him, bind his arms and legs behind his back, hang him by a stout rope from the central pillar, then leave him there to suffer behind the firmly closed door while the two of you return." The herdsmen obeyed their leader's command. They sneaked up behind the goatherd in a corner of the room where he was still ferreting about in search of more weapons. As he came to the door, a helmet in one hand and an old and dilapidated shield in the other, they grabbed him and pushed him screaming to the floor. They then bound his hands and feet behind his back, knotted a long rope to a hook in the ceiling, lashed it around his body, and then hoisted him up the tall pillar until he hung close to the rafters. "I hope you are comfortable up there," said the swineherd. "Sweet dreams!" They closed the door and returned to their posts near Odysseus. Then, unexpectedly, the four of them were joined by a fifth ally, Athena, appearing in the guise of Mentor, son of Alcimus, whom Odysseus joyously recognized as the goddess. When the suitors also identified the new combatant, Agelaus angrily shouted, "Mentor, I advise you not to allow Odysseus to persuade you to make war on the suitors. For if you do, we shall kill you and all your kin, along with this father and son!"

Enraged by such talk, Athena goaded Odysseus towards much greater deeds. "You do not seem to be the man you once were, my friend," she said. "You give no sign of the bravery you displayed at Troy ten years ago. It was thanks to your leadership that the city fell. So, when it comes to defending your own palace and possessions, why waste time and effort fighting the suitors?" Her words were intended to encourage him, for she did not propose to take any part in the battle. Suddenly, she took the shape of a swallow and, like a swallow, perched on the sooty rafters. "The high and mighty Mentor has gone," Agelaus told his friends. "Now the four of them are on their own again, so let us consider our tactics. Do not all throw your spears at the same time. You six over there, go first and make sure you aim straight

"HAVE MERCY ON ME, MY LORD!" HE CRIED, CLUTCHING THE HERO'S KNEES.

for Odysseus. The others will be less of a problem." But Athena interfered with their shots. One stuck in the doorpost, another in the door, the rest hit the wall. Then Odysseus ordered his comrades, "Take careful aim and shoot straight!" All four hit their targets. Odysseus struck Demoptolemus, Telemachus shot Euryades, the swineherd caught Elatus, and the cowherd took out Pisander, who all sank into the dust. When the surviving suitors witnessed the fate of their comrades, they fled to the furthest corners of the great hall, but they soon plucked up enough courage to advance again, bearing spears drawn from the dead. Once again, most of the missiles failed to strike the target, apart from Amphimedon's spear which slightly grazed Telemachus's wrist, while that of Ctesippus scratched the swineherd's shoulder just above the shield. The two friends with minor wounds repaid their would-be killers by destroying them. As the swineherd threw his spear he yelled, "Take that, you ill-bred beast, for chucking a cow's hoof at my master when he was begging in the great hall!"

Eurydamas was struck down by Odysseus, who then killed Agelaus, son of Damastor. Telemachus pursued Leiocritos and thrust a spear through his gut. Then, from up on the ceiling where Athena lurked, came the rattle of her magical but deadly breastplate, which so frightened the suitors that they fled through the hall like children bitten by horseflies or small birds trying to escape the talons of a hawk. Odysseus and his friends leapt down from the threshold and stormed through the hall across a floor flowing with blood, accompanied as they went by the crack of skulls and the sound of death rattles.

One of the suitors, Leiodes, threw himself at Odysseus's feet, clasped his knees, and cried, "Have pity on me! I have never acted in any way to hurt you or your kin. I tried to quiet the others, but they refused to listen to me. My task was merely to pour the libations. Am I sentenced to death just for that?" Odysseus replied threateningly, "If you poured libations for them, you must at least have prayed for them!" With that, he picked the sword of Ageleus, whom he had left to die there on the floor, and used it to slice Leiodes's head from his neck. As it rolled away in the dust, the lips continued to plead for mercy.

Close to the side door stood Phemius the singer, holding his lyre in his hands. Overcome by the fear of death, he wondered if it would be better to sidle out of the narrow door or to plead with Odysseus. He chose the latter, laying his lyre on the ground between the mixing vessel and chair, before throwing himself on the ground at Odysseus's feet. "Have mercy on me, my lord!" he cried, clutching the hero's knees. "Surely you would regret slaying a singer who has delighted gods and mortals. A god was my tutor and, like a god, I shall compose a song in your honor! Your son will tell you that I did not come here of my own free will, but they bullied me into singing for them." Odysseus raised his sword, but hesitated. Then Telemachus interrupted. "Stop, father! Do not hurt him, for he is blameless! And if the herald Medon has not already been slaughtered by you or your herdsmen, then please treat him kindly. He took such great care of me when I was a small boy and always wished the family well." When Medon, hiding under a chair and wrapped in a new ox hide, heard Telemachus pleading on his behalf, he unwound himself and lay at the young man's feet. Odysseus, the irascible hero, could not help but smile. He told the singer and the herald, "You two have nothing to fear, for Telemachus and his pleas has saved your lives. Go and tell them all out there that it is better to be loyal than treacherous." The two hurried out from the great hall and sat down in the courtyard, still trembling with fear.

ODYSSEUS
REUNITED WITH PENELOPE

The secret of an olive tree:
Penelope still has doubts about whether the winner of the competition is really Odysseus.
She tells Eurycleia to make the bed outside the bedchamber. Odysseus then
explains that no mortal can move his bed because he carved it from the trunk of an olive tree.
With the mention of this secret that only Odysseus could have known, all doubts
are resolved. She realizes that Odysseus has truly returned.

Illustration by Newell Convers Wyeth

ODYSSEUS: REUNITED WITH PENELOPE

When Eurycleia, the old and faithful servant, had obeyed Odysseus's call for incense to purify the air, she climbed up to her beloved mistress's chamber to tell her that none other than her husband Odysseus had returned home. The elderly woman was still quick on her feet, although her knees sometimes bothered her.

Stepping up softly to Penelope's couch to awaken her, she said, "Dear child, wake up and see what you have awaited for many years with your own eyes. Odysseus has come home. At last he is here, in the palace! And as for those vile suitors who have plagued you, gobbling up your stores and insulting your son – he has killed the lot of them!"

Penelope rubbed the sleep from her eyes and replied, "You silly old woman, the gods have turned you insane. What made you wake me with a pack of lies, when I was enjoying the most peaceful slumber I have ever had? I have not slept so soundly since Odysseus went away! If anyone other than you arrived with such tales, I would have sent her off with something more than hard words. As for you, I shall overlook your stupidity only on grounds of age. But for now, go back down to the hall and leave me in peace."

"Keep your temper, child," said Eurycleia. "The stranger, the beggar they all sneered at, he is your husband! Your son Telemachus has known for some time, but he was ordered to keep the fact to himself until revenge had been taken on the suitors."

On hearing this, the queen leapt from her couch and clung tearfully to the old servant. "If what you say is true and Odysseus really is here in the palace, tell me how he defeated that great horde of hostile men!"

"I myself neither saw nor heard anything," Eurycleia replied. "We women were ordered to go straight to our quarters and lock ourselves in. We sat there terrified and I clearly heard the sound of cries and groans. Then, when your son finally summoned me, I saw your husband standing there, surrounded by dead suitors piled high one on top of another. Gruesome though it was, my dear, I think it would have pleased you to see them. Now all the corpses have been dragged away and

are lying outside the courtyard gates. Meanwhile, I have overseen the house being thoroughly cleaned and purified with sulfur. Now that there is nothing revolting to see, you can go down safely."

"I still cannot believe it," said Penelope. "It must have been an immortal who slew the suitors. But Odysseus? No! He is far from here. He is no longer alive." "What a doubting heart you have," said Eurycleia shaking her head. "So now I shall tell you of an infallible sign. You already know of the scar caused by a boar spearing his leg with its tusk. Remember, too, that you instructed me to wash the beggar's feet. It was then that I recognized the scar. I wanted to tell you at once, but he clasped me around the throat and would not let me speak."

"Then let us go down," said Penelope, trembling with both hope and fear. The two women walked together down to the great hall and crossed the threshold. There, without saying a word, Penelope sat down opposite Odysseus, studying him in the full light of the hearth fire. He was sitting by a tall pillar, eyes cast down, waiting for her to speak. But astonishment and doubt rendered her speechless. At first she thought she recognized his face, but then her eyes fixed on the beggar's rags he wore. In the end, Telemachus walked towards his mother, half smiling with pleasure, half hostile with rage. He said, "What a disagreeable woman you are, mother! How can you sit there unmoved? Go and sit beside father. Get to know him again. Ask him a few questions. What other woman, whose husband returns home after twenty years of hardship and misfortune, would conduct herself as you do? Do you have a heart of stone?"

"Dear son," Penelope replied. "I am lost in wonder. I am speechless. I can ask him no questions. I cannot look him straight in the eye! But, yes, it is true. He is my own Odysseus who has come back home! We shall soon recognize one another, for we have secret signs which only we understand." Then Odysseus turned towards his son, smiling gently. "Let your mother explore me in her way. Thus far she does not take me seriously as I go about in these unsavory rags. However, we have other matters to consider. A man who has slain another of his own people will flee from home, even if his victim has few others to avenge him.

ODYSSEUS: REUNITED WITH PENELOPE

All through the night, husband and wife
told one another of the endless suffering they
had endured in those last twenty years.

We, however, have killed the pillars of our nation, the noblest young men of the island and its neighbors. What shall we do?"

"Father," said Telemachus. "The decision must be yours. Throughout the world, you are respected as the wisest advisor." "Then I shall tell you what I consider to be wisest," Odysseus replied. "You, the herdsmen, and everyone in the house shall bathe and don your finest clothes. The handmaids too shall wear their best. The singer shall then take up his lyre and play music to which we and our guests will dance. Then any neighbor who happens to be passing will think the feasting continues and rumors of the suitors' deaths will not spread through the city until we have reached our farms in the country. Then a god shall tell us what to do next."

Soon the whole palace rang with the sound of the lyre and with singing and dancing. Residents had gathered on the street outside, saying to one another, "There is no doubt! Penelope has married again and they are celebrating at the palace. What a shameless woman! Could she not have waited for her husband to come home?" Towards evening, the crowd began to disperse. Meanwhile, Odysseus had bathed and anointed himself. Athena had also played her part in his beautification, making his dark hair grow more densely on the top of his head, so that he now rose from the bath, cutting an almost godlike figure. He returned to the great hall, where he seated himself opposite his wife. "What a strange woman you are," he said. "The gods have given you a heart of stone. No other wife would so stubbornly refuse to recognize a husband when he comes home after twenty years of trials and tribulations. I must turn to you, dear faithful Eurycleia, to prepare a couch for me, for this woman's heart is made of iron!"

"You simply do not understand," said Penelope. "Neither pride nor scorn, nor any other such feeling holds me back from you. I know very well how you looked when you sailed from Ithaca. Very well, Eurycleia, please prepare him a couch outside it."

But Penelope's words were meant to test his response, which was merely to look up and glare. "Those were harsh words, woman," he said. "No mortal could move my bed, even one still blessed with his youthful vigor. I built it myself and it has a secret of its own. In the middle of the plot on which we were to build the palace, there stood a fine, shady olive tree, strong and straight as a pillar. So I asked that our home be arranged so that our bedchamber was set around the tree. When the bedchamber had been built from strong stone with a ceiling of fine wood, I cut back the top of the olive tree, then I began to smooth and carve the trunk from the root upwards, so that it formed one bedpost to which others would match. The frame was then inlaid with gold, silver, and ivory, with strong ox hide straps to hold it together. This was our bed, Penelope! I do not know whether or not it still stands, but anyone wishing to move it would have had to chop the tree from its roots."

On hearing this, the queen trembled at the knees as she recognized what these words meant. Weeping, she rose from her chair and ran towards her husband with open arms, kissing him again and again. Then she said, "Odysseus, you have always been the kindest and wisest of men. Please do not be angry with me! The immortal gods caused us to suffer because they believed it best for us both to suffer in our youth and then share a tranquil journey into old age together. Do not begrudge me my failure to immediately welcome you. My heart has been in constant fear that some swindler might try to fool me. Now that you have told me things that only you and I – and our old gatekeeper Actoris, who came with me from my father's house – could possibly have known, my doubts are assuaged. I believe your every word!"

All through the night, husband and wife told one another of the endless suffering they had known in those last twenty years. Penelope could not sleep until Odysseus had given her a full account of all his wanderings. And at last, everyone throughout the palace could enjoy the peaceful rest they longed for to help them recover from the day's harrowing events.

PHILEMON AND BAUCIS

Gods reward true hospitality:
Philemon and Baucis do not know they are hosting Zeus and Hermes in their humble
cottage. The gods thank them by turning their home into a temple for them to look after.
They die together as they wished, transformed into an oak and a linden tree.

Illustrations by Walter Crane and Milo Winter

PHILEMON AND BAUCIS

On a hillside in the land of Phrygia, there stands a thousand-year-old oak tree next to a linden tree of the same age, the two encircled by a low wall. Many branches of these intertwined trees are hung with garlands. Nearby is a shallow, swamp-like lake which once flooded, sweeping away every sign of human habitation. Now, nothing but herons and diving birds can be seen fluttering around the water. Once upon a time, Zeus, King of the Gods, arrived in the neighborhood with his son Hermes, who was carrying with him his staff, but not wearing his winged helmet. Disguised as mere mortals, they set out to test the willingness of the inhabitants to offer them a place to stay, knocking on a thousand doors and begging for overnight shelter. But those people were mean and hard-hearted, and they refused to admit the celestial visitors. Then behold, there came into view a small and lowly hut covered with straw and swamp reeds. This was the humble dwelling of a happy couple, Philemon and his wife Baucis, two simple old people of similar age. It was there they had shared their blissful youth and it was there they had progressed into white-haired old age. This cheerful, warmhearted pair who, though childless, loved each other dearly, made no secret of their poverty, which they found easy to endure as they turned the modest little hut into a home where they could live together.

The tall figures of the two gods came towards the little shack whose low roof and doorway obliged them to stoop as they made their way inside. The kindly couple greeted them warmly, the old man arranging the couch, which Baucis covered with woven fabric, on which they bade the guests to rest. The little old woman bustled towards the fire, rummaged through the still-glowing ash and, with her fragile breath, blew through the smoke to ignite the flames. She then brought chopped wood, which she packed under the little cauldron hanging over the fire. Meanwhile, Philemon returned from their small, well-watered garden with cabbage from which the old woman rapidly tore the leaves. Then, with a two-pronged fork, she lifted down from the room's sooty ceiling a smoked loin of pork (which she had long saved for a special occasion), then carved a small piece from the shoulder and placed it in the simmering water. For fear that the strangers might be bored by the lengthy wait, she made an effort to entertain them with gentle conversation. She also poured water into a wooden trough so that they might bathe their feet. With friendly smiles, they accepted this thoughtful gesture and they soaked their feet in the soothing water while their benevolent hosts tidied the couch. They stood it in the middle of the room, the pillows stuffed with pondweed and the frame made of wickerwork, but Philemon dragged in rugs which only appeared on high days and holidays – and oh, how old and tattered they were, too! Even so, now that the meal was ready, the divine guests were happy to recline on the rugs while they dined. Then with trembling hands, the little old woman took hold of a three-legged table and when it refused to stand firm, shoved a wedge under the shortest foot, and then rubbed the platters with fresh spearmint before bringing the food. The meal consisted of olives, autumnal cornelian cherries preserved in clear, thick juices, as well as radishes, endives, cheese, and eggs cooked in the warm ashes. Baucis served all the food in earthenware pots, among them a brightly colored pitcher and delicate goblets, smoothed inside with yellow wax. The wine poured by the honest host was neither too old nor too sweet. Now, however, an aroma of hot victuals wafted from the stove and goblets were pushed to one side to make room enough for sweetmeats. Nuts, figs, and crinkled dates were brought, together with two small baskets of plums and fragrant apples, nor was there a lack of purple grapes from the vine, while a resplendent off-white honeycomb graced the center of the table. Nonetheless, the finest seasoning to the meal lay in the generosity and decency that shone from the kind, friendly faces of the courageous old couple.

While they all were feasting on food and wine, Philemon noticed that, despite constantly refilling goblets, the pitcher was never less than full to the brim. It was then he recognized with amazement and awe whom he was sheltering. Full of fear, arms upraised, eyes downcast, he begged his lifelong companion to assure him that their visitors had looked graciously upon the meager meal and were not angered by such pitiful hospitality. Alas, what could they possibly offer their celestial guests? "Of course!" It occurred to them. Outside in the tiny stable was a

PHILEMON AND BAUCIS

single goose which they could immediately sacrifice. The two of them hurried through the door, but the goose moved a great deal faster. With much squawking and flapping of its wings, it escaped the old couple by running back and forth. Finally, it ran into the house and hid behind the immortals, as if begging them for protection. This was granted by the guests, who also sought to calm their elderly hosts. Speaking softly and with a smile, they said, "We are gods! We returned to Earth to study the spirit of hospitality among mortals. We found your neighbors to be despicable, for which they will not escape punishment. But you must leave this house and follow us up the mountain, so that you, the innocent, will not suffer with the guilty." Both obeyed and, supported by their staffs, struggled wearily up the steep mountainside. Still an arrowshot away from the highest peak, they turned and, looking in fear at the view, saw that the flooded valley had been transformed into a rolling sea, but their little house was still standing. They stood in amazement, mourning the fate of others, and behold! The wretched little hut had been changed into a soaring temple, where beneath a roof of shimmering gold lay a marble-covered floor. And then Zeus, his face lit by a benevolent smile, turned

towards the old couple, both trembling with unease, and said, "Tell me, thou honest old man, and thou, his beloved spouse, what do you both wish for?" Only a few words were exchanged between Philemon and his wife before he spoke. "We would be glad to be your priests and caretakers of yonder temple. And since we have lived together in harmony for so long, let us each die within one hour of the other. Thus, I shall never have to look upon my wife's grave, nor shall she have to gaze upon mine." Their wish was granted. Together they watched over the temple for as long as they lived. And finally, as they stood side by side before the sacred steps, bent with age and years, thinking about their wonderful destiny, Baucis saw her Philemon, and Philemon his Baucis, vanish among the greenery. Already shady treetops could be seen growing around each of their faces and then upwards into the sky. "Farewell, my dearest one!" "Farewell, my love!" They called to one another as long as they were capable of speech. Thus was the fate of the venerable couple; he became an oak, she a linden, and even in death they stood harmoniously side by side, as inseparable as they had been in life. The gods cherish the pious. Honor is due to those who behave with honor.

ARACHNE

Arrogance never pays:
Although her weaving and embroidery skills are famous far and wide,
Arachne should have known better than to challenge Athena at the loom. The goddess
graciously concedes Arachne's talent but is angered by the mockery of the gods in the
pictures Arachne weaves. She punishes Arachne by turning her into a spider.

Illustration by Walter Crane

In Hypaepa, a small city in Lydia, there lived a maiden of lowly birth, Arachne by name. Her father, Idmon of Colophon, was a dyer in purple, while her mother, carried away by early death, was also the daughter of humble parents. Nevertheless, the name of Arachne was esteemed in Lydian towns and cities, for she surpassed all other mortal weavers with her artistry and diligence. Even the nymphs from the vine-covered slopes of the Tmolus Mountains and from the River Pactolus came to the maiden's modest abode to see and marvel at her work. Never were art and beauty so perfectly matched. Whether she was spinning coarse wool, pulling threads finer and finer, turning the spindle with nimble fingers, or embroidering with a needle, it always seemed as though she had been trained by Pallas Athena herself. But Arachne didn't want to hear this. Instead, she often declared, "I did not learn my art from the goddess. Let her come and compete with me. If she wins, I will tolerate any punishment!" Athena listened with indignation to her arrogance, then disguised herself as a little old woman, her brow encircled by gray hair, and her withered hands grasping a walking stick. Thus transformed, she entered Arachne's cottage, declaring, "Old age does not mean adversity; with the passing years our skills mature. Therefore, do not spurn my advice! Seek renown as the mortal who best understands the art of weaving wool, but yield to the goddess with humility. Beg her to forgive your disrespectful language and she will certainly overlook your demand." Seething with anger, Arachne let the threads unravel, and spoke in a voice quivering with rage, "Old woman, you are dimwitted; your mind has been enfeebled by the burden of years. It is not wise to live too long. Go and preach your nonsense to your daughter. I do not need your advice and I shall ignore your warning. Why has Pallas Athena not come here herself? Why does she avoid competing with me?" The goddess's

"I DID NOT LEARN MY ART FROM THE GODDESS. LET HER COME AND COMPETE WITH ME."

patience was at an end. "She is already here!" she announced, suddenly standing there in her divine form. The nymphs and Lydian women present fell at the feet of the goddess in homage; Arachne alone did not tremble. A fleeting blush colored her defiant countenance as she boldly held to her decision and, driven by an even more ridiculous desire for fame, she hurtled towards her impending fate. The daughter of Zeus gave no further warning but stood ready for the fight.

At once, each placed her loom in a separate spot and both enthusiastically set their highly skilled hands to work, ingeniously interweaving purple and a thousand other colors, as well as gold thread, to bewilder the unaccustomed eye. Soon wondrous images sprang up before the astonished gaze of the onlookers. Athena depicted the Acropolis and her own legendary dispute with the god of the sea over the control of Athens. Twelve gods, venerable and divine beings, with Zeus among them, were present. Here, Poseidon could be seen plunging his huge trident into the rock, from which sprang forth a torrent of salt seawater. The divine artist herself also appeared in the tapestry. Armed with shield and spear, a helmet on her head and the fearsome aegis on her breast, she was shown striking the earth with the point of the spear. An olive tree sprang from this point, to the amazement of the gods and to the salvation of the land. Thus Athena wove her own victory into the textile. In the four corners she also worked four examples of human arrogance, whose perpetrators were to suffer the vengeance of the gods and meet a sad end. In the first corner King Haemus and Queen Rhodope of Thrace can be seen. Their excessively high spirits led them to call themselves Zeus and Hera, for which they were turned into high mountains. In the second corner, the ill-fated mother of the Pygmy people, whom Hera defeated, was turned into a crane doomed to fight against her own children. In the third corner there appeared Antigone,

ARACHNE

the charming daughter of King Laomedon of Troy, who so prided herself on her beauty and especially that of her splendid curly hair, that she compared herself to Hera. But the Queen of the Gods turned her tresses into snakes which bit and tormented her, until out of pity Zeus recreated the unfortunate young woman as a stork, which still gleefully crowed about its beauty. Finally, Pallas Athena depicted Kinyras as he wept over the fate of his daughter. Her pride had inflamed the wrath of Hera, who turned the young woman into a flight of stone steps leading up to her temple. Her father threw himself down on to them, covering the hard-hearted marble with his hot tears. Athena had woven all these images into the tapestry, surrounding them with olive leaves.

By contrast, Arachne beguiled her audience of mortal women as she covered her tapestry with images in which she strove to ridicule the gods, especially Zeus, who was represented as a bull, then as an eagle and a swan, then as a lascivious satyr, or transformed into a blazing fire or a shower of gold.

Each image was surrounded by a garland of ivy, sprinkled with flowers. When the artist completed her work, even Pallas Athena herself could not reproach her, even though she was outraged at the images that revealed Arachne's blasphemous lack of respect. In anger she tore the irreverent tapestry apart and struck the haughty young woman three times on the forehead with the weaver's shuttle she still held in her hand. This the unfortunate maiden could not bear. Seized by madness and despair she threw a rope around her neck and hanged herself. She was already swinging in the air when the goddess, stricken by pity, lifted her down from the suffocating noose and said, "Live, but hang, you reckless creature, and may your whole species be thus punished, down to the last grandchild." With these words, the goddess left, having sprinkled a few drops of magic herbs onto Arachne's face. At once, the maiden's hair, nose, and ears disappeared, and she shrank into a tiny, ugly creature. As a spider, to this day, she practices the ancient art, one thread after another.

MIDAS

Greed can be life-threatening:
Dionysus grants King Midas one wish. He asks for everything he touches to turn
to gold and his wish comes true. That gold can be a curse soon becomes apparent when
everything Midas tries to eat or drink is accordingly immediately turned to gold. He begs
Dionysus to save him from certain death and the god frees him from the spell.

Illustrations by Arthur Rackham and Milo Winter

MIDAS

Page 261
"Make it so that everything my body touches turns into glittering gold."

Right
And behold, a green twig from an oak tree turned to gold.

Once upon a time, the mighty Dionysus, the Greek God of Wine, wandered into Asia Minor accompanied by his maenads and satyrs. There he and his entourage strolled across the vine-covered heights of the Tmolus Mountains. But the old drunkard Silenus was missing, left behind having drunk too much wine and fallen asleep. The slumbering elder was found by Phrygian peasants, who garlanded him with flowers and led him to their King Midas. The king himself reverently greeted the friend of the celestial god, receiving him with pleasure and regaling him with festive feasts for ten days and nights. On the eleventh morning, the king brought his guest to the Lydian realm, where he handed him over to Dionysus. Delighted at the return of his old comrade, the god asked the king to select a gift he would like to receive. To which Midas replied, "May I ask, great Dionysus, that everything my body might touch will turn into glittering gold?" The god was saddened at not having been met with a better choice, but he signaled that the wish be fulfilled. Pleased with his covetous gift, Midas hurried away and immediately tried to find whether the promise would stand the test, and behold, a green twig

from an oak tree turned to gold. Then a stone he lifted from the ground became a sparkling gold nugget. He broke the ripe ears of grain from the stalk and reaped gold; fruit he plucked from the tree gleamed like the Apples of the Hesperides. Utterly enchanted, he ran into his palace. His fingers barely touched the doorposts before they glowed like fire; even the water in which he rinsed his hands turned to gold. Beside himself with joy, he ordered the servants to prepare him a delectable meal. Soon the table stood ready, loaded with succulent roast meat and loaves of white bread. He then reached for a loaf and the gift of the goddess Demeter turned as hard as stone; he thrust the meat into his mouth and shimmering metal rattled between his teeth; he took up the goblet to sip some fragrant wine and liquid gold slid down his throat. It then became clear to him what an appalling gift he had asked for; so rich and yet so poor, he cursed his folly. Never again could he appease hunger or thirst; a horrible death was certain. In despair, he beat his forehead with his fist. Horror of horrors! Even his face shone and glistened like gold. Full of fear, he lifted his hands to Heaven and implored, "Have pity, Father Dionysus! Forgive me, a foolhardy sinner, and deliver me from this glittering evil!" Dionysus, the kindly deity, heeded the plea of the repentant fool and broke the spell, then said, "Go to the River Pactolus and follow it to its source in the mountains. There, where bubbling water gushes from the rocks, dip your face into its cool flow to wash away the shining varnish. Thus the guilt will also be borne away with the gold." Midas obeyed the divine command and behold, that very moment, the spell was lifted from him and the power to produce gold poured into the river, which has carried the precious metal in abundance ever since.

From that day on Midas despised all riches. He left his sumptuous palace and happily roamed through woods and meadows in admiration of Pan, God of Nature, whose favorite haunts were mountain caves. At heart, however, the king was still as foolish as ever and soon laid hands on a gift he would never be rid of.

In the Tmolus Mountains, the cloven-footed Pan used to entertain the mountain nymphs by performing his roguish songs on a reed pipe. One day he had the audacity to challenge Apollo himself to a competition. Tmolus, the aged God of the Mountains, his azure hair and temples garlanded with oak leaves,

"Forgive me, a foolhardy sinner, and deliver me from this glittering evil!"

sat on the mountainside to judge the contest, surrounded by charming nymphs and mortal men and women, including King Midas, who had come to listen. Then Pan began to play on his syrinx flute, bringing forth boisterous, rowdy sounds from the instrument. Midas harkened with glee. When Pan finished, Apollo stepped forward in his long, purple robe, his golden locks wreathed with laurels, his ivory lyre in his left hand, his countenance and demeanor full of godlike grandeur. He touched the strings, creating sounds that filled the listeners with rapture and great admiration. And Tmolus, an erudite judge, declared him the victor. While all those present unanimously applauded his decision, Midas could not control his prattling tongue and loudly disputed the verdict, claiming that Pan deserved the prize. Then Apollo stepped imperceptibly towards the ridiculous king and seized him by both ears. With one gentle pull he threw them into the air, and behold, they became pointed and covered themselves with tufts of gray hair. As he could not bear the thought of a human being with such

IT THEN BECAME CLEAR TO HIM WHAT AN APPALLING GIFT HE HAD ASKED FOR; SO RICH AND YET SO POOR, HE CURSED HIS FOLLY.

silly features, in one simple movement the god made the ears flexible at the base. Two long donkey's ears adorned the head of the poor king, who was bitterly ashamed of the humiliating embellishment.

He sought to cover his shame and conceal his embarrassment from the world by wearing a huge turban. But nothing could be hidden from the servant who cut his hair. Having barely caught sight of his master's new adornment, he immediately longed to uncover the secret. But since he did not dare reveal it to another human being, he went to the riverbank where he dug a hole in the ground, into which he whispered what he had discovered. Then he carefully refilled the hole with water and left the spot, reassured. But soon there sprang up a thick forest of reeds which rustled so beautifully when stirred by a gentle breeze, whispering softly but distinctly to each other, "King Midas has donkey's ears!" Thus the secret was divulged.

HYACINTHUS

A god mourns:
Hyacinthus, son of the king of Sparta, is a favorite and lover of Apollo.
While the boy is happily engaged in a throwing contest with the god, a ricocheting
discus strikes him dead. Apollo cannot save Hyacinthus but makes the flower known
as hyacinth bloom every spring as an eternal memorial to the unfortunate youth.

Illustration by Walter Crane

HYACINTHUS

As pale as the stricken one, Apollo came running and gathered the dying boy in his arms.

Hyacinthus was the youngest son of King Amyclas of Laconia. Phoebus Apollo caught sight of the handsome young man and became deeply enamored of him. Indeed, he even considered leading him up to Mount Olympus, so that he would constantly be close by. But sad fate begrudged the mortal such veneration and swept him away in the flower of his youth. Often Apollo would leave behind the sanctity of Delphi and head toward the banks of the River Eurotas near the wall-less city of Sparta, there to delight in the company of his favorite. Forgetting lyre and bow in favor of their jovial games, he saw no harm in taking Hyacinthus hunting amid the rugged heights of the Taygetos Mountains. One day around noon, when the sun cast its burning rays downwards, they shed their attire, anointed their bodies with oil and prepared to throw the discus. Apollo was the first to take up the heavy disk, steadying it with his forearm before hurling it into the heavens with such force that it tore a cloud apart. It took some time for the round lump of ore to fall back to earth. Eager to follow his divine master's example, Hyacinthus leapt forward to grab the disk. But it rebounded from the rugged ground and alas! struck the beautiful child in the face. As pale as the stricken one, Apollo came running and gathered the

dying boy in his arms, immediately attempting to warm his stiffening limbs, wipe the blood from his terrible wounds and apply healing herbs to prevent the departure of his beloved's soul. But it was all in vain! Suddenly, the youth's moribund head drooped downwards like stem of a delicate flower broken in a garden, sinking limply and languidly on to the breast of Apollo, who in turn called him by the most affectionate names, bathing his darling with his falling tears. Oh, how could he call himself a god if he could not die with, or instead of, his dearly beloved? Suddenly, he exclaimed, "No, sweet child, you shall not die entirely. My songs shall sing of you while you, in the guise of a flower, shall proclaim my grief." Thus said Apollo and behold, from the streaming blood that turned the grass red sprang a flower with the somber sheen of Tyrian purple and lily-shaped blooms growing from a single stalk while, written in clear script on every leaf, was the lament of the god, "Ah, woe is me!" Thus, every springtime there appear hyacinths, the flowers named after the god's favorite. And like the young man himself, they die soon afterwards, a symbol of the transitory nature of all Earth's most beautiful things. However, every summer in Laconia, the feast of Hyacinthia was held in honor of Hyacinthus and his celestial friend to mourn the fate of the boy who died too young and to joyously celebrate his deification.

ORPHEUS AND EURYDICE

An opera libretto:
Orpheus, a singer and musician, loses his beloved wife too soon.
He charms flora, fauna, and mortals by singing and playing the lyre. Since the gods
also find his music irresistible, he implores them to return Eurydice to him. They grant
his wish. He is allowed to lead her out of the underworld, but is forbidden to look
back before he has left it. Orpheus, unable to resist temptation, turns around too soon.
Eurydice's shade vanishes for eternity.

Illustration by Edmund Dulac

The unrivaled singer Orpheus was the son of the Thracian king and river god Oeagrus and the muse Calliope. Apollo, the God of Music himself, had made him the gift of a lyre which Orpheus played to accompany the beautiful songs his mother taught him. Birds came through the air, fish swam through water, animals scampered through the forest, and even trees and rocks drew near to listen to such wondrous sounds. His wife was the enchanting naiad, Eurydice, and they loved each other most tenderly. But alas, their happiness was all too short. Scarcely had their joyous wedding songs been sung when early death carried away the radiant young bride. Playing and strolling through the green meadows with her special friends from among the nymphs, the fair Eurydice was bitten on her delicate heel by a poisonous adder lurking hidden in the grass and fell dying into the arms of her terrified playmates. The hills and valleys resounded endlessly with the sobbing of the nymphs, while Orpheus bemoaned his grief in melancholy laments, and the little birds and the wise stags and roe deer mourned with the bereaved spouse. But his pleas and tears did not bring back his lost beloved. He then took an inconceivable decision: he vowed to descend into the gruesome realm of the shadows to incite the saturnine king and queen to restore Eurydice to him. He stepped down through the Tainaron gate to the underworld. There, the shades of the dead hovered above the living, but he strode onwards through the horrors of the netherworld, until he stood before the throne of the pallid Hades and his hard-faced consort. There he seized his lyre and sang to the sweet sound of the strings, "Oh rulers of the subterranean empire, permit me to speak the truth and graciously hear my plea! I am not here driven by curiosity to look upon Tartarus, nor to shackle the three-headed dog. Alas, no! It is because of my wife I approach you. Poisoned by the bite of an adder, my beloved died in the bloom of youth. She was my pride and joy for but a few days. Behold, I sought to bear the immeasurable grief, against which I as a man have long struggled. But love has broken my heart. Without Eurydice I cannot live. So it is here, in these abhorrent halls of death, in the silent desolation of your domain, I implore you, oh terrible, holy gods of death, give my dear wife back to me. Set her free and once more restore to her the life that withered all too soon! But if this cannot be, take me also to rest with the dead, for I shall never return to the living without her." Behold, the bloodless shades heard and wept. Ill-fated Tantalus no longer pursued the water as it slipped beyond reach, Ixion's wheel ceased to hurtle around, the daughters of Danaus abandoned their futile toils and leaned listening against the urn, and even Sisyphus forgot his tribulations and sat upon the implacable rock to hear the plaintive song. Then, or so it is said, tears even ran down the cheeks of the redoubtable Furies, and for the first time, the regal rulers themselves were moved with compassion. Persephone summoned the soul of Eurydice, who approached with uncertain steps. "Take her with you," said the queen of the dead, "but beware, only if you refrain from casting even a simple glance at her as she walks behind you, until you have passed through the gate to the underworld. For if you look at her too soon our generosity will be withdrawn."

Silently and speedily the couple continued through the darkness, surrounded by the foreboding of the night. Then Orpheus was seized by inexpressible longing to hear the breathing of his beloved or the rustle of her garments, but he was encircled by

SILENTLY AND SPEEDILY THE COUPLE CONTINUED THROUGH THE DARKNESS, SURROUNDED BY THE FOREBODING OF THE NIGHT.

Page 269
Overwhelmed by fear and love, unable to control himself, he dared to throw a fleeting glance at the one for whom he had longed.

silence, deathly silence. Overwhelmed by fear and love, unable to control himself, he dared to throw a fleeting glance at the one for whom he had longed. Oh, such torment! She drifted back into the unspeakable depths, her sad eyes fixed upon him, full of tenderness. In desperation he stretched his arms towards her as she vanished. But all in vain! For the second time she had died without even a whimper – could she have lamented being so deeply loved? Already she had almost disappeared from view. "Farewell, farewell!" These words resounded from afar. At first, Orpheus stood rigid with grief and desperation before tumbling back into the dark chasms; but now Charon stood in his way, refusing to ferry him across the black River Styx. For seven days and nights the wretched mortal sat there, shedding countless tears, pleading to the gods of the underworld for mercy, but they remained implacable, refusing to relent for a second time. Grief-stricken, he returned to the world above to live all alone in Thrace's tranquil mountain forest. There he remained in solitude for three years, avoiding all human society. The sight of women was loathsome to him, for it caused the image of his beloved to return and hover around him. All his sighs and songs were devoted to her as, in her memory, he wrung sweet, plaintive sounds from his lyre.

One day, the divine singer sat on a green, unshaded hill and began his song. Soon, the forest was in motion, the mighty trees moving ever closer until he was shaded by their branches. Then came the creatures of the forest to hear him, while merry woodland birds circled above as they listened to these wonderful sounds. Then swarms of Thracian maenads came careering across the mountains, celebrating the famous feast in honor of Dionysus. They loathed the singer who, since the death of his wife, had scorned all women. "Behold the one who reviles us!" screamed the first of the furious women, and in a flash they rushed ferociously upon him, attacking him with stones and wands of fennel. For a long time the loyal animals protected their beloved singer, but as his melodious notes were gradually drowned out by the ranting and raving of the frenzied women, they fled terrified into the woodland undergrowth. Then one of the stones struck the unfortunate singer in the temple. He collapsed, bleeding, onto the green grass. Alas! Through the mouth that delivered many a song, his soul skimmed past the rocks and the mountain wilderness and fled away.

Barely had the murderous mob disappeared when the birds flew past, weeping as they sadly approached the cliffs and creatures of the natural world. The nymphs of the springs and trees hastened together, clothed in black, and together they mourned Orpheus as they buried his mutilated limbs.

But his head and lyre were caught up by the strengthening flow of the River Hebros and carried midstream. Still an even sweeter lament sounded from the strings and from the lifeless tongue, while the riverbanks responded with melancholy echoes. Thus the current carried the head and lyre of Orpheus out to sea and to the shore of the island of Lesbos, whose pious inhabitants rescued both. The head they buried and the lyre they hung in a temple. It is because of this that the island has produced such splendid poets and singers, and even nightingales have sung more sweetly than elsewhere so as to honor the grave of the divine Orpheus. Even so, his soul drifted down to the shadowlands. There he was reunited with his beloved and there they dwelt together, blissfully entwined in the Elysian Fields, united for all eternity.

CEYX
AND HALCYONE

Apart forever, together for eternity:
Ceyx wants to travel to the oracle of Apollo in Asia Minor.
His wife, Halcyone, fears he might die. Ceyx indeed drowns at sea.
When Halcyone learns of her husband's death in a dream, she wants to throw
herself into the waves. The gods, however, take pity on them and
transform them both into kingfishers so they can always live as lovers.

Illustration by Helen Stratton

CEYX AND HALCYONE

Ceyx, son of the evening star and the nymph Philonis, was so alarmed by ominous prophesies that he decided to journey across the sea to Claros in Asia Minor, where there stood a famous oracle of Apollo. He was bound by the deepest love to his loyal wife Halcyone, daughter of the wind god Aeolus. She attempted to dissuade him from his intentions with complaints and gentle reproaches, or at least to persuade him to take her with him on the perilous journey. Although in his innermost heart he was touched by her words and tears, he did not depart from his plan and attempted to console her. "Long though any delay may be for both of us," he said, "I swear by my radiant father that I shall return before the second orbit of the moon." Then he prepared the vessel with everything needed on the voyage and launched it into the sea. On his departure, Halcyone could not hide her unspeakable pain. "Farewell" was all she could say before sinking senseless to the shore. Ceyx would have liked to stay longer, but scarcely had the young oarsmen set the ship underway than the sea began to seethe. No longer could he linger and so he hurried on board. When Halcyone lifted her eyes wet with tears, she saw her beloved husband standing in the stern of the ship, waving her a final farewell. She did likewise until the ship's white sail disappeared from view. Returning to her lonely house, she took to her bed bewailing her husband's departure.

Meanwhile he sailed further on to the high seas. A gentle wind began to blow, the oars were withdrawn, and a favorable breeze swelled the sails. The voyage had already reached halfway and the ship was sailing at equal distance from both shores when behold, towards evening the fearsome Euros, God of the East Wind, blasted from the south, crowning the waves with white foam and raising a violent storm. "Lower the topsails!" bellowed the helmsman. "Furl all the sails tight to the yards!" But his words were left unheard against the howl of the wind and the thunder of the waves. Now each man hurried to do what he judged best: one pulled in the oars, another plugged the oar ports. Here the sails were torn away, there the inflowing floodwater was scooped back out into the sea. Amid this confusion the wind blew at ever-increasing speed, churning up the ocean bed. The ship's captain gave up all hope, admitting that he no longer knew what he should order his men to do, or forbid them from doing. Now black masses of cloud enveloped the ether, leaving all but the darkness of night, lit only by juddering bolts of lightning. Thunder crashed, one strike after another, the waves billowed ever higher, deluging the ship with brine. Crewmen screamed out loud. Timbers were threatening to split when a colossal wave plunged into the hold. Many sailors were in despair: one wept; another stood motionless, as if turned to stone; another expressed envy of those fortunately laid to rest on land; another called upon the gods to rescue him, in vain raising his arms to the invisible sky; one recalled his loved ones at home, his aged father, his gentle wife, his thriving children. Ceyx thought only of Halcyone, repeating her name again and again. While in his heart he longed to be with her, he was glad that she was far away. Oh, how deep were his desires to return to the shores of home and see her face again. He stretched his dying hands to the land where she lived but in the impenetrable darkness he did not know which way to turn. Then the shattered mast came crashing down on to the wheel. The wave stood up straight like a huntress proud of her kill as the vessel sank to the seabed. Many of the sailors were caught up in the whirlpool and returned lifeless to the surface of the water. Ceyx held a paltry piece of wood in the hand that once held his scepter, calling "Halcyone!" Again he called "Halcyone" as his weary arm grew weaker. "Halcyone," he sighed as the waves crashed above his head; and the last word from the lips of the drowning man was "Halcyone." His celestial father, who was not permitted to leave the firmament, hid his face in black clouds so as not to see his beloved son die.

Meanwhile, unaware of the disaster, Halcyone counted down the days and nights before her dear husband's homecoming. She had already set out the garments they both would wear, and she did not forget to make sacrifices to the gods, especially Hera, pleading for her to bring her beloved spouse home and in good health. Hera watched in sorrow and called upon Iris, the messenger of the gods, saying, "Hurry to the court of the god of sleep. Bid him send the waiting Halcyone a dream in the shape of the departed Ceyx, so that he himself can tell her of his death." Immediately Iris donned her cloak of many colors and

CEYX AND HALCYONE

She walked out onto the seashore to visit the place from where she had bidden her beloved a final farewell.

hurried along the sparkling rainbow to the god's cliff dwelling. Far away on the western edge of the earth's disk, there stood a mountain from where the god of sleep ruled. Never did Helios's rays stream in; a dark mist rose from the floor, enveloping everything in twilight.

No sound, neither the barking of dogs nor human speech disturbed the never-ending stillness. Only a gentle stream flowed with a soporific murmur around the entrance to the cave; on its banks there sprang up countless fragrant herbs, from which the night distilled calming juices. The door of the dwelling stood open, with no creaking hinges. Deep inside the innermost chamber stood an ebony couch covered with sumptuous pillows. There the god rested his weary limbs while around him lay his own offspring – dreams in many shapes and forms.

As Iris entered the grotto, the glitter of her garments immediately illuminated the entire house. The god of sleep drearily raised his eyes, falling back to sleep again and again, nodding his head as if drunk, then leaning on his arm while he composed himself. "What kind of message do you bring, sparkling Iris?" he finally asked. The gods' messenger quickly fulfilled her duty and immediately hurried back to Olympus, for she could no longer endure the stupefying scent that penetrated the whole cave. Then, from his flock of a thousand children, the god of sleep chose Morpheus to carry out the divine command, above all because of his ability to imitate any mortal in gait and voice, shape and face. The old god sank back, once more burying his head in the soft pillow while Morpheus flew through the night on silent wings. Leaning over the bed of the slumbering Halcyone, he took on the form of the drowned Ceyx. Deathly pale, naked with dripping hair and beard, tears streaming down his cheeks, he asked, "Do you, poor woman, still recognize your Ceyx, or has death transformed my features? You believe you

know me! Alas, I am not Ceyx. No, I am but his ghost. I am dead, beloved. My dead body lies adrift in the Aegean Sea, where the storm wrecked our ship. Therefore, dress in widow's weeds and shed tears for me, for I cannot be sent unmourned into the sorrowful underworld." Trembling and awakened by her own sobs, the widow stretched her arms towards him. "Oh, stay! Why must you flee from me?" She cried as the vision disappeared, "Take me with you!" As she gradually reawakened, she struck at her face, tore at her golden curls, and ripped her robe, screaming in unending misery.

With the approach of morning, she walked out on to the seashore to visit the place from where she had bidden her beloved a final farewell. As she looked with tearful eyes into the blue distance, far away from the shore there suddenly appeared what seemed to be a human body. The closer it was washed by the waves, the more uncertain her feelings became. But then it floated close to land. "It is he!" screamed the ill-fated woman, her hands outstretched towards the body of her dear husband. "So you have returned to me, you poor, sad creature. Now I shall return to you." As she sought to throw herself into the sea, behold, wings lifted her, wistfully wailing, into the air and she fluttered like a bird close to the water and soared, sobbing, onto her dead spouse's breast. And was it not true that he could feel the presence of his loyal wife? Indeed he could, for the gods in their mercy changed him into a different creature, thereby giving him a new life. Transformed into kingfishers, the two spouses still remain faithful to their old, tender love and continue to live inseparably side by side. Every year in midwinter, seven calm, windless days return, when Halcyone sits brooding in a floating nest on the smooth, mirror-like surface of the sea. For at this time her father Aeolus keeps the winds at home so as to grant his grandchildren peace and protection.

APPENDIX

C·E·BROCK

ARTIST BIOGRAPHIES

Constance N. Baikie
(dates unknown)

Born in Glasgow, Constance N. Baikie (born Turner-Smith) is known only through the works written in the fields of ancient history and archaeology by her husband, James Baikie (1866–1931), a Scottish writer, university professor, and Egyptologist. James Baikie's books addressed a youthful readership, and Constance's illustrations made her husband's writings come vividly alive for young readers. His best-known works include titles such as *Ancient Egypt* (1916), *Ancient Greece* (1924), *Ancient Crete* (1924) and *Ancient Rome* (1925). The illustration in this book of Daedalus and his son (p. 59) was taken from Baikie's *Ancient Greece*.

Other books written by James Baikie and featuring illustrations by his wife are *The Ancient East and its Story* (1910), *Egyptian Papyri and Papyrus-hunting* (1925), and *Wonder Tales of the Ancient World* (1915).

Charles Edmund Brock
(1870–1938)

Charles Edmund Brock was the eldest of four brothers, all of whom were artists. Like his brother Henry, who was five years younger, Charles Edmund was a successful and well-known book illustrator. He was also a celebrated landscape, portrait, and genre painter whose fame was at its zenith in the first third of the twentieth century. His career began with drawings in India ink. Stylistically revealing the influence of Hugh Thomson, they illustrated Thomas Hood's comical poems, which were still extremely popular in the late nineteenth century. Twenty-three at the time, Charles Edmund Brock made such a strong impression with those drawings that a commission to illustrate Swift's *Gulliver's Travels* (1894) immediately followed. His illustrations for Jane Austen's *Pride and Prejudice* (1895) were even more of a hit. He subsequently produced a vast number of illustrations for works by distinguished nineteenth-century authors. Prime examples of his illustrations were for classics of English and Scottish literature by Charles Dickens, William Makepeace Thackeray, and Robert Louis Stevenson.

The brothers' prolific output can be attributed in part to the very well-equipped studio they shared. Props they owned included antique furniture and a private collection of historic costumes, which enabled them to produce an impressively large number of illustrations in a short amount of time for books, illustrated weeklies, newspapers, and the like. The brothers were well organized and executed commissions promptly for *Punch*, *Cassell's Children's Annual*, *Cassell's Family Magazine* and *The Graphic*. And the range of subject matter and motifs addressed by Charles Edmund Brock was extremely broad – to which the illustrations he did with his brother, Henry Matthew Brock, for *Through the Bible* by Theodora Wilson give eloquent testimony.

The colored illustrations reproduced here (pp. 61, 140, 164, 176, 278, 319) exemplify Charles Edmund Brock's style. They are from Eva March Tappan's *Stories from the Classics*, published in 1907 as the third volume of *The Children's Hour*, the ten-volume series she edited. Although the Brock brothers had a family style, Charles Edmund was widely regarded as a perfectionist. His linework and expression were viewed as particularly sensitive and harmonious; his execution was always extremely precise and finer and more accurate than that of his brother, Henry Matthew Brock. In these watercolors, the descriptive powers of Charles Edmund Brock's palette along with his linework underscores the expressivity of his figures. So dynamic are their facial expressions and gestures that the characters depicted almost seem to be in motion.

Page 276
Virginia Frances Sterrett
Having overpowered the Minotaur and found his way from the heart of the labyrinth, Theseus returns to Ariadne, 1921

Left
Charles Edmund Brock
A dolphin miraculously carries Arion and his lyre to safety after he was kidnapped by pirates, 1907

Henry Matthew Brock
(1875–1960)

Although Charles Edmund Brock made his name as the more con-
scientious and perfectionist of the two brothers, his younger brother,
Henry Matthew, was also noteworthy for his creative drive and ability
to turn a motif into a picture. A fellow painter, Alfred Bestall, observed
this while adding skeptically that Henry Matthew Brock had indeed
made impressive increases in productivity over the years, but had done
so by losing sight of the need for a distinctively individual artistic signature. Henry Matthew survived his elder brother by more than two
decades, remaining extremely prolific until he went blind in 1950. After
training at the Cambridge School of Art, Henry Matthew Brock, like
his brother, illustrated numerous children's books while still a young
man, including *Robin Hood and the Men of Greenwood* (in collaboration with Walter Crane) as well as English classics of the Victorian
and Edwardian eras, on which he also worked with jointly his brother.
Henry Matthew Brock greatly esteemed the work of his colleagues
such as Arthur Rackham, Edmund Dulac, and Sir William Russell Flint,
all of them distinguished exponents of the European art of book
illustration.

Now Henry Matthew Brock's illustrations from more than
2,000 publications can be seen along with work by his brothers
Charles Edmund and Richard Henry in the H. M. Brock Collection
at the University of Reading in England.

Zdeněk Burian
(1905–1981)

Zdeněk Burian was born in the Moravian town of Kopřivnice,
Austria-Hungary, on 11 February 1905. His talent as a draftsman was
recognized and fostered while he was still a young boy. He entered the
Prague Academy of Fine Arts at fourteen but left the institute quite
soon without taking a diploma to earn a precarious livelihood as a day
laborer. During that early period Burian spent a great deal of time working outdoors, which was highly beneficial to the studies of nature he
was doing as a self-taught artist. He also taught himself a range of drawing and painting techniques. In 1921 his first illustrations were published
in *Dobrodružství Davida Balfoura* (*Kidnapped: Being Memoirs of the
Adventures of David Balfour in the Year 1751*) by Robert Louis Stevenson.

Burian was not only an accomplished painter but also worked quickly, a skill of great interest to publishers. After commissions for various
journals and periodicals, by the 1930s he was able to support his family
– he had married in 1927 – as a book illustrator. Numerous adventure
and science fiction classics by Rudyard Kipling, Jules Verne, and even
Edgar Rice Burroughs were published with illustrations by Burian.
The work reproduced here also showcases Burian's skills. The dramatic
situation he created by skillfully deploying composition, palette, and
differences in scale is in stark contrast to the gaping stupidity which is
writ large on Cyclops's face (p. 192).

Burian was not only a distinguished illustrator of books for children
and adolescents. He was also known for the paleontological reconstruc-
tion drawings on which he collaborated with leading paleontologists of
his day, continuing to work in this field until he died in 1981. Published
in many books and scientific journals, they still play a major role in
shaping our perception of prehistoric natural phenomena. *The Lost
Worlds of Zdeněk Burian*, edited by Judith Schalansky in 2013, provides
an excellent overview of the body of work produced by an illustrator
whose importance cannot be overstated.

Zdeněk Burian
*Zeus casts down his lightning bolts
to wreck the ship of Odysseus and
his companions,* 1934

Right
Walter Crane
Cradling Medusa's head and aided by
a helmet of invisibility, Perseus evades
the remaining Gorgons, 1893

Walter Crane
(1845–1915)

Born in Liverpool in 1845, the English artist and illustrator Walter Crane continued to influence generations of book illustrators with his innovative children's books well into the twentieth century. A leading exponent of the Arts and Crafts movement, he set new standards in book design.

Like most members of that movement, Crane was also very active politically. In line with his commitment to the international Socialist movement, he viewed his book illustrations as an important contribution to public education. The Arts and Crafts movement had taken up the cause of making all areas of life beautiful for everyone. It used a holistic approach which entailed viewing life and art as a complete work of art. This included all modes of expression related to design, specifically the decorative arts.

A member of the Socialist League since 1885, Crane was interested not only in painting and sculpture but in all art forms, including stained-glass windows, wallpaper, and tapestries as well as textile design. Both as an illustrator and a painter, Crane drew on a wide variety of sources for inspiration, such as medieval manuscript illumination, Japanese colored woodcuts, and early Italian Renaissance painting as well as the Pre-Raphaelites.

Crane's career began with an apprenticeship to the celebrated wood-engraver William James Linton. By the age of twenty, Crane had collaborated with Edmund Evans, a masterly specialist in the then new full-color woodblock printing process, to produce his first books of children's song and verse. The success of Crane's children's books was chiefly due to high quality standards and affordable pricing.

The children's books Crane illustrated between 1865 and 1875 earned the genre unprecedented appreciation. He represented an entire generation of artists who developed new ideas of book design and, thanks to the great advances made in printing in England, also had the opportunity to put those ideas into practice. A few more remarkable works of Crane's warrant further attention, including his illustrations for the Oscar Wilde collection of children's stories entitled *The Happy Prince and Other Tales* (1888) and his much lauded illustrations for Edmund Spenser's epic poem *The Faerie Queene* (1895–1897), not to mention his illustrations from Greek mythology, which reveal the depth of his teeming imagination by confronting readers not only with great mythic heroes and numinous mortals such as Pandora (pp. 36, 282), the first woman, but also showing them touching figures such as the elderly lovers Philemon and Baucis (p. 251) and Odysseus as a beggar (p. 234).

Above
Walter Crane
The evils of the world spill out from
Pandora's box, 1893

Edmund Dulac
(1882–1953)

Edmund Dulac's signature as a designer and stylist is remarkable and might at first glance seem to differ markedly from that of English contemporaries. Sensitive, even occasionally exuberant, handling of color is a pivotal feature of his brilliantly expressive approach to his art. Born in Toulouse in 1882, Dulac developed a keen interest in Oriental art, especially Persian miniatures, which shaped his early work. A prolific designer, caricaturist, painter, and illustrator, Edmund Dulac moved to London in 1905 after desultory university studies in Toulouse and three years' training at the art academy there. His first commissions in London were for *The Pall Mall Magazine*, followed by fifty watercolors to illustrate *Stories from the Arabian Nights* (1907). A year later Hodder & Stoughton published an edition of *The Tempest* illustrated with forty Dulac watercolors. After his foray into Shakespeare, Dulac returned to his early love, Orientalism, for an illustrated edition of *The Rubáiyát of Omar Khayyám*, before turning to great American Gothic writers with an illustrated edition of Edgar Allan Poe's poems in 1912 and Nathaniel Hawthorne's *Tanglewood Tales* in a 1918 edition.

However, Dulac was not only famous for his drawings, watercolors, and paintings. The range of his work is vast and diverse, also encompassing both theater masks and costumes and interior design, such as the smoking room he designed for the transatlantic liner RMS *Empress of Britain*. He was also a prolific designer of banknotes and postage stamps.

A noted *bon vivant*, Dulac was not only a gourmet cook but also engaged enthusiastically with Flamenco dancing, a passion that would ultimately ensure he "died happy" of a heart attack at seventy after overindulging in a Flamenco session.

The art critic Ann Conolly Hughey identified four underlying features characteristic of Dulac's work: sensational colorism, stunning design, Orientalism, and humor. These four defining features are also immediately recognizable in the illustrations of his that are reproduced here.

Herbert Granville Fell
With the task completed, Perseus brandishes the Gorgon's head at his wedding feast, 1910

Herbert Granville Fell
(1872–1951)

Born in London in 1872, Herbert Granville Fell began his career with academic training at the Heatherley School of Fine Art in London. Afterwards he studied art in Paris and Brussels as well as various academies in Germany. Although he at first attracted attention as an illustrator, he soon felt an urge to try his hand at other, albeit related, occupations. He was not long in expanding his range of activities to include art criticism.

Fell also successfully edited a number of upmarket art and women's magazines: he was editor of *The Connoisseur* for sixteen years until he died in 1951; he edited *The Strand Magazine* from 1910 until 1912; he also edited popular women's magazines, such as *The Ladies Field*, which he headed for twelve years (1907–1919), and *The Woman at Home* (1924–1928).

He evidently had organizational and managerial skills. He was only twenty-eight when he was appointed in 1900 to the new Royal Albert Memorial College in Exeter as its first director. The College was a merger of the School of Science and the School of Art, where he was head of the drawing, painting, and design departments.

His sideline, illustrations for various publications between the mid-1890s and the mid-1910s, also attracted a great deal of attention and acclaim. Works he illustrated during that period include *The History of Ali Baba and the Forty Thieves* (1895) and *The Book of Dragons* (1901). Apart from illustrations for *Wagner Heroes* by Constance Maud, published in 1895, illustrations for books from the Bible represented a focal point of his work: the Book of Job was published in 1896 and *The Song of Salomon* in 1897. Fell also addressed Greek historiography adapted for child readers, illustrating *Wonder Stories from Herodotus* in 1900. The illustrations of Fell's reproduced here (pp. 284, 321) came from *A Wonder-Book and Tanglewood Tales* (1910), a children's classic by Nathaniel Hawthorne that ran to numerous editions. The drawing proves what art critics still confirm: Fell, a versatile prodigy, is not in the slightest overshadowed by distinguished contemporaries in his field. After all, the influence of Edward Burne-Jones (pp. 4, 23) and Walter Crane, Art nouveau and Jugendstil can be seen in Fell's work, like that of so many of his fellow illustrators when illustration was at its zenith as an artform. Thus, we can see echoes of the art he had become familiar with when he spent all those years studying art in Brussels, Paris, and Germany.

William Russell Flint
*After the killing of the suitors, Odysseus
and Penelope are reunited at last,* 1924

John Flaxman
(1755–1826)

The second son of a molder of plaster casts, John Flaxman not only inherited his father's name, but evidently his great artistic talent as well. Born in York, the younger Flaxman died in London at the age of seventy-one after an impressive career. A sickly child with a hunchback, Flaxman was a self-taught artist who learned to read and draw from his father. Flaxman followed in his father's footsteps, at first making tombstones. To earn a secure livelihood, at the age of twenty he became an employee at the pottery run by Thomas Bentley and Josiah Wedgwood in 1775 and remained there for twelve years. Financial support from Wedgwood also later enabled Flaxman to spend time in Italy. Other distinguished artist friends and supporters of Flaxman's were William Blake, with whom Flaxman was friends all his life, as well as Thomas Stothard and George Romney. As a child Flaxman was enthusiastic about ancient Greek and Roman art. By the time he was twelve years old he was receiving commissions for drawings and plaster casts, which were also exhibited. Yet he had to wait a long time before he was able to study ancient art on site. At the age of thirty-two he finally left for a grand tour of Italy, where he spent most of his time in Rome. Although he had initially planned to stay two years in Italy, he ended up staying for seven (1787–1794). The years in Italy were a highly productive period in his life, when he also did the outline drawings illustrating the *Iliad* (pp. 161, 167, 169) and the *Odyssey* (pp. 191, 208, 213) reproduced in this book, with which he established an international reputation. Pure line drawings, they are harmonious and elegant with movement rendered so convincingly and body proportions so consistently that Flaxman deserves to be viewed as a groundbreaking draftsman and one of the finest masters of line of the eighteenth and nineteenth centuries. Of all artists, he perhaps came closest to translating Johann Joachim Winckelmann's ideal of noble simplicity and quiet grandeur to his chosen medium. Some may argue that neo-Classical art increasingly exaggerated Enlightenment ideals to transmogrify them into timeless beauty. Unsurprisingly, however, the Romantic art critic August Wilhelm Schlegel went into transports of delight over Flaxman's dexterous linework and exclaimed in wonder about the English artist's illustrations from his Roman period "that so much Soul can dwell in so few and so delicate lines."

The drawings reproduced here are affecting and their beauty is captivating. Take time to linger over them and enjoy them.

William Russell Flint
(1880–1969)

Born in Edinburgh in 1880, Sir William Russell Flint received a broad-based education, at first in Portobello, then in Edinburgh at Daniel Stewart's College, followed by a six-year apprenticeship as a lithographic draftsman. He took evening courses on the side taught by the Scottish painter Charles D. Hodder. Flint afterwards traveled in the Netherlands and Italy for study purposes. He also took courses at the Hammersmith School of Art and was instructed in watercolor techniques at Thomas Heatherley's school.

From 1903 until 1907 Flint was employed as an illustrator for *The Illustrated London News* – the first weekly in the world of its kind – before earning a reputation as a watercolorist and book illustrator. His work can be admired in the 1907 edition of H. Rider Haggard's *King Solomon's Mines*, W. S. Gilbert's collection of four opera librettos published as *Savoy Operas* (1909), Thomas Malory's *Le Morte d'Arthur* (1910/11) and in a 1912 reissue of Geoffrey Chaucer's *Canterbury Tales*. In 1912 Flint was awarded a silver medal at the Paris Salon.

After serving as a naval officer in World War I, Flint returned to painting, becoming one of the most respected landscape artists of his generation. He showed work regularly at the Royal Academy and was elected president of the Royal Society of Painters in Water Color in 1936. Knighted in 1947 for services to art, Flint remained active as an artist for the rest of his life, dying in London on 30 December 1969.

Some of the illustrations reproduced here were taken from the first edition (1912) of Charles Kingsley's *The Heroes, or, Greek Fairy Tales for My Children*. Although Flint might seem to have cared little about characterizing figures as individuals, he is adept at capturing the aesthetic qualities of the scenes from literature he is illustrating. Some examples: the outlines of Danae's body shimmering softly through her robes (p. 49); the sinuous figure of Medea as she hands Theseus the cup of poison as well as the intricate detailing of the setting, such as the mosaic in the background and the bedstead in the foreground (pp. 126/27); the dramatic heightening of Theseus subduing the Minotaur (p. 129), which Flint has staged by thrusting the combatants into a triangular composition aslant the picture plane, and, of course, the superb modelling of the anatomically perfect bodies in this watercolor. All these qualities make clear why Flint is regarded as a true master of the exacting technique of painting in watercolors.

ARTIST BIOGRAPHIES

Henry Justice Ford
(1860–1941)

Born in London in 1860, Henry Justice Ford was the son of Katherine Mary Justice and William Augustus Ford, a lawyer who was better known as a cricketer. After achieving a first-class degree in the Classical Tripos (Latin, Greek, ancient history) at Clare College, Cambridge, Ford went on to train in art at the Slade School of Fine Art in London and Herkomer's Art School in Bushey, Herts. By 1892 he was able to begin showing his history paintings and landscapes at the Royal Academy of Arts.

Ford became famous for his collaboration as an illustrator with Andrew Lang, a Scottish man of letters who traveled extensively throughout Europe to collect fairy tales and folklore, which he published in twenty-five volumes as the *Fairy Books* (1889–1913), all of them illustrated by Henry Justice Ford. Numerous elements of those illustrations were also used in the *Tales of Troy and Greece* (1907) as recounted by Andrew Lang, from which some of the illustrations reproduced here have been taken. Ford was an expert at depicting mythic beasts and monsters, such as Scylla. By contrast, let us recall the scene in which Paris, son of the king of Troy, is gravely wounded by a poisoned arrow and implores Oenone for an antidote although he had once abandoned her for Helen of Troy (p. 171). Here the nymph is stylized in such a way that she is, from the aesthetic standpoint, reminiscent of the female figure type made famous by Edward Burne-Jones, the "last of the Pre-Raphaelites" and a friend of Ford's. However, the pictorial invention is distinctively Ford's, in line with the artist's approach to rendering scenes from literary templates. This is shown in the figural composition, which is centered on Paris's outstretched left arm and bandaged hand. Oenone's left hand, with which she gathers the folds of her dress, rests, descriptively rather than fortuitously, on her pubic mound. Oenone will refuse her unfaithful lover's last wish although she will later regret it. And her expression reveals conflicting emotions – superb narrative illustration with more than a hint of psychological depth.

Ford spent some of his last years in Dorset at Dunshay Manor, an estate owned by George Spencer Watson, a friend and colleague, and then at Langton Matravers on the isle of Purbeck. Ultimately, he moved north, dying at Mickleover in Derby, little more than six miles from Repton, his old school.

Clément Gontier
(1876–1918)

Clément Gontier was born in Lavaur, a small town nearly 25 miles northeast of Toulouse, on May 15, 1876. His father was a wheelwright and his mother a housewife. This was a humble background that did not make him seem predestined for a career in painting. Overcoming that disadvantage, he succeeded in being admitted to the École des beaux-arts in Toulouse. After his studies there he went to Paris, where he continued to study painting under the tutelage of the celebrated history painter Jean-Paul Laurens. In 1900 Gontier became a pupil of the painter and etcher Jean-Joseph Benjamin-Constant.

Gontier's career began with the competition for the Prix de Rome in 1901. He was awarded second prize for his *Christ guérissant les malades* (*Christ Healing the Sick*, Musée du Pays Vaurais, Lavaur), which failed to secure him the grant he needed for a sojourn at the French Academy in Rome, but did garner favorable notice in the Paris press. History painting played a large role in Gontier's work, although he was unable to target a wider public with it over the long term and could not earn a living from history painting alone. Hence Gontier was forced to turn to more lucrative genres. In 1904 he was awarded third prize at the Salon des Artistes Français for *La vertu domestique* (*Domestic Virtue*), a genre scene. His Impressionist flower still lifes were also attuned to changes in taste and were universally popular.

Gontier is only known as an illustrator for the twenty-four color plates he did for a French edition of the *Iliad* that was published in 1911. Here the impressive qualities that meet the eye are his assured linework and the bold palette he used in his *Abduction of Helen from Cythera* (p. 145).

After serving at the front in World War I, Gontier died of the Spanish flu in a military hospital in Castres in 1918.

Henry Justice Ford
Theseus finds the Minotaur at the center of Daedalus's labyrinth and stalks him from behind with weapons drawn, 1907

Merlyn Mann
(active 1910–1937)

The autobiography of M. M. Kaye, the British children's author, describes Merlyn Mann as a young illustrator gifted with such a distinctive style that she would go on to greatness.

Merlyn Mann was one of many artists to illustrate Nathaniel Hawthorne's popularizing accounts of the Greek myths. *A Wonder-Book and Tanglewood Tales*, published by J. M. Dent & Sons, combines Hawthorne's collected myths for children. The 1937 edition includes four color plates and eight full-page black-and-white illustrations by Mann, one of which is reproduced in the present book (p. 79). Jason is depicted accomplishing the second task he was set by King Aeetes. The scene is set after Jason sows the dragon's teeth in a grove sacred to Ares, and armed soldiers are shown springing up from the ground and attacking one other.

Mann also illustrated *The Best Poems of 1934* (1934), an anthology edited by Thomas Moult and published by Jonathan Cape.

Fortunino Matania
(1881–1963)

Born in Naples in 1881, Fortunino Matania was the son of the painter and illustrator Edoardo Matania and lost no time in following in his father's footsteps. Fortunio Matania was only fourteen when his first book illustration was published. After studying art in Paris, Milan, and London, and serving in the army in Italy, Matania returned to London in 1902, remaining there for most of his life. He died in 1963. In London he was on the staff at *The Sphere*, an illustrated weekly for which he was a war correspondent during World War I. Hundreds of detailed, realistic watercolors and drawings document events at and behind the front. Based on his own and others' experience, they evoke the horrors of war unretouched. Matania was again behind the lines during World War II, prolifically furnishing well-known British and American papers and journals with memorable illustrations, which were often gruesomely realistic yet untainted with defeatism.

A specialist in historical painting of all kinds, Matania also addressed numerous motifs from ancient history and literature, as exemplified by the gouache reproduced here, which is captioned *Helen of Troy Watching the Battle between Menelaus and Paris before the Walls of Troy* (pp. 148/49). Apart from Helen and two serving maids, we see King Priam seated on his throne, two of the "oldest and wisest Trojan elders" and, in the background, the Achaeans and Trojans ready for battle. Helen is the dominant figure in this detailed, subtly colored, and exquisitely composed scene, so much so that the action central to the plot, the battle of which she is the cause, has been left out altogether – a brilliant sleight of hand freeing Matania to focus on what seems to have mattered most to him: Helen's legendary beauty.

Newell Convers Wyeth
On Mount Parnassus, Odysseus prepares to kill the boar as it wounds him at the knee, 1929

ARTIST BIOGRAPHIES

Willy Pogany
(1882–1955)

Willy Pogany was born in Szeged, Austria-Hungary, on August 24, 1882, and spent his early childhood there. The family later moved to Budapest where Pogany enrolled as an engineering student but dropped out after only a year to devote himself from then on to what he had loved doing most since childhood: drawing and painting. He briefly attended art academies in Budapest and later in Munich before going on to Paris for two years. There he managed to sell work for the first time: to *Le Rire*, a satirical magazine with a substantial focus on the arts, although he barely managed to eke out a meager existence. Moving on to London, he only meant to stay there briefly before emigrating to the U.S. Caught up in the surging demand for book illustrations sparked off by the 1905 publication of the Washington Irving tale *Rip van Winkle* illustrated with Arthur Rackham drawings, Pogany began to receive quite large commissions as an illustrator in London. Designing the entire book production – text and illustrations – of Samuel Taylor Coleridge's long poem *The Rime of the Ancient Mariner* in a 1910 edition represented a breakthrough that brought him acclaim from a broader public.

In 1914 Pogany finally made it to New York and soon his illustrations were adorning the covers of prestigious journals and magazines (including *Metropolitan Magazine*, *Harper's Weekly*, *American Weekly* and *Theatre Magazine*). From 1917 until 1921 he worked as a stage set and costume designer for the Metropolitan Opera. In 1922 he was commissioned to create a mural for the children's theater endowed by August Heckscher in New York. Pogany spent the 1930s and 1940s in Hollywood, where he worked as art director for several film studios. He returned to the East Coast to spend his last years in New York, where he died in 1955.

His pen drawings are still highly regarded. Two of them are reproduced here from *The Golden Fleece and the Heroes who lived before Achilles*, published in 1921 (pp. 74, 75).

Arthur Rackham
In a land of plenty, and before Pandora has opened the box, children frolic in an apple tree, 1922

Arthur Rackham
(1867–1939)

By the early twentieth century Arthur Rackham was a successful illustrator, a darling of the critics, and adored by a legion of devoted fans. His professional breakthrough came in 1900 with the publication of the *Fairy Tales of the Brothers Grimm*, which ran to numerous revised editions over the years. In 1909 it was reissued with new illustrations along with an edition of Swift's *Gulliver's Travels*, also illustrated by Rackham. By then Rackham's status as the paramount book illustrator of his generation in the English-speaking countries was uncontested and he was already exerting a considerable influence on his fellow illustrators. Rackham's illustrations lead viewers into the darkest corners of mythology and legend, where adventure is interwoven with dream and reality in occasionally spectral imagery.

Eerily gnarled trees and grimacing primordial figures rendered in earthy, dull browns and reds sent appreciative shivers down the spines of generations of readers and made their creator rich. The illustrations reproduced here showing Heracles and Cerberus (pp. 118/19) and Philemon and Baucis (p. 294) attest to his quality as an illustrator. His representation of Phineus and the Harpies (p. 71) as well as the battle between Heracles and the Hydra (p. 110) reveal another facet of Rackham as an illustrator: the probing psychologist gifted with empathy. Rackham's sensitive eye for the soul and the depths it can plumb transcends the dramatic narrative of the literary tale to place the illustration as an art form on an equal footing with the text.

Rackham illustrated numerous bestsellers in a booming market for children's books, including an edition of Lewis Carroll's *Alice's Adventures in Wonderland* (1907), as well as Shakespeare plays and Dickens stories (*A Christmas Carol*, 1915). Two of the illustrations reproduced here (pp. 71, 110) were taken from *The Greek Heroes*, the English translation of *Griechische Heroen-Geschichten*, which the German statesman and scholar Barthold Georg Niebuhr had written for his son. The German original had been published as far back as the 1820s, but the groundbreaking Rackham illustrations were a crucial factor in the success of the English edition, which Cassell published in 1910. Rackham's career as a book illustrator coincided with the emergence of the halftone reprographic technique in book printing. Permitting exceptional faithfulness to detail and color, this printing process was ideally suited to his works, rendering them with the utmost accuracy. His imitators may eventually have managed to shrug off his influence, yet for generations of readers Rackham's inimitable style would remain as unforgotten as the timeless tales on which his illustrations were based.

Thomas Heath Robinson
(1869–1953)

Thomas Heath Robinson was born in Islington, London, in 1869, the eldest of six children born to Thomas Robinson, an engraver, and Eliza A. Robinson, born Heath. His younger brothers Charles and William, born in 1870 and 1872 respectively, were also illustrators. At sixteen Thomas enrolled in the Islington School of Art and afterwards became an assistant to his father. In 1893 Thomas received his first commission: a series of drawings for a story by the popular novelist Mary Elizabeth Braddon, which was published that year in the *Pall Mall Magazine*. Heath Robinson's career was put on a successful trajectory by his first book illustrations. In 1895 George Allen & Sons published Frank Rinder's *Old World Japan. Legends of the Land of the Gods* boasting thirty-four superb black-and-white illustrations by Heath Robinson that were reminiscent not only of Japanese woodcuts but also the work of Robinson's contemporary, Aubrey Beardsley. This initial success would be followed by numerous illustrations for books and magazines. In the first decade of his career, Robinson was one of the most important English illustrators of his day, due partly to the broad range of techniques he employed, including his first forays into color illustration. The work reproduced here from Charles Kingsley's *The Heroes, or, Greek Fairy Tales for my Children* dates from that decade (p. 327). In 1901 Robinson married Edith Emma Barnett, with whom he had four daughters. The family had lived in Hampstead since 1902 but moved to Pinner, Middlesex, in 1906. The outbreak of World War I so sharply reduced the demand for his work that by 1920 Robinson was forced to move into social housing. However, his financial situation improved markedly after he received numerous commissions for illustrating children's books, and the family moved back to Pinner in 1926. After his wife died in 1940, Heath Robinson moved to St. Ives in Cornwall, where he remained until his death in February 1953.

Artuš Scheiner
(1863–1938)

Artuš Scheiner was born in Benešov, Bohemia (about 22 miles southeast of Prague), on October 28, 1863. A clerk at the Prague revenue office, he managed to turn a hobby into a career. By 1897 his drawings were being published in Czech art, entertainment, and satirical magazines. The first book of fairy tales he illustrated was published in 1902: *Růženka a Bobeš* (*Sleeping Beauty and Bobeš*), with black-and-white drawings executed in a sinuously elegant Jugendstil style that brought popularity and more commissions. He went on to illustrate fairy tales by Hans Christian Andersen, Božena Němcová, and Karel Jaromír Erben. In 1919 a romance by Julius Zeyer, *Román o věrném přátelství Amise a Amila* (roughly: The Romance of the True Friendship between the Knight Amis and Amil, 1904) was published with Scheiner's enchantingly subtle erotic drawings.

Artuš Scheiner had an unerring feel for the fantastic and dramatic, as the works shown here attest. The most impressive of the Scheiner illustrations reproduced here is surely his *Niobe* (p. 106), whose grief at the slaughter of her children by Artemis and Apollo is shown in a mountain setting in which the figure melds with the rocky summit in a brilliant display of consummate painterly skill. The depth of Niobe's grief is echoed by the monumentality of this montiform figuration, whose ceaselessly flowing tears transform as if by magic into a realistically evoked rushing mountain stream.

Scheiner did not live to see the Germans march into Prague – he had died there three months before the invasion on December 20, 1938.

Arthur Rackham
Philemon and Baucis, rewarded for their good and hospitable nature, are transformed by the gods into an oak and a linden tree, 1928

ARTIST BIOGRAPHIES

Virginia Frances Sterrett
(1900–1931)

Virginia Frances Sterrett was born in Chicago, Illinois, in 1900. After her father's early death, she moved with her mother and sister to live with relatives in Missouri and later to Kansas. Virginia drew constantly even in early childhood. As a teenager she won three first prizes in a competition at the Kansas State Fair, an event she would describe as one of the most encouraging she had experienced in her life.

In 1915 the family returned to Chicago, where Sterrett attended high school. She then worked in the advertising division of a department store, where the managing director was so entranced by her drawing skills that he ensured she was admitted to the School of the Art Institute of Chicago. Sterrett was even given a scholarship but had to leave the Institute a year later because her mother's health was so poor her daughter was forced to support the family by working for advertising agencies.

Sterrett must indeed have been a darling of the gods, who gave everything to those they loved, as Goethe put it, "all joys, boundlessly/ all griefs, infinitely, all." Another lover of the classics, Lord Byron, quoted a Menander fragment: "... whom the god loves dies young." At nineteen Sterrett was given a death sentence. She learned that she had contracted tuberculosis, but shortly afterwards she was granted the opportunity of fulfilling her lifelong dream. She was commissioned by the Penn Publishing Company to illustrate the fairy tales written by Sophie Rostopchine, Comtesse de Ségur. The English version of her *Old French Fairy Tales*, published in 1920, made Sterrett famous overnight as a children's book illustrator, and her next commission was soon to follow: illustrating Nathaniel Hawthorne's *Tanglewood Tales for Boys and Girls* (1921). Her illustrations, executed in color as well as black-and-white, are stylistically Art nouveau. The selection reproduced here vividly demonstrates how her delicate yet vibrant handling of color and line is an ideal vehicle for whisking youthful readers away to the world of Greek mythology as revisited by Hawthorne.

In 1923 the family moved to Altadena in southern California, where Sterrett, whose health was deteriorating rapidly, was soon admitted to a sanatorium. By then she was only able to work on her illustrations for short periods at a time. This circumstance explains why it took five years for her next, and last, masterpiece to be published: the *Arabian Nights* (1928), conceived as a children's book yet equally captivating for adults, with sixteen illustrations in color and twenty in black-and-white. A teeming artistic imagination was free to take flight.

Sterrett died of tuberculosis on June 8, 1931. A moving obituary in the *St. Louis Post-Dispatch* evokes her art and her tragically short but productive life: "She made pictures of haunting loveliness, suggesting Oriental lands she never saw and magical realms no one ever knew except in the dreams of childhood... In the imaginative scenes she set down on paper, she must have escaped from the harsh actualities of existence."

Helen Stratton
(1867–1961)

The daughter of an army surgeon, Helen Stratton was born on April 5, 1867, in Chhatarpur in the state Madhya Pradesh, India. While she was still a baby, her father retired and the family left for England to live in Bath. In 1891 Stratton lived in Kensington and attended art school, where she discovered an affinity for the Art nouveau style represented by the Glasgow School of Art. Remaining unmarried, she lived for years with her widowed mother and her siblings in Kensington, working as a book illustrator and painter. She returned to Bath in the 1930s.

Her first success was a commission for illustrating *Songs for Little People*, a book of poems for children by Norman Gale published in 1896. Two years later she drew 167 illustrations for *Beyond the Border*, a collection of fairy tales by Walter Douglas Campbell. Stratton was best known for the boldly imaginative pen drawings with which she illustrated classical fairy tales, such as the Brother Grimm collection and the fairy tales Hans Christian Andersen wrote. The high point of Stratton's career as a book illustrator is represented by the more than 400 drawings she did for an edition of Andersen's fairy tales published by George Newnes in 1899. Later Stratton also worked in color, for instance, illustrating Agnes Grozier Herbertson's *Heroic Legends* (1908) and Jean Lang's *A Book of Myths* (1915), from which the watercolor reproduced here (p. 274) was taken. Her illustrations for the George MacDonald fantasy novels for children, *The Princess and the Goblin* and its sequel *The Princess and Curdie* (1912), were particularly popular. Helen Stratton died at the age of 95 in a retirement home in Bath on June 4, 1961.

ARTIST BIOGRAPHIES

Sybil Tawse
(1886–1971)

Sybil Tawse was born in Sunderland, northeast England, on September 26, 1886. She received many scholarships during her time as a student at the Lambeth School of Art and the Royal College of Art in London. Almost forgotten now, Sybil Tawse embarked on a successful career in the "Golden Age" of book illustration and poster art. In 1908 she illustrated *Anne of Green Gables*, a children's novel by the Canadian writer Lucy Maud Montgomery. In 1914, eight full-page illustrations in color by Sybil Tawse featured in a new edition of *Cranford*, a loosely structured novel by Elizabeth Gaskell published in installments by Charles Dickens between 1851 and 1853. Depicting village life in Victorian England, *Cranford* was reissued several times in the twentieth century and was adapted for the third time as a BBC film in the early twenty-first century.

The Sybil Tawse illustrations provide readers with a chance to identify with the characters in the novel, most of whom are female. This was possible because she individualized the characters and lovingly rendered them in vivid detail in the context of the social tensions arising from an increasingly industrialized country. Another nineteenth-century classic of English literature illustrated by Tawse was also written by a woman: George Eliot. A 1929 edition of *Silas Marner*, a realistic formation novel with interwoven fairy-tale elements that is still widely read, was published with Tawse's illustrations.

The illustration by Tawse (p. 92) reproduced here depicts another female icon who has been introduced in line with the best mythological and iconographic tradition: Medea. The heroine is shown subduing the Cretan bronze giant, Talos, by "pulling the plug on him" – in her right hand she is holding the nail that stops the lifeblood from draining out of the artery in his leg (in the Gustav Schwab text Talos bleeds to death from injury). The characterization is remarkable for the cool assurance, the casual elegance, with which the delicate figure of Medea triumphs over the robotic monster.

Gustaf Tenggren
(1896–1970)

Born in 1896 in Magra, a small town in western Sweden, Gustaf Tenggren had a variegated career that led him from the "Golden Age" of book illustration (roughly 1890–1920) to the hub of early animated cartoon film in Hollywood, and ultimately to a successful life in the U.S. as an illustrator of children's books.

Tenggren's talent was discovered while he was still very young, and it secured him a scholarship to the Valand Academy of Fine Art in Gothenburg. In 1917 he was commissioned to illustrate a popular series of fairy tales, *Bland tomtar och troll* (Among Gnomes and Trolls), stepping in to replace the legendary Swedish illustrator John Bauer. In the early 1920s Tenggren moved to New York, where he illustrated a number of popular children's books, including *Grimms' Fairy Tales* (1922) and *Mother Goose* (1929), and received lucrative advertising commissions.

Tenggren's imaginative, richly detailed style of illustration is reminiscent of the work of earlier luminaries such as Arthur Rackham and Kay Nielsen. The Walt Disney Company must have had something similar in mind when it engaged Tenggren as the art director for the first Disney animated cartoon film, *Snow White and the Seven Dwarfs*, in 1936. Tenggren stayed at Disney for three years, working on seven classic productions, including *Pinocchio* (1940), *Fantasia* (1940), and *Bambi* (1942).

After his stint at Disney, Tenggren's style underwent a radical change. Although he had been hired for his European style in the Rackham manner, he now made a U-turn to cultivate a simple, linear style that he would retain for the rest of his career. Beginning in 1942, he spent the next twenty years collaborating on *Little Golden Books*, a children's book series that targeted a mass market, contributing almost a title a year. The illustrations chosen for reproduction in this book clearly demonstrate the stylistic turnaround described above, thus revealing Tenggren's astonishing artistic range.

A mere glance at the number of bestsellers Tenggren collaborated on indicates that he was probably the most successful Swedish book illustrator of all time. Tenggren remained a popular and prolific artist in his chosen medium into the mid-1950s, continuing to illustrate numerous books for children and adolescents.

Gustaf Tenggren
Heracles looks to Atlas, the bearer of the sky, and asks for his help in claiming the three golden apples, 1930

ARTIST BIOGRAPHIES

Salomon van Abbé
As Pegasus flies above the three-headed chimera, Bellerophon prepares to administer the fatal blow, 1949

Harry George Theaker
(1873–1954)

Born in Wolstanton, Staffordshire, Harry George Theaker came from a family of English artists. His father, George Theaker, was also an active painter and was the headmaster of the Burslem School of Art for twenty-five years.

After studying art at the institute his father headed, Harry George Theaker continued his academic training at the Royal College of Art in London and afterwards in Italy. Like his father and his brother, Charles Edmund, Harry George Theaker frequently worked for the Wedgwood Institute in Burslem as a designer of the exquisite porcelain for which it is known. Noteworthy in the present connection are Theaker's designs for transfer printing, for which he drew on John Tenniel's legendary illustrations for *Alice in Wonderland* and *Alice Through the Looking-Glass.*

Theaker's main professional focus was on painting and book illustration. He had a marked preference for motifs from faraway lands and exotic civilizations, which he satisfied by illustrating collections of stories about them such as *Children's Stories from the Arabian Nights* (1914), *Tales and Legends from India* (n. d.) and N. Kato's *Children's Stories from Japanese Fairy Tales and Legends* (1918).

In the 1920s he received commissions to illustrate new editions of classic English stories for children, including E. C. Vivian's *Robin Hood* (1918) and *The Water-Babies* by Charles Kingsley, a perennial favorite in England. Toward the end of that decade, which had been so productive for Theaker as a book illustrator, he illustrated Jonathan Swift's *Gulliver's Travels* (1928) and provided illustrations in color for *Grimms' Fairy Tales* (1930). The year before he had even contributed to an edition of Cervantes' *Don Quixote*, a touchstone work for ambitious illustrators.

The illustration reproduced here was taken from the Prometheus myth (p. 325) as retold by Blanche Winder in *Long, Long Ago: Stories from the Classics* (1923), a title richly endowed by forty-eight Theaker illustrations in color. The picture narrates the fate of Prometheus and the desperate situation he was in after Zeus sentenced him to be chained to a rock high above an abyss. Every day Zeus sent an eagle to Prometheus to devour the captive Titan's liver, which constantly regenerated so that the gruesome spectacle could begin again in an endless cycle. Prometheus would not be freed until Heracles came to his rescue, allegedly 30,000 years after the sentence was so cruelly inflicted on him. Theaker's take on the story seems to anticipate Prometheus' liberation. Heracles is seen rushing forward from a distance to slay the eagle and unchain Prometheus. We are spared the sight of the blood-thirsty eagle savaging Prometheus, although the bird is hovering over him about to attack. The palette of the picture projects an overall hopeful mood. We suspect, or at least hope, that a good outcome is imminent.

Salomon van Abbé
(1883–1955)

Salomon van Abbé, born in Amsterdam on July 31, 1883, was the son of a Dutch diamond merchant. When he was five years old the family moved to England, where van Abbé received comprehensive schooling in art at the London County Council School of Photoengraving and Lithography. He at first worked as an illustrator for newspapers, but switched later to portraits and genre paintings (police, judges, and family scenes). He also designed numerous book dust jackets for, among others, works by Dorothy Sayers and Agatha Christie from the "Golden Age of crime fiction." In his later years van Abbé turned to illustrating children's books, where he could draw on a lifetime of experience in deftly capturing fleeting poses, gestures, and facial expressions, a skill which came in handy when he addressed Nathanial Hawthorne's *The Paradise of Children* in *A Wonder-Book for Girls and Boys,* from which the gouache reproduced here (p. 18) was taken. Epimetheus is shown on the right and, in the center, Pandora, who has just opened the fateful "box" for the second time. This time, Hope, "a sunny and smiling little personage," as described in the volume preceding Hawthorne's better known *Tanglewood Tales*, emerges from it to console the children. Two aspects of van Abbé's handling demonstrate how he succeeded in faithfully rendering and aesthetically heightening the literary template. Hope's wings are "colored like the rainbow" and she tells them, "I am partly made of tears as well as smiles." The light green of Hope's dress is the result of mixing blue and yellow, the colors of Pandora and Epimetheus. In embracing the playmates, Hope has become a synthesis of the two. This interpretation is reinforced by the figures' poses: Epimetheus is holding his arms out straight while Pandora's are bent to match Hope's.

Patten Wilson
(1869–1934)

From the mid-1890s to the late 1920s, Patten Wilson was a leading exponent of a new English approach to the art of illustration. Being commissioned to work for *The Yellow Book* admitted him to a circle of distinguished artists who were making a groundbreaking contribution to book design. Co-founded by Aubrey Beardsley, who was its first art editor, *The Yellow Book* was a sumptuously illustrated quarterly periodical that in its heyday set new aesthetic standards in publishing a diverse range of literary genres, illustrations, and art reproductions. As the Bodley Head publisher's prospectus claims for the first volume, it is "... a book that every book-lover will love at first sight; a book that will make book-lovers of many who are now indifferent to books." That is literally what Patten Wilson did on the dust jacket of *The Gorgon's Head* (1912) from Nathanial Hawthorne's *Tanglewood Tales* reproduced here (p. 19 l.). A reader is shown entering the stage represented by the book, as we are invited to enter a new world. The door to it has opened a crack, and Wilson lets us peer through it and, in doing so, grasp the content of the book thus tantalizingly disclosed.

Patten Wilson began his career by enrolling at the Kidderminster School of Art. He soon realized that he would not be able to sufficiently pursue his interests there, and dropped out to teach himself to draw by copying Albrecht Dürer's work and making many studies of animals and plants. Executed in faithful detail, those early studies soon attracted attention from fellow artists as well as publishers and art critics. Wilson spent the 1890s consolidating a distinctive signature of his own, which is convincingly displayed in an edition of Samuel Taylor Coleridge's poems he illustrated (1898). Other notable mature works by Wilson are his illustrations for a Complete Works of Shakespeare (1899) and for an edition of the Dickens *A Child's History of England*, which was published by J.M. Dent in 1902. In later years, Wilson's popularity underwent a steady decline, although he was still receiving occasional commissions in the early 1930s.

Milo Winter
(1888–1956)

Born in Princeton, Illinois, in 1888, Milo Winter trained as an artist at the renowned School of the Art Institute of Chicago. A few months after he graduated in 1912, he had found a distinguished publisher for *Billy Popgun*, an adventure story he had written and lavishly provided with fantastic color plates and black-and-white illustrations. Unsurprisingly, viewers are reminded of great English and American names in book illustration, such as Arthur Rackham and Maxfield Parrish. Winter did not become famous solely for his animals and mythic beasts as encountered in *Billy Popgun*, but also for his detailed and anatomically correct human figures as shown by the illustrations he did for the *Windermere* series published by Rand McNally, which featured such classics for children and adolescents as *Gulliver's Travels*, *Alice in Wonderland*, *Robinson Crusoe*, *Twenty Thousand Leagues Under the Sea*, *The Three Musketeers*, and *Treasure Island*, as well as the Nathanial Hawthorne *Wonder-Book*, from which the illustrations by Winter reproduced here were taken. Apart from a noticeable fondness for detail, the most striking feature here is Winter's ability to stage his figures effectively and lend them remarkable powers of expression through his handling of body language and facial expression, as well as the overarching pictorial composition.

Winter was an extremely accomplished illustrator with a consummate mastery of technique. He always exploited techniques fashionable at the time to push his handling of the medium to the extreme. They included the scratchboard technique, by means of which a picture is created by removing a layer of color with sharp scratching tools instead of additive color – Winter illustrated Virginia Moe's *Animal Inn* (1946) with scratchboard pictures.

From 1947 until 1949 Winter was employed by Field Enterprises as the art director for their *Childcraft* anthology. He transferred to another publishing house, Silver Burdett, where he also served as art director. In the early 1950s he moved to New York, remaining there until he died in 1956.

Patten Wilson
His one wish granted by Dionysus,
King Midas sits in his treasury to count
his spoils, 1890

ARTIST BIOGRAPHIES

Max Wulff
(1871–1947)

Max Wulff was a Berlin painter, printmaker, and illustrator who trained at the art academies in Berlin and Munich. The books he illustrated for children and adolescent readers include novels, tales, and fairy tales by James Fenimore Cooper, Jules Verne, Johanna Spyri, Sophie Wörishöffer, Else Ury, Wilhelm Hauff, and the Brothers Grimm. Less well-known are Wulff's illustrations for books with historical content for young readers, such as the work of Fritz Skowronnek from the Masurian region of Poland. Wulff motifs from children's books published by Meidingers Jugendschriften Verlag, like many of the above, are also featured on poster stamps, which are "postage stamps" measuring 7 x 5 cm used by publishers for advertising. From today's standpoint, Wulff squandered his talents on illustrating publications such as *Helden der See: Heldentaten unserer Marine 1914/18* (Heroes of the Sea: Our Navy's Heroic Feats 1914/18, 1934), which are highly problematic from a historical standpoint.

Like the illustration reproduced here (p. 163), which was taken from M. von Witzleben's *Griechische Geschichte* (a history of ancient Greece for children and adolescents), Wulff's work is distinguished by a skillfully balanced handling of color. His portraits of Ludwig van Beethoven and Arthur Schopenhauer show that he could work independently in other genres.

Newell Convers Wyeth
With a flash of her staff, the enchantress Circe transforms Odysseus's companions into swine, 1929

Newell Convers Wyeth
(1882–1945)

The most important U.S. book illustrator of his day was also one of the most prolific: the illustrations for more than 100 books and over 3,000 paintings laid the foundation for a lasting reputation. Newell Convers Wyeth was born in Needham, Massachusetts, on October 22, 1882. His talent was discovered early on and his parents sent him to the Mechanics Arts School in Boston, where he was advised to study book illustration at the Eric Pope School of Art. At eighteen, Wyeth went to Wilmington, Delaware, to study with Howard Pyle, one of the most successful illustrators of his day, who would found the celebrated Brandywine School of Art. It is to Pyle's credit that Wyeth, after only a few months under his tutelage, received his first commission. N. C. Wyeth's first illustration graced the cover of the February 21, 1903 edition of the *Saturday Evening Post*. His *Bronco Buster* attracted requests for more cover pictures with "Old West" motifs. At Pyle's urging, Wyeth traveled to Colorado and Arizona to familiarize himself more thoroughly with the "Wild West."

On his return, Wyeth painted his first book illustrations for the *Scribner Classics* series. Robert Louis Stevenson's *Treasure Island* was published in 1911 with illustrations made from seventeen Wyeth oil paintings on canvas that deftly captured dramatic moments of the story and draw the reader into it. Wyeth had a sure eye in calculating the effect to be achieved by painting pictures in quite large formats (measuring roughly 47 x 32/38 inches) for subsequent reduction to book-page size. He would retain this method of working for future projects, such as the *Odysseus* illustrations reproduced here.

After marrying Carolyn Bockius – four of their five children also became artists – Wyeth lived and worked in the country at Chadds Ford, Pennsylvania. At his study there he produced numerous paintings unrelated to book illustration. In the 1910s and 1920s they showed the influence of American Impressionism, but from the 1930s on they belong stylistically to American Realism. N. C. Wyeth hoped to escape the constraint of having to illustrate books for a living. He compared illustration unfavorably to painting, conceding that an illustrator's creative powers drew on the same source as those of a painter, but the profound difference between the two lay in the fact that the illustrator subjected his inspiration to a particular purpose whereas the painter could carry his inspiration into the infinite. This, according to Wyeth, was why the illustrator's work was a handicraft.

Wyeth was killed on October 19, 1945, when his car stalled on a railroad crossing and was hit by a train.

ARTIST BIOGRAPHIES

Alexander Zick
(1845–1907)

Alexander Zick had a lot to live up to. Born in Koblenz on December 20, 1845, he was the son of the painter Gustav Zick and the grandson of Konrad Zick, another painter, and the great-grandson of Januarius Zick, a celebrated painter and architect. His great-great-grandfather was the fresco painter Johann Zick. With such a family history, there was never a question of Alexander Zick becoming anything but a painter. He was sent first to train in Paris. The six months he spent in the studio of the famous history painter Alexandre Cabanel were formative. All his life Zick would remain indebted to Cabanel's academic aestheticism. The work of genre painter Ludwig Knaus, a protégé of Alexander Zick's at the Düsseldorf Academy, exerted no stylistic influence on Zick during his time at the Düsseldorf school. Zick was at the Düsseldorf Art Academy from 1865 until 1872 but his studies were interrupted by service in the Franco-Prussian War. In 1872 Zick returned to Koblenz and Clemens Brentano's collection of fairy tales *Gockel, Hinkel und Gackeleia* (roughly: The Rooster, the Hen and Their Chirping Chick) was published in an edition illustrated with woodcuts by Alexander Zick. Critical acclaim for Zick boiled down to Brentano's tales "being poetry that defied illustration." Little is known about Zick's Koblenz period, but he must have decided there to concentrate on book illustration as his chief art form. After moving to Berlin with Ludwig Knaus's assistance, Zick's career in illustration took off in 1880 and he was as successful as he was prolific. Thanks to the aestheticism mentioned above, Zick was commissioned to illustrate the 1890 edition of the myths of classical antiquity retold by Gustav Schwab, from which the illustrations reproduced here (pp. 134, 306) were taken. Because such subject matter was unrelated to genre painting, it perfectly matched his inclinations and aptitudes.

Above
Alexander Zick
The fire-stealing Prometheus suffers his eternal punishment, 1890

Right
Newell Convers Wyeth
Penelope mourns for the absent and estranged Odysseus, 1929

306

THE ILLUSTRATOR

Clifford Harper
(* 1949)

Clifford Harper, who is one of Britain's best-known contemporary illustrators, is famous chiefly for his inimitable black-and-white style. His linework, and the enormously expressive quality of his illustrations, so reminiscent of poster art, lend his drawings a dynamic quality. Above all, however, Harper is a past master at reducing art to the essential, making what is to be conveyed immediately obvious.

Born in Chiswick, London in 1949, Harper came from a humble background; his mother was a cook, and his father a postman. Harper was expelled from school at age thirteen as he became increasingly involved with 1960s anarchist ideas. For some time, Harper lived in a commune in an old farmhouse in Cumberland, and in 1969, he moved to Eel Pie Island, which was in the Thames in London. There he founded a commune in the Eel Pie Island Hotel, a dilapidated nineteenth-century building that by 1970 housed the largest hippie community in the United Kingdom. The commune fell apart, however, after the hotel burned down in a fire in 1971. Since 1974, Harper has lived in Camberwell, south London.

Harper has never had any formal training in art, and appears to have taught himself the basics of his trade while working at a printer's. In the early 1970s, Harper worked as an illustrator for anarchist underground newspapers and magazines, as well as various political groups.

Over time, however, he developed a style that was distinctively his own. At first he worked in a manner strongly reminiscent of George Grosz and Félix Vallotton, but his technique later showed the influence of Frans Masereel's woodcuts, although Harper has never worked in that particular medium. Instead, he draws with pen and ink, and his meticulously handled hatching is often the result of reworking with a scratch knife.

In the 1980s Harper became known to a broader public through the illustrations he did for major British newspapers. In 1996 he began to illustrate the *Guardian* column "Country Diary," and from 1999 to 2002 he illustrated "The Last Word" column, written for the paper by the philosopher A. C. Grayling.

The vignettes Clifford Harper has drawn for this book are much more than mere typographic ornaments, and recall the illustrations he drew for a new edition of Ernst Gombrich's *A Little History of the World* (2005). Executed in a clear, expressive visual idiom, they draw viewers into the stories being told, usually via devices that only seem simple at first glance. Yet they are so ingeniously interlocking in composition that the perils faced by the *Argo*, cradled between Scylla and Charybdis (p. 86), leap from the page.

Right
Henry Matthew Brock
As the magic of Medea and the sounds of Orpheus's lyre put the guarding serpent to sleep, Jason claims the Golden Fleece from the tree at Colchis, 1928

Pages 310/11
William Russell Flint
Penelope is mocked by impatient suitors, 1924

W.RVSSELL FLINT MCMXIV

GLOSSARY

Achilles
Son of Peleus, king of Phthia in Thessaly, and the sea nymph Thetis. He is the most important hero in Homer's *Iliad*. He kills Hector in hand-to-hand combat. Achilles' heel is his only vulnerable spot, but Paris hits him there with an arrow, fatally wounding him.

Agamemnon
King of Mycenae and field commander of the Greek forces in the Trojan War. He is the brother of Menelaus, king of Sparta and husband of Helen of Troy.

Andromache
Wife of the Trojan hero Hector, and mother of his son, Astyanax.

Antigone
The daughter of Oedipus and Jocasta, who was both his wife and his mother.

Aphrodite
The goddess of love, beauty, and lust. She was the daughter of Uranus, or of Zeus and Dione.

Apollo
The god of light and the arts and prophecy, he was the son of Zeus and Leto. He is the twin brother of Artemis and protector of the oracle at Delphi.

Ares
God of war and son of Zeus and Hera. He had a love affair with Aphrodite, who was married to Hephaestus, the god of fire.

Argonauts
The company that travelled on the Argo with the hero Jason when he sailed to Colchis. Their goal was to steal the Golden Fleece, which was guarded by a dragon.

Artemis
Goddess of the hunt and wooded regions and twin sister of Apollo. Her parents are Zeus and Leto. A silver bow and arrows are her principal identifying attributes.

Athena
The goddess of wisdom, art, science, and crafts. The daughter of Zeus, she was born from her father's head fully armed. The city of Athens is named after Athena and she is its patroness. The best-known temple to her is the Parthenon on the Acropolis in Athens. The most famous representation of her in antiquity was a colossal gold-and-ivory statue by Phidias, which stood in the Parthenon and was as tall as the interior chamber itself.

Atlas
A Titan who carries the vault of heaven at the westernmost point in the known world in Gibraltar.

Bellerophon
A Corinthian hero, he killed the Chimaera with the help of the winged horse Pegasus.

GLOSSARY

Page 312
Henry Matthew Brock
*Closely pursued by two vengeful Gorgons,
Perseus bolts away in the winged sandals
lent to him by Hermes,* 1928

Right
Virginia Frances Sterrett
*Arriving at Circe's palace, the voyagers
stare in wonder at her opulent quilt,* 1921

Calypso

A sea nymph who lives on the island of Ogygia. She holds Odysseus captive for years as her lover until Zeus orders her to release the hero so he can return to the family he yearns for in Ithaca.

Castor

Twin brother of Pollux and, like him, went on the Argonaut expedition to the Golden Fleece.

Cerberus

A monster with three dog's heads that guards the entrance to the Underworld. He is briefly brought to the upper world by Heracles.

Chimaera

A hybrid fire-breathing beast that has a lion's head on a goat's body and a snake as its tail. It was slain by the Corinthian hero Bellerophon. Its monstrous siblings are Cerberus, the Hydra, and the Sphinx.

Chiron

The most famous of the Centaurs, hybrid creatures whose upper halves are human with the bodies and legs of horses. Chiron was the mentor of heroes, including Achilles and Jason.

Circe

The daughter of Helios, the sun god, and Perseis, daughter of Oceanus. When Odysseus arrivers at Aeaea, her island, on his way home from Troy, Circe transforms some of his companions into swine. With divine help, Odysseus forces the enchantress to turn them back into humans.

Colchis

Land between the Caucasus and the east coast of the Black Sea that is ruled by King Aetes. He is the owner of the Golden Fleece, which is guarded by a dragon, but is stolen by Jason with the aid of Medea, the king's daughter.

Crete

The largest Greek island. The most famous mythical king of Crete is Minos, for whom Daedalus built the labyrinth to house the Minotaur. Theseus slays it with the help of Ariadne, the king's daughter.

Daedalus

Celebrated artist, engineer, architect, and inventor. He built the labyrinth to house the Minotaur for Minos, king of Crete. In an attempt to escape from the labyrinth on wings made from feathers and wax, his son, Icarus, plunges into the sea and drowns.

Demeter

Goddess of fertility, the earth, and grain. She bears a daughter, Persephone, to her brother, Zeus. Demeter is also the mother of Plutus, the personification of wealth.

GLOSSARY

Walter Crane
The naval Battle of Salamis, contested between the Greeks and the Persians in 480 BC, 1913

Erechtheum
A temple on the Acropolis in Athens. Built between 420 and 406 BC, it stands on what is said to have been the site of the palace of Erechtheus, mythical king of Athens. The Erechtheum is best known for its atrium, which is supported by six caryatids, columns in the form of standing young women. They are believed to represent the six daughters of Erechtheus.

Erechtheus
Reared by the goddess Athena, he was a mythical king of Athens. He slew Eumolpus, who had invaded Athens. The Erechtheum is said to have been built on the site where Poseidon, father of Eumolpus, struck down Erechtheus with his trident in front of his palace on the rocks of the Acropolis.

Eros
Personification of lust and romance and companion of Aphrodite. Although insignificant as a cult figure, Eros is popular in art, music, and literature.

Europa
Daughter of Phoenician king Agenor. Inflamed with passion, Zeus transformed into a bull and abducted her to Crete. The continent of Europe is named after her.

Eurydice
A Thracian Dryad, whom Orpheus married on his return from the voyage of the Argonauts.

Gaia
The personification of the Earth. She gave birth to Erechtheus, who was raised by the goddess Athena.

Golden Apples of the Hesperides
The Golden Apples of the Hesperides (nymphs of the setting sun) grew on a tree was guarded by Ladon, a dragon. One of the Labors of Heracles was to pick these apples.

Golden Fleece
The golden fleece of a ram that could fly and speak. With Medea's help, Jason the Argonaut stole the fleece in Colchis.

Hades
God of the Underworld and elder brother of Zeus.

Hector
Eldest son of King Priam of Troy and commander of the Trojan forces. Hector killed Patroclus, Achilles' friend, and was slain by Achilles in hand-to-hand combat before the city walls.

Helen of Troy
Daughter of Zeus and Leda. Helen is the most beautiful woman in the world. She married Menelaus, king of Sparta and brother of Agamemnon. The Trojan War breaks out after Paris abducts her and takes her to Troy. The war ends ten years later with the destruction of Troy, and Helen returns to her husband, Menelaus.

Helios
God of the sun. He drives the fiery chariot of the sun drawn by four horses across the sky.

GLOSSARY

Charles Edmund Brock
*Polyphemus searches for the ram
in his cave,* 1907

Hephaestus
The god of fire and the forge, he is a son
of Zeus and Hera. The weapons carried by
Achilles and the armor he wears in battle
against Hector before Troy were made by
Hephaestus.

Hera
Wife of Zeus, king of the gods, and also
his sister.

Heracles
Son of Zeus and Alcmene. A hero famed for
his enormous strength, Heracles performed
many arduous tasks during his lifetime. After
his death he was taken into the Olympic pantheon and made immortal. His best-known
attribute is a lion's skin.

Hermes
Messenger of the gods as well as the god
of travelers, merchants, and thieves. Hermes
also accompanies the souls of the dead to
the Underworld.

Homer
Often called the earliest Western poet,
although no biographical data such as a place
of birth or death are known. He is widely
regarded as the author of Western epics. Possibly dating from the eight century BC, the
Iliad and the *Odyssey*, popularly attributed to
Homer, relate episodes from the Trojan War
and Odysseus's protracted journey home from
the war.

Hydra
A serpent-like monster with multiple heads.
If one head is cut off, two new ones grow to
replace it. The Hydra was a sister of the Sphinx,
the Chimaera, and Cerberus. She was slain
by Heracles.

Icarus
Son of Daedalus. He receives wings constructed of feathers and wax from his father
so they could flee Crete. While crossing the
sea, Icarus shrugs off his father's warnings and
flies too close to the sun. The wax melts and
he falls into the water.

The *Iliad*
Attributed to Homer and called the earliest
European epic poem, it may have been composed in the eighth century BC. In 15,693 lines
of hexameter, the plot covers only fifty-one days
of the Trojan War, which lasted for ten years.
It focuses on the wrath of Achilles aroused
by a quarrel with Agamemnon and the death
of Hector. The end of the Trojan War is not
described in the *Iliad*.

Jason
A king's son from Iolcus in Thessaly, he leads
the Argonauts on the expedition to Colchis to
steal the Golden Fleece. Jason marries Medea
after she helped him to procure the Fleece,
but does not remain faithful to her.

Medea
Daughter of Aetes, king of Colchis. Medea
falls in love with Jason when he arrives with
his band of Argonauts to steal the Golden
Fleece. She uses magic to help Jason accomplish this perilous feat, flees with him, and
marries him.

GLOSSARY

Herbert Granville Fell
Heracles paddles his way towards
Atlas as he bears the sky aloft, 1910

Medusa

One of the three Gorgons, terrifying creatures with serpents in place of hair. A glance at a Gorgon turns anyone to stone. Her sisters, Stheno and Euryale, are immortal, but Medusa dies when she is decapitated by Perseus.

Meleager

The son of the king of Calydon and an Argonaut. He slew the huge Calydonian boar that was rooting up the fields in Calydon and killing humans and animals.

Menelaus

King of Sparta and husband of Helen of Troy. When Paris exploits his hospitality and abducts Helen, taking her to Troy with him, war breaks out between the Greeks and Trojans. After it is over, Menelaus returns to Sparta with Helen. The commander of the Greek forces is Agamemnon, Menelaus's brother and king of Mycenae.

Midas

Mythical king in Phrygia. Coveting riches causes his downfall. Dionysus fulfils his wish that everything he touches turn to gold, even food and drink. Dying of thirst and starvation, Midas begs the god to reverse the spell.

Minos

King of Crete and son of Zeus and Europa. He has Daedalus build the labyrinth, in which the Minotaur is kept. The Minoan civilization is named after the mythical king. The best-known Minoan ruin is the Palace of Knossos, which is so full of nooks and crannies that it resembles a labyrinth.

Niobe

Wife of Amphion, king of Thebes, with whom she had seven sons and seven daughters. She taunts Leto about having only two children – Apollo and Artemis – while she has fourteen. To punish Niobe for her arrogance, Apollo and Artemis kill all her children.

Odysseus

King of Ithaca, Odysseys is one of the best-known heroes of the Trojan War. His defining character traits, intelligence and craftiness, are proverbial. Constructing the Wooden Horse that deceives the Trojans and brings about the fall of Troy is his idea. After ten years of adventurous wanderings, Odysseus returns home to his wife, Penelope, and his son, Telemachus.

The *Odyssey*

The second epic poem attributed to Homer. Shorter than the *Iliad*, it comprises 12,109 hexametric lines recounting the wanderings of Odysseus on his way home from Troy.

Oedipus

Son of the king of Thebes. A string of fateful events turns Oedipus into the ultimate tragic figure. He accidentally kills his father and unknowingly marries his mother. On realizing what he has done, Oedipus blinds himself and goes into exile. He also defeats the Sphinx by solving its riddles.

Olympus

The light-filled dwelling of the Greek gods. Mount Olympus lies near the eastern coast of Thessaly and, at 9,570 ft, it is the highest peak in Greece. It has been equated with the home of Zeus and the pantheon of gods since the fifth century BC.

GLOSSARY

Artuš Scheiner
Odysseus and his companions take cover in the cave of the cyclops Polyphemus, 1920

Orpheus

Singer and poet from Thrace, husband of Eurydice. He enchants gods and mortals, flora and fauna by singing and playing his lyre. On the voyage of the Argo, he sings even more sweetly than the Sirens.

Pandora

Formed of clay by Hephaestus, Pandora is ordered by Zeus to avenge the theft of fire by Prometheus. As a reward she is given a box containing all the evils of this world as well as hope. She opens the box and the evils are released, but Pandora keeps hope inside, leaving the world without it.

Pandora's Box

Contains all evils known to man, including hard work, disease, and death. They are released into the world when Pandora opens the box.

Paris

Son of Priam, king of Troy. Paris decides the beauty contest between the goddesses Hera, Athena, and Aphrodite in favor of Aphrodite, goddess of love and beauty. As his reward, Aphrodite promises him the world's most beautiful woman. Paris chooses to abduct Helen, wife of Menelaus, king of Sparta. The Trojan War breaks out because he takes her to Sparta.

Parthenon

Temple dedicated to Athena, patron deity of Athens. Built on the Acropolis in Athens between 447 and 438 BC, the Parthenon is probably the most important temple of ancient Greece, indeed of all classical antiquity, with its architecture and celebrated sculptural decoration. A colossal gold-and-ivory statue of Pallas Athena by the sculptor Phidias once stood inside it.

Patroclus

Friend of Achilles and his companion-in-arms at Troy. Wearing Achilles' armor, he fights against the Trojans, at first with success, but Hector kills him and takes the gleaming armor as the spoils of war. Driven made by grief, Achilles avenges his friend and kills Hector.

Pegasus

A winged horse that springs fully formed from the Gorgon Medusa's neck after Perseus decapitated her. Pegasus is the steed ridden by Bellerophon in his battle against the Chimaera.

Penelope

Married to Odysseus, the proverbial faithful wife. During the twenty years her husband is away, she keeps her many suitors at a distance by employing a ruse: She tells the men she will select a suitor when the cloth she is weaving is finished. During the night she unravels the cloth she has woven all day. Odysseus returns in time.

Perseus

Son of Zeus and Danae. Perseus is the slayer of the Gorgon, Medusa.

Pollux

Twin brother of Castor and, like him, went on the expedition of the Argonauts to Colchis.

GLOSSARY

Polyphemus

One-eyed giant and son of Poseidon and the sea nymph Thoosa. Polyphemus kept Odysseus and some of his companions captive in his cave and ate six of them. Odysseus uses a trick to save himself and the remaining captives.

Poseidon

God of the sea and brother of Zeus. His best-known attribute is the trident. He can cause earthquakes and floods by driving it into the ground.

Priam

The last king of Troy and the father of Hector and Paris.

Prometheus

A member of the race of Titans. He angers Zeus by bringing fire to mankind against the will of the king of the gods. Prometheus is punished by being fettered to a rock in the Caucasus.

Sphinx

A winged monster with a lion's body and the head of a woman, she is the sister of the Hydra and the Chimaera. On a mountain near Thebes, she asks riddles to travelers, and kills them if they fail to answer correctly. She is defeated by Oedipus.

Styx

The river that flows between the world of the living and Hades, the underworld.

Telemachus

Son of Odysseus and his wife, Penelope.

Theseus

Son of Aegeus, king of Athens, and later king himself. Theseus sails to Crete to kill the Minotaur in the labyrinth built by Daedalus. Ariadne, daughter of the Cretan king, helps him escape.

Thetis

Daughter of Nereus, Old Man of the Sea. She is Achilles' mother.

Troy

City at the entrance to the Hellespont (the Dardanelles) and the center of Priam's kingdom. Troy is destroyed at the end of the Trojan War.

Wooden Horse / Trojan Horse

A colossal horse constructed of wood, in which Greek heroes are concealed. After hauling the horse into Troy, the unsuspecting Trojans celebrate what they think means victory over the Greeks. At night the concealed warriors climb out of the wooden horse and destroy the city.

Zeus

Head of the Greek pantheon of gods, king of the gods. Zeus is a son of the Titans Cronus and Rhea.

SELECTED BIBLIOGRAPHY

Archäologisches Landesmuseum Baden-Württemberg (Ed.), *Troia. Traum und Wirklichkeit*, Exh. cat. Stuttgart, Braunschweig, Bonn, 2001/2002. Stuttgart, 2001

Brinkmann, Vinzenz (Ed.), *Athen. Triumph der Bilder*, Exh. cat. Frankfurt am Main, Liebighaus, 2016. Petersberg, 2016

Brinkmann, Vinzenz (Ed.), *Medeas Liebe und die Jagd nach dem Goldenen Vlies*, Exh. cat. Frankfurt am Main, Liebighaus, 2018. Munich, 2018

Brinkmann, Vinzenz and Ulrike Koch-Brinkmann (Eds.), *Bunte Götter. Die Farben der Antike. Golden Edition*, Exh. cat. Frankfurt am Main, Liebighaus, 2020. Munich/London/New York, 2020

Evers, Daniela, *Die schönsten Sagen des klassischen Altertums. Zur Bedeutung und Funktion der Bearbeitungen antiker mythologischer Erzählungen in der Kinder- und Jugendliteratur des 19. Jahrhunderts.* St. Ingbert, 2001

Groß, Jonathan, *Antike Mythen im schwäbischen Gewand. Gustav Schwabs Sagen des klassischen Altertums und ihre antiken Quellen.* Göttingen, 2020

Kerényi, Karl, *Die Mythologie der Griechen. 1. Die Götter- und Menschheitsgeschichten.* Munich, 2003; 2. *Die Heroen-Geschichten.* Munich, 2004

Lücke, Hans-K. and Susanne, *Antike Mythologie – Ein Handbuch. Der Mythos und seine Überlieferung in Literatur und bildender Kunst.* Hamburg, 1999

Lücke, Hans-K. and Susanne, *Helden und Gottheiten der Antike – Ein Handbuch. Der Mythos und seine Überlieferung in Literatur und bildender Kunst.* Hamburg, 2002

Ranke-Graves, Robert, *Griechische Mythologie. Quelle und Deutung.* Hamburg, 2003

Rutenfranz, Maria, *Götter, Helden, Menschen. Rezeption und Adaption antiker Mythologien in der deutschen Kinder- und Jugendliteratur.* Frankfurt am Main, 2004

Schwab, Gustav, *Die schönsten Sagen des klassischen Altertums. Nach seinen Dichtern und Erzählern*, 3 vols. Stuttgart, 1838–1840

Schwab, Gustav, *Die schönsten Sagen des klassischen Altertums.* Stuttgart, 2009

Taplin, Oliver, *Feuer vom Olymp. Die moderne Welt und die Kultur der Griechen.* Hamburg, 1991 (original edition: *Greek Fire.* London, 1989)

Wünsche, Raimund (Ed.), *Mythos Troja*, Exh. cat. Munich, Antikensammlung und Glyptothek, 2006/2007. Munich, 2006

EDITORIAL NOTE

The texts printed here are a selection of myths translated from *Sagen des klassischen Altertums* by Gustav Schwab (1792–1850), from the Gütersloh/Leipzig edition of 1888. Some myths have been partially abridged.

NOTES TO THE INTRODUCTION

1 Hermann Hesse, *Eine Literaturgeschichte in Rezensionen und Aufsätzen*, Schriften zur Literatur, vol. 2, Frankfurt am Main, 1970, p. 258f.

2 "Orpheus im Tiergarten. Kindheit in Berlin und die ersten drei Bücher", in: *Die Zeit*, no. 25, June 19, 1952.

3 Plutarch, *Alexander* 15: Dryden translation.

Thomas Heath Robinson
As the Argonauts sail inexorably toward the island of sirens, Orpheus strums his lyre to ward off their song, 1905

INDEX

INDEX

Page 328
Virginia Frances Sterrett
The sea nymphs collect shells and prepare necklaces for Persephone at the bottom of the ocean, 1921

Right
Patten Wilson
As Heracles enquires after the golden apples, Atlas, carrier of the heavens, prepares a ruse, 1914

PHOTO CREDITS

Newell Convers Wyeth
Telemachus mounts the chariot of Nestor before a setting sun, following his visit at Pylos, 1929

Illustrations listed by artist

Baikie, Constance N. 59
Brock, Charles Edmund 61, 140, 164, 176, 278, 319
Brock, Henry Matthew 91, 309, 312
Burian, Zdeněk 12, 192, 281
Crane, Walter 36, 234, 251, 252, 255, 259, 267, 282, 283, 316
Dulac, Edmund 39, 77, 269
Fell, Herbert Granville 284, 321
Flaxman, John 105, 161, 167, 169, 191, 208, 213
Flint, William Russell 25, 49, 51, 52/53, 56, 63, 64, 67, 89, 126/27, 129, 181, 183, 184, 198/99, 202, 232/33, 287, 310/11
Ford, Henry Justice 54, 55, 98–101, 144, 171, 179, 215, 241, 288

Gontier, Clément 145, 155, 159, 160
Harper, Clifford 3, 30/31, cover, back cover, front- and endpapers, all chapter openers and glossary symbols
Mann, Merlyn 79
Matania, Fortunino 148/49
Pogany, Willy 74, 75
Rackham, Arthur 17, 21, 71, 110, 118/19, 261, 263, 264, 293, 294
Robinson, Thomas Heath 327
Scheiner, Artuš 106, 133, 137, 322
Sterrett, Virginia Frances 41, 43–46, 81–84, 95, 125, 197, 201, 276, 297, 315, 328
Stratton, Helen 274
Tawse, Sybil 92

Tenggren, Gustaf 2, 33, 103, 121, 123, 298
Theaker, Harry George 325
Van Abbé, Salomon 18, 301
Wilson, Patten 19 l., 302, 331
Winter, Milo 19 r., 34, 113–115, 254, 336
Wulff, Max 163
Wyeth, Newell Convers 1, 189, 195, 207, 211, 219, 222, 224, 228, 238, 243, 249, 290, 305, 307, 332
Zick, Alexander 134, 306

THE AUTHOR

Michael Siebler studied classical archaeology and wrote his doctoral thesis on the Roman god Mars Ultor. After receiving his PhD, he initially worked at the German Archaeological Institute in Damascus, and has taken part in several excavations, including at Olympia. He was later a research associate at the Institute for Classical Archaeology at Mainz University and then a long-standing features editor at the *Frankfurter Allgemeine Zeitung*. He currently works as a freelance writer, and is the author of TASCHEN's *Greek Art* and *Roman Art* (both 2007).

ACKNOWLEDGMENTS

We are much indebted to the institutions and private collections mentioned in the captions and photo credits for their kind support of our publication.
We especially would like to thank the author Michael Siebler for his explanatory texts, and Clifford Harper for his expressive illustrations of the myths.
We would also like to extend our thanks to Lioba Waleczek for her support with the artist biographies featured in this volume.

IMPRINT

Cover, back cover, front- and endpapers:
Clifford Harper

Page 1
Newell Convers Wyeth
*Imprint design for the edition of Homer's
Odyssey illustrated by Wyeth, showing
Zeus, King of the Gods, launching lightning
bolts from each hand,* 1929

Page 2
Gustaf Tenggren
*As punishment for the theft of fire,
Prometheus is bound to a cliff for
eternity,* 1950s

Page 4
Edward Burne-Jones
The Baleful Head, gouache on paper,
ca. 1876
*Perseus and Andromeda view Medusa's
gaze from the reflection of an octagonal
well.*

Pages 6/7
Abraham Ortelius
The map Argonautica, *from a supplement
to* Theatrum Orbis Terrarum, *illustrating
the key stations of the Argonauts' voyage
across the Mediterranean and the Black
Sea,* 1604

Page 336
Milo Winter
*The winged horse Pegasus in flight, from
the illustrated edition of* A Wonder-Book
by Nathaniel Hawthorne, 1913

**EACH AND EVERY TASCHEN BOOK
PLANTS A SEED!**
TASCHEN is a carbon neutral publisher. Each
year, we offset our annual carbon emissions
with carbon credits at the Instituto Terra, a
reforestation program in Minas Gerais, Brazil,
founded by Lélia and Sebastião Salgado. To
find out more about this ecological partner-
ship, please check: www.taschen.com/
zerocarbon
Inspiration: unlimited. Carbon footprint:
zero.

To stay informed about TASCHEN and our
upcoming titles, please subscribe to our free
magazine at www.taschen.com/magazine,
follow us on Instagram and Facebook, or e-mail
your questions to contact@taschen.com.

Project management: Mahros Allamezade,
Tom Pitt-Brooke, Cologne
Translation: Jolene Lighthizer, London
(texts by Michael Siebler); Isabel Varea-Riley,
Cambridge/UK (texts by Gustav Schwab)
Art direction: Andy Disl, Los Angeles,
Birgit Eichwede, Cologne
Production: Daniela Asmuth, Cologne

© 2021 TASCHEN GmbH
Hohenzollernring 53, D–50672 Köln
www.taschen.com

ISBN 978-3-8365-8472-2
Printed in Slovakia